Boswell-Hardeman Discussion

on

Instrumental Music in the Worship

Conducted in the Ryman Auditorium,
Nashville, Tenn., May 31 to
June 5, 1923

ISBN 1-58427-023-3

Guardian of Truth Foundation
P.O. Box 9670
Bowling Green, Kentucky 42102

FOREWARD

The *Guardian of Truth Foundation* takes great pleasure in bringing back into print the *Boswell-Hardeman Discussion* on instrumental music in the worship. This debate is the classic on this question, and has been for nearly sixty-years the book to read for the best arguments on both sides of this controversy. It has long been out of print, but calls for it are made on a regular basis.

There was a need for this debate sixty years ago and that need is just as much present today as then. The Christian Church then had men who would publicly affirm that instrumental music in worship is scriptural. Boswell had twenty-two speeches in which he diligently labored seeking to prove by the scriptures that mechanical music in worship to God is right. Hardeman denied this. The entire record is here for your honest investigation. Is instrumental music in worship "Christian liberty"; "only an opinion"; or is it really authorized by the scriptures? This work will immeasurably assist you in finding the right answers covering this question.

Eternal vigilance is the price that must be paid to keep the church, its work and worship, pure as the scriptures of God guides it to be. The present generation, while enjoying *scriptural worship*, must consider more than the present; what future there might be ought to receive a spiritual legacy from us who go before. The need is great and the hour is late for watchmen on the walls of Zion who know the difference between human opinions and divine legislation.

Words of sincere appreciation are hereby given to brother Bill Draffen and his good wife, Nancy, for making possible this edition.

Earl E. Robertson, President
Guardian Of Truth Foundation
April 29, 1981

CONTENTS

INTRODUCTION

As I was one of the moderators of the Boswell-Hardeman debate, I was asked to write an introduction for this book. This debate was held in the Ryman Auditorium, in the city of Nashville, May 31 to June 5, 1923. The debate was five sessions of two hours each, and from six to seven thousand people were present at every session. There was, perhaps, more interest shown in this debate, especially by those who do not use the instrument of music in worship, than has been shown over the discussion of any religious question which has ever been held in the city of Nashville. I have been especially requested to give the facts which led up to the discussion and how an agreement was reached on the proposition for debate. In order to get these facts before the readers of the book, I can do no better than quote from the files of the Gospel Advocate.

There appeared in the Gospel Advocate of May 18, 1922, the following:

THE COMMISSION ON UNITY

BY F. B. S.

Recently I received the following communication:

WEST NASHVILLE, TENN., May 1, 1922.

Dear Sir and Brother:

We sent you last year a copy of O. E. Payne's book on the church-music question for your consideration and to be returned after reading. We have not yet received the copy sent you, so we are writing to request the return of the same. Fraternally,

THE COMMISSION ON UNITY.

I wonder who appointed this Commission on Unity or who has any right to make suggestions as to how unity can be brought about or maintained. If this commission has been appointed by any one or by any church, I would like to know who or which, because that individual or church should know what this commission is doing to promote unity. But if it is a self-appointed commission, as I believe it is, I have as much right to offer suggestions as any one. If this commission is calling in O. E. Payne's book on the church-music question in order to destroy it, it is working on the right line, and I want to commend them; but if it is calling in these books in order to give them to others and thus continue their circulation, I suggest a change of name for the commission. It should be called "The Commission on Division" instead of "The Commission on Unity." I doubt whether one church in fifty in this country uses the instrument in their worship. If this book is circulated and read and changes no one, it could not assist in bringing about unity, because we already have unity on that question in most of the churches in these parts; but if it changes some one and makes him believe that he ought to have the instrument in worship, cannot this commission see that this would bring about division? The instrument would be forced into the worship by these new converts made by Payne's book, which would drive out those it did not convert, and thus we would have division instead of unity as a result of this work. Surely this commission could not hope to change every one on this question with this book and thus get every one wrong; but if it did not change all, but changed any, it would cause division instead of unity. Why is it necessary to have a commission in order to circulate O. E. Payne's book on the church-music question? Is it possible that those who are doing this work are ashamed to come out in the open and do it as individuals, or are they trying to make the impression that some church or association of men and women are behind them in their divisive work? We know it is not necessary in this city to have the instrument in order to have unity on the music question, for it was demonstrated in the recent meeting at the Ryman Auditorium that even those brethren who use the instrument can unite with those that do not and sing without the instrument, for they did it in that meeting. The only way to have unity on this question is to stop circulating such literature as O. E. Payne's book and cease to encourage such a commission as the one that has sprung up in West Nashville.

I cannot comply with the request herein made to return the copy of the book claimed to have been sent to me, as I have no recollection of having seen it, and no member of my family remembers anything about it; but I will agree to send a copy of M. C. Kurfees' reply to O. E. Payne's book, if the commission will agree to use it as an antidote to the Payne poison. If this commission is true to its name and is really a commission on unity, it will accept this proposition and will circulate this reply to Payne's book by Brother Kurfees as extensively as it circulates the Payne book; but if this commission is not true to its name, then the church where the individuals composing the commission hold membership should promptly withdraw from them, in harmony with the plain command of the apostle where he says: "Mark them that are causing the divisions and occasions of stumbling, contrary to the doctrine which ye learned: and turn away from them." (Rom. 16: 17.)

While the foregoing says nothing about a debate, it was

really the foundation for further correspondence, out of which grew the Nashville debate on the church-music question.

In the Gospel Advocate, issue of June 1, 1922, the following appeared:

THAT COMMISSION ON UNITY, AGAIN.

BY F. B. S.

My former article on the above subject, two weeks back, drew from Brother John B. Cowden the following letter:

WEST NASHVILLE, TENN., May 18, 1922.

Dear Brother Srygley:

I notice what you have to say in this week's Gospel Advocate in regard to the Commission on Unity, and I write to give you some information that I thought was generally known. There is so little contact between those that use and those that do not use instrumental music in the church that we often misunderstand each other for this reason. There is no shame nor secrecy about the Commission on Unity. It has been at work here in Tennessee for four or five years, and nothing has been done "in a corner."' The original personnel of the same was Carey E. Morgan, E. J. Barnett, A. Preston Gray, W. J. Shelburne, John B. Cowden; and others since have identified themselves with us. I can furnish their names, if you wish them. It is not an organization at all, but a mere association of the friends of unity. It was not appointed by any church or organization and does not represent any. It is open to all Christians; the only requirement for membership is to believe in and work for the unity of the church. We would be glad to have you or any other friend of unity associated with us in the work.

Now, in regard to O. E. Payne's book, we proceed on the hypothesis that there can be no unity until our divisive differences are settled, and settled right. Accordingly, we send out all the light we can get on these matters. If you will furnish us the books, as others have O. E. Payne's, we will be glad to send out a copy of M. C. Kurfees' reply with every copy of Payne's book that we send out. We have no desire to suppress or destroy this reply, as you appear to have toward O. E. Payne's book. We want the whole truth on this subject (all that can be said on both sides) known, and we are willing to leave conclusions with the people. With all thinking, truth-loving people, Payne's book stands or falls on its own merits, and so does Kurfees' reply.

If you care to know anything about my individual work in the interest of unity, you can ask any one that has attended one of my meetings in the interest of Christian unity; or, better still, you can attend one yourself and get the information first-hand. I expect to hold such meetings all this summer near Nashville; and, if you think it worth while, I would be glad for you to attend one, if you find it convenient and desirable.

The book intended for you must have gone astray or was not sent at all. The fact is, we did not expect to have to request the return of these books, so a rather loose record was kept of the books sent out. We beg your pardon for bothering you with the request to return.

Of course, you will publish this letter in the Gospel Advocate, since the lack of this information places us in a false light before your readers.

Yours fraternally,

JOHN B. COWDEN.

Brother Cowden is correct when he says there is little contact between those who use the instrument in worship and those who do not use it. What, I ask, is the cause of this division, misunderstanding, and lack of contact between those who use the instrument and those who do not? Is it not the use of the instrument in the worship? Then why does the Commission on Unity not strike at the cause and remove it? Why continue to circulate O. E. Payne's book? The commission cannot hope to remove the instrument by circulating a book that advocates its use in the worship.

I am glad to learn the personnel of the commission. I felt at the time that the main leaders of the commission were members of the Vine Street Christian Church, but I did not know that one of the charter members was their preacher, Brother Carey E. Morgan; but in Brother Cowden's letter to me, Brother Morgan heads the list. Brother Cowden says this commission "is not an organization at all, but a mere association of the friends of unity. It was not appointed by any church or organization and does not represent any." Perhaps not, but it is true that any church ought to have some jurisdiction over its members. If the elders have no rule or right to counsel and control the members of their congregation, they ought to have. In my former article I advised the church where the individuals composing this commission hold membership to withdraw from them on the ground that they are causing division and not unity in circulating O. E. Payne's book. The church should first admonish these brethren to cease their divisive work, and, after proper admonition, if they will not stop the work that is causing division, they should be made to feel the enormity of their sin. Suppose the church has not authorized this commission. As a matter of fact, the most active members of the commission are members of the Vine Street Christian Church; and unless this church condemns the course of these men in some way, they will be partakers of their sin.

I cannot understand how Brother Carey E. Morgan can consistently circulate O. E. Payne's book, because, if I remember correctly, O. E. Payne takes the position in this same book that the Greek word "psallo," from which we sometimes have the word "sing" in our English Bible, means to sing accompanied with an instrument as certainly as the word "baptizo" means to immerse. If this is true, then no man can "psallo" without an instrument. But Brother Morgan did sing in the Auditorium meeting without an instrument, for I sat by him and heard him; but, if O. E. Payne is correct, he no more obeyed God in that singing than one would to be sprinkled instead of immersed. The very fact that those brethren sang with us in that meeting without the instrument is proof that they do not believe O. E. Payne's book as a whole. This is another reason why they should cease circulating the worthless thing. It cannot be true if they are right in their practice; and since it is causing division, it ought to be prohibited.

But Brother Cowden says if I will furnish M. C. Kurfees' reply to O. E. Payne's book as others have the book itself, this commission will send out the reply with every book. That seems to be a fair proposition on its face; but why place such a financial burden on me, when by stopping the circulation of the book the reply to it would be unnecessary? Others are furnishing these books, are they? Who is furnishing this cause of division to these brethren? Surely the preacher is not appropriating any of the funds of the church for such a purpose. The brother says: "We have no desire to suppress or destroy M. C. Kurfees' reply to the Payne book." Of course, you ought not to desire to destroy the antidote to the poison, when you are circulating it; but if you would destroy the poison, the antidote would be useless, as it would not be needed.

Brother Cowden says if I care to know more of his individual work in the interest of unity, I can inquire or attend his meeting myself. No, I was not inquiring about his individual work, but I was inquiring about the Commission on Unity. Brother Cowden says it has been at work here in Tennessee four or five years, but what has it accomplished on that subject? Where has it brought about union? Surely it is about time to disband this commission on the ground of a failure to function. What a pity that Brother Cowden will not give himself to the work of preaching the gospel and establishing churches instead of going from place to place and disturbing our churches over the use of the instrument in the worship, when he himself admits the instrument is unnecessary to acceptable worship? No wonder, Brother Cowden, I had not heard of your work, because it is of no benefit to any one; for it consists mainly in circulating a worthless book, to the neglect of the things that make for peace.

Since writing the foregoing a good brother has agreed to furnish a copy of Kurfees' reply to the Payne book to every one to whom this commission sends the Payne book, provided a list of the names is sent to this office. Since Brother Cowden says the light on the subject is what he wants the people to have, this brother further agrees to furnish a good man to discuss the question with any good man the commission may name that will affirm their practice on the use of the instrument of music in the worship. This would give all seekers after the truth on this question the opportunity of hearing both sides of the subject; and then, to make all this information permanent, this brother further agrees to bear half the expense of printing this discussion in book form, and then both sides can be circulated together. What say you, Brother Cowden? Please send the list to me at this office, and your decision on the discussion, and I will see that the proper man gets it. We shall see what we shall see.

In this communication we have the debate mentioned for the first time. It will be noted that the publication of the debate in a book is also mentioned in the foregoing article. A certain brother was to bear half the expense of the publication of the book, and the inference is clear that those who use the instrument were to bear the other half of the expense and aid in the circulation of the book. After this, the understanding was clear that these brethren who use the instrument in their worship were to pay half the expense of the stenographic report of the debate and the publication of the same. This understanding continued till the debate began, when quite suddenly some of them decided they had no interest in the publication and that they already had all the expense with it that they were willing to bear. This move on their part left J. C. McQuiddy the sole owner and publisher of the book.

On June 15, 1922, the following appeared in the Gospel Advocate:

WILL THERE BE A DISCUSSION ON THE MUSIC QUESTION?

BY F. B. S.

My last article on the Commission on Unity drew from Brother John B. Cowden the following letter, which we gladly give to our readers:

WEST NASHVILLE, TENN., June 7, 1922.

Dear Brother Srygley:

Your reply and proposition through the Gospel Advocate to discuss the church-music question has been received and considered. As you doubtless know, those in Tennessee using instruments in the church have been averse to any joint public discussion of this question on the grounds of Tit. 3: 9, or at least they regard the question *per se* of not sufficient importance to discuss; but this question has become so involved with the question of fraternity, which we do regard worth contending for, that we are disposed to accept your proposition as a doubtful yet possible step toward the restoration of fraternity between those that use and those that do not use instruments in the church. We have tried everything else without bettering the situation; and, for my part, I am ready to try this. However, there are many that doubt the wisdom of any such discussions, who must be considered. I have shared this view in the past, but I am now inclined to think otherwise with respect to the church-music question. Of course, I can speak for no one except myself, and would not presume to act on my own views without advising with others interested. The State Convention of Tennessee churches meets this next week at Ovoca, so I shall bring your proposition up for consideration there; and I will do what I can to get them to accept your proposition; and I feel reasonably sure that it will be accepted, because there is a growing desire in the churches to see this thing threshed out that all may see the grains of truth on both sides. Although religious debates are often fratricidal in their nature and results, yet they are sometimes necessary to put an end to fratricidal warfare. They also help to clear the religious atmosphere, and this is needed in Tennessee. Whether this discussion will have these desired results, I know not; but I am willing to try it out, and will advise with the brethren at Ovoca to this end; and some concerted decision and action will be taken and forwarded to you. At any rate, "we shall see what we shall see."

Fraternally,
JOHN B. COWDEN.

Yes, I knew these brethren were averse to a joint public discussion of this question, but I did not know why they were averse to it. Brother Cowden says here that one reason is on the grounds of Tit. 3: 9. Well, I must say that if Tit. 3: 9 forbids such a discussion, it would not only be grounds for an aversion to it, but it would be the end of it with me. While I would like to hear such a discussion, I would not be willing to disobey the apostle Paul in order to hear it or be a party to any such disobedience.

But I have looked at the passage very closely, and I cannot see one word in the verse that forbids such a discussion. In fact, the apostle was not on that subject. The verse referred to here reads: "But shun foolish questionings, and genealogies, and strifes, and fightings about the law; for they are unprofitable and vain." If any one is fighting about the law, it is Brother Cowden in this case; but I do not see what the law has to do with it. "The law" here evidently refers to the law of Moses. I have known all the time that the only authority these brethren have for instrumental music in worship was in the law of Moses; but this is not the brother's point, as his letter shows. He says they "regard the question *per se* of not sufficient importance to discuss." I cannot understand how the brother can say that and continue to circulate O. E. Payne's book, for O. E. Payne says in this same book on page 172: "We must unite in agreeing that if we forego musical instruments we cannot conform to the divine injunction to *psallein*." And yet Brother Cowden says the question is not of sufficient importance to discuss. Then it is of little importance, according to Brother Cowden, for people to conform to a divine injunction. It is bad for any one to even feel that way about a divine injunction, much less express it in words. Brother F. W. Smith tells me that Brother Cowden told him he fully indorsed Payne's position in his book, and the fact that he circulates the book proves Brother Smith did not misunderstand him, and yet it is of little importance with Cowden and his coworkers.

But Brother Cowden says he has tried everything else but a debate without making it any better. Then I was right last week when I said his Commission on Unity was doing no good; for, according to his own statement, he has made it no better. I wonder now what these brethren who have sent Brother Cowden out think about continuing him, when by his own statement he is doing no good and is ready to come to my position. I have said all the time this is the way to do it. Let these brethren affirm their practice on the scripturalness of instrumental music in the worship and stand up like brave men and try to defend it.

But Brother Cowden and O. E. Payne are not alone in their contention that the Bible requires the use of the instrument in the worship; for the *Christian Standard* of June 3, speaking editorially in regard to O. E. Payne's book, "Instrumental Music in the Worship," says: "The author has made an exhaustive research of the meaning of the word *'psallo,'* precisely as Campbell and others have made the same investigation in regard to *'baptizo.'* The result is an overwhelming conviction that not only was instrumental music allowed in the worship of the primitive church, but that it was positively enjoined." How, then, brethren believing this can say it is a matter of little importance is more than I can understand.

I am glad Brother Cowden is to take this question to the convention and not decide it for himself alone; for while we are anxious to convert Brother Cowden and make a useful man out of him, yet we want the interest and attendance of others. Now, Brother Cowden, do all you can to get your brethren at Ovoca to defend their practice. We will wait with interest their decision. I have more interest in this coming convention than any that has been held by these erring brethren for a long time, for it is to decide whether we are to have a joint public discussion or not. If they decide to do so, write or wire me immediately.

This quotation from the Gospel Advocate was followed two weeks later with the following:

GOOD NEWS FROM OVOCA.

BY F. B. S.

It will be remembered that Brother John B. Cowden, in a letter to me of June 7, promised to submit to the convention which was to meet in Ovoca the question as to whether they would indorse a debate on the instrumental-music question in the worship of God. It seems from the following letter that they have agreed to indorse and encourage such a discussion, and there appears to be nothing to do now but arrange the preliminaries. But here is his letter, with my reply:

WEST NASHVILLE, TENN.

Dear Brother Srygley:

After advising with the brethren in convention at Ovoca and others interested, the Commission on Unity accepts your challenge and proposition to discuss the church-music question on two essential conditions—namely, that the discussion be in every way fraternal and becoming Christians, and that it be thorough and carried into every community where either party thinks it wise to have it, the choice of place to alternate, until the field has been covered, or both parties are satisfied to close the discussion. A committee from the Commission on Unity is ready to meet a like committee from you to arrange details.

Yours fraternally,
JOHN B. COWDEN,
Secretary of the Commission on Unity.

NASHVILLE, TENN., July 5, 1922.

Mr. John B. Cowden, West Nashville, City:

Dear Brother: Your letter was forwarded to me at Chicago, but I had left there before its arrival, and it has been returned to me today. I am glad that your brethren are willing to discuss their practice on the instrumental-music question; and while I am not able to select a like committee, I have selected the following brethren: S. H. Hall, H. Leo Boles, and F. W. Smith.

You can easily get in touch with these brethren at any time by calling at the Gospel Advocate office. At any time you wish a meeting between these brethren and your committee, please advise with any one of them and a meeting can be easily arranged. If you could have a meeting of your committee with these brethren any time between now and Saturday noon, I could also be present in the meeting; but as I will be out of the city much of the time holding meetings for the next few months, I am glad to leave the matter in the hands of these brethren, and I feel that they are so well known by all brethren through this part of the country that there will be no objections to any arrangement they may make. It might be well to have also a written discussion between one of your brethren and one of ours who opposes the instrument in worship, provided such a discussion could be published in one of your papers as well as in one of ours. Since you suggest "that it be thorough and carried into every community," a written discussion would help to do that.

Please give this matter your immediate attention and have your committee meet with our brethren at the earliest date possible. I can assure you that many of my brethren will be glad to hear such a discussion. As you insist, let there be nothing done or said in the discussion that is not becoming to Christians. Let us hear from the committee at once as to what it proposes to do. I am certainly glad that there is a prospect of an honest, fair discussion of the real difference between those who use instrumental music and those who do not. I shall always be glad of the part that I have taken in this matter, and I sincerely hope that it will result in many learning the truth on the subject of how to worship God.

Please communicate with the brethren herein named.

I am, very truly yours,
F. B. SRYGLEY.

From this letter of Brother Cowden we have a right to expect that these brethren will discuss their practice in using instrumental music in the worship on its merits, and we are all fortunate in having the privilege of hearing their proof in the presence of an opponent who will have the opportunity to examine it, and let us see if their conclusions follow from a fair and impartial interpretation of the word. All great questions that have been settled right have been settled by discussion. There is no reason why there should be any prejudice against honorable controversy conducted in the spirit of the Master. I am glad that these brethren have decided to stand up like brave men and defend their practice in an open, fair discussion of the question before the public. If I have done anything to bring about this condition, I am proud of it, and I pray that we may all learn the truth and practice it. We shall keep the readers of the Gospel Advocate informed as to the outcome of this matter.

Up to this time everything seemed to be progressing fine, but about the time the foregoing article appeared in print the two committees had a meeting and failed to agree on a proposition. To give the result of the first meeting, I quote again from the Gospel Advocate of July 20, 1922:

WILL THEIR COURAGE FAIL?

BY F. B. S.

In last week's issue of the Gospel Advocate I gave the readers the benefit of Brother John B. Cowden's letter in which he asked for a committee to meet his Commission on Unity to arrange the preliminaries for a public discussion on the question of instrumental music in the worship. Brother Cowden asked that the two committees meet on Saturday morning at the study of the Vine Street Christian Church. I was present in that meeting, but was disappointed when I saw that the courage of the Commission on Unity had oozed out and they were not willing to affirm that the New Testament commands the use of instruments in the worship of God. Brother Cowden was the spokesman for his commission, and we saw that his bravery was gone and he was back in his old rut that the instrument is a nonessential. He opened the meeting by telling us that the Commission on Unity had been insisting on unity on essentials, but excluding nonessentials. We saw at once that he was back on his old cry of "nothing in the instrument." We asked him for a proposition for discussion, and he presented this: "Instrumental music is scripturally permissible in the church." We could all see that this proposition was the old joke of the instrument as an aid to the singing, but no part of the worship. We very promptly gave the Commission on Unity to understand that this was no longer the issue, but that since O. E. Payne had written his book and had tried to prove that "psallo" meant to sing accompanied with an instrument, and John B. Cowden, J. B. Briney, and the rest of the debaters had indorsed the book, they must prove that the New Testament requires the instrument in worship or repudiate their commendation of the Payne book.

I have before me a folder advertising O. E. Payne's book, "Instrumental Music Is Scriptural," in which John B. Cowden is quoted as saying: "Your book on the church-music question is the most exhaustive, thorough, and convincing treatise of the subject, or, indeed, of any other subject, that I have ever seen. In my investigation I had but touched the hem of the garment, not dreaming that the confirming facts were so many and convincing. What Alexander Campbell did for the baptism question, you have done for the music question—settled it. The pity is that some one did not make this research and publish the facts while the people were open to conviction." I wonder if Brother John thinks that Alexander Campbell settled the baptism question by proving it is "scripturally permissible?" Mr. Campbell proved that baptism is commanded in the New Testament; and if Mr. Payne has settled the instrumental-music question as Campbell did the baptism question, he has proved that the New Testament commands the use of instruments in the worship. I really believe that when Brother Cowden wrote that, he thought Payne had proved it; but now it looks like he has fallen back to the "hem of the garment" again.

Mr. Payne also quotes from Brother J. B. Briney, of whom he says: "In all the world, no man is regarded as more competent to speak on this question than J. B. Briney. As editor, logician, and debater, he has no living peer." This man without a "living peer" says of O. E. Payne's book: "The author aims to prove that instrumental music in Christian worship is scriptural; and when I say that his effort is a complete success, I state the case conservatively. Mr. Payne builds his argument almost exclusively upon the meaning of the Greek word 'psallo,' which occurs in some form five times in the New Testament, and hence the Scripture sanctions the doing of whatever this word meant when the New Testament was written. The author first points out how the meaning of the Greek word 'baptizo' (baptize) is ascertained, and by the same method he demonstrates (I use the term advisedly) that when the New Testament was written 'psallo' carried with it the idea of the use of the instrument of music. This he does, first, by such an array of Greek lexicons as I have never seen assembled in the support of the meaning of any other word."

Now you have it, according to the great debater, J. B. Briney, "demonstrated." More evidence brought to its support than to that of any other subject, not even baptism itself excepted. I suppose, after this demonstration and all this evidence, Brother Briney would be ashamed to ask us to affirm that the use of instrumental music in the worship is sinful. Is that the way he debates baptism? Does he wait until some one will affirm it is a sin to be baptized, or does he go forward like a man and prove his proposition that the New Testament commands it? Why not do likewise in the discussion of the instrumental-music question, which has "been demonstrated," and when it has far more proof in its favor?

Brother Payne also quotes from S. S. Lappin, a former editor of the *Christian Standard*, the following: "'Instrumental Music Is Scriptural' is by far the best treatment of the subject I have ever seen. It takes the dilemma by both horns, beards the beast in his lair and tells him to begone. It puts the other fellow on the defensive." Very well, we are perfectly willing to be on the defensive; but Brother Cowden is evidently afraid that Payne's hold on the beast will slip, and so he is not willing to risk it by signing a proposition that sets forth O. E. Payne's position.

Mr. Payne in his book says: "In the previous chapters it has been demonstrated that, to him who correctly understands the New Testament, God has not carelessly left any room for doubt or uncertainty. Just as there was no occasion for disagreement as to the meaning of the Greek verb 'baptizo,' I shall now as completely demonstrate that neither is there the slightest ground for misgiving as to the meaning of the Greek verb 'psallo' as it came from the inspired writers." I wonder if Mr. Payne and Brother Cowden are still going over the country affirming that baptism is "scripturally permissible," or are they, like true men, preaching that baptism is commanded in the New Testament? Why not do the same thing about instrumental music, since Payne says he has "demonstrated" it, and that the evidence "is stronger" for the instrument than it is for baptism?

Now, Brother Cowden, since you have over your own signature indorsed O. E. Payne's book and your Commission on Unity has circulated it, come up like a man and affirm his teaching. We will not ask you to prove that Payne "demonstrated" its use in the New Testament, but you ought to affirm that the New Testament commands instrumental music in the worship of God. They all raised a shout of rejoicing over Payne's book when it first appeared. It was the last word on the subject, beyond even Brother Cowden's dreams. Payne's book proved that the New Testament taught instrumental music clearer than it did immersion. We had a right to expect that these brethren would throw down their former contention that the instrument is only an aid to the singing, but no part of the worship. Now Brother Cowden says that a few of his brethren will accept O. E. Payne's contention, but the large majority will not. One of his committee said right out that he would not. It is only an aid, or permissible, with him. It seems that a majority of them are afraid "the beast will not begone." He is bearded all right, but they are afraid the beard will pull out. Will some one help Brother Payne turn the beast loose? Brother Cowden is evidently afraid to fool with him, with the hold Brother Payne has on him. Come on now, brethren, and debate the issue that you yourselves have made by indorsing and circulating O. E. Payne's book—the New Testament commands the use of instrumental music in the worship of God. You know this is Payne's position in his book, "Instrumental Music Is Scriptural."

In justice to Brother Cowden, I will say that in the meeting of these committees he said he was willing for the proposition to read, "Instrumental music is scriptural," but he would not add "in the worship of God." Of course, this would only give grounds for quibbling. What we want is the instrumental-music question in worship affirmed;

and since Brother Payne has "demonstrated" the use of the instrument in the New Testament worship by the meaning of the word "*psallo,*" we must insist that they meet this issue or repudiate O. E. Payne and his erroneous contention. We have Payne's position, brethren, in black and white, and your own indorsement of it over your own signature. You must not allow your courage to evaporate, but come like brave men and defend the issue.

O. E. Payne in his book further says: "Since it seems probable that he pursued the study far enough to make sure that there was pay dirt if he would but delve deeper, it is a cause for regret that J. Carroll Stark failed to go to the bottom of the question. He sought a debate years ago with R. B. Neal in which he would affirm, 'The New Testament authorizes the use of instruments.' Long afterwards he concluded his handsome book, 'The King and His Kingdom,' thus: 'V. That in the distinction made by Paul between *hymns* and *psalms* he *authorized* the use of instrumental music in the worship of the church. . . . VI. That it is positively *commanded* by the apostle and authorized by the Holy Spirit under the gospel dispensation. This should end the controversy. Where God speaks, we will speak.' " (O. E. Payne's book, pages 25, 26.) From this quotation it seems that J. Carroll Stark was braver when he had just begun to feel that he had struck "pay dirt" than these brethren are when they get to the bottom of the mine. What is the matter with the hole, brethren, that you have lost your courage? If the New Testament has spoken on this subject as you say it has, why not embody it in your proposition and affirm that the New Testament teaches the use of instrumental music in the worship of God? I am sorry for you, brethren; but you have put yourselves in this predicament by indorsing and circulating O. E. Payne's book.

Is it possible that what they heralded abroad as their success will prove their greatest handicap? Let us stand, brethren, on our rights, and let these erring brethren worry with the difficulty into which O. E. Payne has placed them. He says instruments of music are commanded in the New Testament in the very meaning of the word "psallo," and they have indorsed his book. Now let them wriggle. Why should we worry?

Everything seemed to be off, and it looked like the debate was gone; but in the meantime Brethren S. H. Hall and J. J. Walker, of East Nashville, perfected an agreement to hold a "joint study" on the church-music question, in which Brother Walker agreed to give his very best reasons for believing that instrumental music in church worship is scriptural. At the close of this "study," or debate, the "Commission on Unity" circulated a poster in which they expressed a willingness to debate the question, and submitted the following propositions, either one of which they would affirm: (1) "Instrumental music is scripturally permissible," or (2) "Instrumental music in the church is scriptural." To this poster I made the following reply in the Gospel Advocate of October 26, 1922:

WHAT WE HAVE SEEN.

BY F. B. S.

At the close of the Hall-Walker discussion at the Ryman Auditorium on the night of October 10, Brother John B. Cowden circulated a poster in which he seeks to make the impression that I shut him out of the Gospel Advocate because I saw something that I did not want the public to see. If this is true, I do not know it, and I have a better chance to know it than he has. He says in this poster that the essentials of the discussion had been agreed to, and refers to his own statement in the Gospel Advocate of June 1 and July 13. I do not know what he calls the "essentials" of a debate, but I do know that I never agreed to debate either of the two propositions he mentions. I know, furthermore, that our correspondence came up over O. E. Payne's book and the position he takes in that book on the music question, which is as quoted by me in the Gospel Advocate of June 15: "We must unite in agreeing that if we forego musical instruments we cannot conform to the divine injunction to *psallein.*" (O. E. Payne's book, page 172.) The brother says in his poster: "We did not agree to discuss O. E. Payne's book." I am not asking you to discuss the book or defend it, but to affirm the position which Mr. Payne takes in his book. You have been circulating the book, and gave it your public indorsement over your own signature. Writing to O. E. Payne, John B. Cowden said: "Your book on the church-music question is the most exhaustive, thorough, and convincing treatise of the subject, or, indeed, of any other subject, that I have ever seen. In my investigation I had but touched the hem of the garment, not dreaming that the confirming facts were so many and so convincing. What Alexander Campbell did for the baptism question, you have done for the music question—settled it. The pity is that some one did not make this research and publish the facts while the people were open to conviction." With this most fulsome indorsement by John B. Cowden before me, I had a right to expect that he would defend the position which O. E. Payne takes in his book, when he says that Payne settled the question. Well, if he settled it, as Brother Cowden says, he settled it by proving that one cannot obey the divine injunction to *psallein* without the use of a musical instrument. But Brother Cowden says he will not defend O. E. Payne's position in debate; then he ought to defend what he said to Payne. When I get so I cannot defend what I said, I will apologize for saying it. But the brother says O. E. Payne is able to defend his own book. Well, John B. Cowden ought to be able to defend what he has said about the book. Brother, I am not asking you to defend Payne, but I am asking you to defend your statement. You say Payne is able to take care of himself; then you ought to be able to take care of yourself also. I must say if O. E. Payne is able and willing to defend himself, he beats John B. Cowden.

The propositions submitted by Brother Cowden are indefinite, and a debate on such propositions would be largely over the meaning of the propositions. One of the first rules of honorable controversy is that the terms of the propositions should be so clearly defined that there can be no misunderstanding respecting them. His first proposition is: "Instrumental music is scripturally permissible." There might be some misunderstanding over what is meant by "permissible," or there might be some misunderstanding over when instrumental music is permissible. That proposition did not state when it is permissible or how it is permissible. I judge that it is permissible in some places myself, and there are many places and times when it might be permissible, and neither I nor any other man would care anything about whether it is or is not permissible. The other proposition is nearly as bad: "Instrumental music in the church is scriptural." This proposition does not say what is meant by the "church." The word "church," to some, simply means a meetinghouse. Whatever the brother means by it, he does not mean the worshiping assembly; for he says in the same poster that he will not affirm that it is scriptural in the worship, for that would make it an integral part of the worship. From that statement I conclude that he does not use the word "church" in the sense of a worshiping assembly. Then, what does he mean by it? Cowden says I ought to deny his proposition or accept it; but I beg his pardon, for I could not do either. It looks like he stated his proposition that way on purpose so I could not deny or accept. Your Brother Gast debated this proposition with me in Portsmouth, Ohio, June 27-30: "Instrumental music is scriptural in the worship of God." I told him he was a braver man than his brethren were in Tennessee.

Again, the brother says: "O. E. Payne's book has nothing to do with this discussion (except possibly you fear the facts therein contained)." Why should I fear these facts in your hands when you do not believe them yourself? At least, you do not believe them strong enough to affirm one of them—namely: "No one can obey the divine injunction to *psallein* without the use of the musical instrument." It was my contention throughout our entire correspondence that you ought to affirm that instrumental music is scriptural in worship; and when you flatly refused to do this, I told you that that was all I had asked you to do and that my part of the matter was done and you could call the committees together and see if they could agree on some other proposition for a debate; but, instead of doing that, you got out a poster, I suppose, hoping that you could create the impression that you were very anxious for a debate, but that we had all got afraid of you and quit.

Brother Cowden in his poster further says: "As to my rejection of the phrase, 'in the worship,' from our statement, *Instrumental music is scriptural,* this makes instrumental music an integral part of worship, which no church that I know anything about does." Now, if that is true, then no church you know anything about believes O. E. Payne's book, which you said was the "most exhaustive, thorough, and convincing treatise of the subject, or, indeed, of any other subject," you ever saw; and Brother J. B. Briney said of Payne's book:

> The author aims to prove that instrumental music in Christian worship is scriptural; and when I say that his effort is a complete success, I state the case conservatively. Mr. Payne builds his argument almost exclusively upon the meaning of the Greek word "psallo," which occurs in some form five times in the New Testament, and hence the Scripture sanctions the doing of whatever this word meant when the New Testament was written. The author first points out how the meaning of the Greek word "baptizo" (baptize) is ascertained, and by the same method he demonstrates (I use the term advisedly) that when the New Testament was written "psallo" carried with it the idea of the use of the instrument of music. This he does, first, by such an array of Greek lexicons as I have never seen assembled in the support of the meaning of any other word.

Notice, Brother Briney says: "The author aims to prove that instrumental music in Christian *worship* is scriptural; and when I say that his effort is a complete success, I state the case conservatively." But Brother Cowden says no church believes that instrumental music in worship is scriptural; then no church believes what J. B. Briney says Mr. Payne proves completely. I am sorry for you, brethren, but you did it yourselves. Now we have it, Brother Cowden, in your Brother Briney's own words: "Instrumental music in Christian worship is scriptural." He is a better debater than you are, and these are his own words. Remember, now, I am not asking you to defend Payne's book—I know you cannot do that; but will you defend J. B. Briney's statement of the question?

Again, the brother says: "But your committee refused to consider either of these statements, and offered instead four statements, or, rather, one statement in three forms—namely, that instrumental music is demanded, commanded, or authorized in Christian worship. We thereupon resented their offering of these statements as offensive presumption on the grounds that every person and party have the right to make their own statements of their faith and practice, and we claimed this just right, and resented their effort to deprive us of it. If we do not know what our faith and practice is, then we are not capable of discussing this question; and if we know, and would not state it correctly, then we are not worthy of discussing it. Either view was an offense; and there was no other view to take." I know you pretend it is a great offense to ask you to affirm that instrumental music is scriptural in worship, but Brother Briney says O. E. Payne proved it. Do you believe Brother Briney was right when he said that? If so, why take offense at me for asking you to affirm it in debate? And if not, why don't you say that Briney was wrong and that Mr. Payne never proved any such thing?

But hear another wail from the poster: "Note from the above that the proposition made and accepted was that we affirm our practice, and you deny the same, and vice versa." Yes, there is where the trouble always arises, because when you try to state your practice you always try to do it so no one can deny your proposition, and then hope to make some one believe you want to debate and no one will debate with you. Now let me try it with this statement before me; and to get exactly straight, I will try the "vice versa" first. We practice singing in Christian worship, and, while I do not expect my brother to deny my proposition, it is all the music we practice; so I will state in regular form an affirmative proposition which I am willing to sign:

Proposition 1. Singing is scriptural in Christian worship.

____________________________Affirms.

____________________________Denies.

Proposition 2. Playing an instrument is scriptural in Christian worship.

____________________________Affirms.

____________________________Denies.

I go to your meeting when you have met to engage in Christian worship, and you are doing this very thing—playing an instrument. Now, are you doing an unscriptural act? If so, why don't you quit? If not, why don't you affirm it? If John B. Cowden will sign the above propositions, I will undertake to have them signed in proper order. But as I am sure he cannot sign the first, for he believes it as well as I do, yet he ought to sign or get some one to sign the other, and this will be better than writing posters for free distribution.

Yes, Brother John, I wrote that letter, and you knew I wrote it, and if it was not signed it was an oversight, which you could have easily learned; but he perhaps thought that to talk about an anonymous letter would help his sensation. You would know who wrote this without my signature, but to be orderly I will let it go at the beginning of the article.

Brother Cowden either swallowed his objection to making instrumental music an integral part of worship or hushed about it, and we finally agreed on the proposition that "instrumental music in church worship is scriptural." The Commission on Unity called Brother Ira M. Boswell to take the affirmative of the proposition, while the brethren unanimously agreed that N. B. Hardeman should defend the negative. John B. Cowden was Brother Boswell's moderator, while the writer was the moderator for Brother Hardeman. The president moderator was Judge Ed. McNeilly. A good spirit prevailed throughout the entire discussion. A careful reading of the book will show the arguments relied on by each man. As far as I know, the oral discussion did no harm, but great good, and it is to be hoped that the printed book will be of great service to those who would learn the truth on the subject of how to praise God in the songs of Zion. It is a great pity that the instrument of music was ever introduced into the few churches in Nashville that use it. We who do not use the instrument in our worship are a power in this city as it is; but if those who use it were with us, we could do almost anything through Christ, who strengthens us.

F. B. SRYGLEY.

16 Academy Place, Nashville, Tenn., April 4, 1924.

RULES OF THE DISCUSSION

JUDGE ED. L. MCNEILLY, Chairman Moderator:

Ladies and Gentlemen: The importance of the question for consideration and discussion to-night is attested by the splendid audience that is assembled here, and also by the high character and the distinguished ability and the great learning of the two speakers who will participate in this debate.

Before entering upon the discussion proper, it is important that I should lay before this body the rules and principles which will govern the discussion; and for this reason I shall refer to some of the sections of the articles of agreement under which the contestants have been brought together.

It is agreed that at this time—from May 31 to June 4, 1923—five nights are to be used, in which, on each night, there will be two-hour sessions, two thirty-minute speeches each night by each speaker; the affirmative to lead, the negative to follow; the last night the affirmative to have fifteen minutes' extra time after the second negative speech of that evening, and the negative to have ten minutes' rejoinder, in which no new material shall be noticed, after the rejoinder fifteen-minute speech, which will close the discussion. It is also agreed that Hedge's "Rules of Controversy" are to govern each speaker in the discussion, and that three moderators are to be selected, who shall enforce the rules of Hedge's logic for controversy and see that each speaker is governed by the rules of honorable controversy. The affirmative is to select one moderator and the negative to select one, and these two moderators are to select a third moderator, who shall act as chairman, with power to vote in case the other two moderators fail to agree on any point of order, the third moderator not to be a member of either of the religious bodies engaged in the discussion.

Elder Cowden represents the affirmative side; Elder

Srygley represents the negative side. These two gentlemen have selected me to act as the third moderator, and my duty in ruling upon any question of order will only arise when these two respective moderators are unable to agree. They will raise all questions of order that should be settled before the speakers will be allowed to proceed, in the event such a point of order is raised.

The question that is presented for discussion will be governed as provided in the agreement in its presentation by Hedge's "Rules of Controversy." These rules are few and very simple, and I will read them to the audience in order that they may be clearly understood.

Rule 1.

Proposition: "Instrumental music in church worship is scriptural."

Rules 2, 3, 4, 5, 6, 7.

These are the rules under which this debate will be conducted. The proposition I will repeat: "Instrumental music in church worship is scriptural." The affirmative of this proposition will be maintained by the Rev. Dr. Ira M. Boswell, and the negative of the proposition will be advanced and defended by N. B. Hardeman. These two gentlemen will have the discussion, in which the affirmative will open with one speech. It will be replied to by the negative, and then the meeting will be turned over for a few minutes for devotional purposes, and then the two concluding speeches will be heard and the audience dismissed with prayer.

I now have the pleasure and the distinguished honor of introducing to you the first speaker of the evening, Rev. Ira M. Boswell, who will maintain the affirmative in this proposition.

THE NEW TESTAMENT MEANING OF PSALLO
THE WORD OF GOD FOR INSTRUMENTAL MUSIC

THE AFFIRMATIVE POSITION To Sing With or Without Instrumental Music	THE NEGATIVE POSITION To Sing Without Instrumental Music	NEUTRAL WITNESSES
PROOF	PROOF	The
1 THE PRIMARY MEANING OF WORD (a) To touch, pluck, twang, etc. (b) To play on a stringed instrument	1 THE PRIMARY MEANING OF WORD	1 Primary Meaning of Word
2 LEXICOGRAPHERS Bullinger; Trench; Liddell and Scott; Robinson; Donegan; Yonge; Bagster; Green; Greenfield; Young; Parkhurst; Harper; Thayer; Souter; Smith, etc.	2 LEXICOGRAPHERS	2 Lexicographers
3 CONTEMPORARY WRITERS The Septuagent; 150 B.C.; Strabo, 24 B.C. Plutarch, 85 A.D.; Clemens of Alex., 190 A.D.; etc	3 CONTEMPORARY WRITERS	3 Contemporary Writers
4 SCHOLARS Perrin, of Yale; Robertson, of Southern Baptist Seminary; Gotthiel, of Columbia; Hutton, of Toronto University; Bacon, of Yale; Summers, of Sheffield, England; Dahl, of Yale; Hodge, of Princeton; Ropes, of Harvard; Eakin; Hiendricks; Dickinson, Pearson, Goodspeed, Tolman, Parrock, etc.	4 SCHOLARS	4 Scholars
5 TRANSLATIONS Peshito Syriac; Coptic; German; Norwegian; Swedish; English; Moffat's; Twentieth Century; Rotherhams; etc.	5 TRANSLATIONS	5 Translations
6 COMMENTARIES Alford; Ligtfoot; Henry; Schatt; Vincent; Moule; Meyer; Weymouth; etc.	6 COMMENTARIES	6 Commentaries
7 BIBLE USAGE Ps. 33:2; 71:22; 98:5; etc.	7 BIBLE USAGE	7 Bible Usage

BOSWELL-HARDEMAN DISCUSSION

ON

INSTRUMENTAL MUSIC IN THE WORSHIP

BOSWELL'S FIRST SPEECH

(Thursday, May 31, 1923.)

President Moderator, Moderators, Brother Hardeman (I trust that I may say without any limitation whatsoever), *Brothers, and Sisters:* Just here let me offer a word of explanation—not in the sense of criticism, but that I may put myself right—that is, I never refer to myself as "Doctor." Other people call me "Doctor;" and I suppose, as the people make the colleges, the people have the right to confer degrees; but I am not a "Doctor," nor do I claim to be a "Reverend." I am not saying this as criticizing the moderator for referring to me as "the Rev. Dr.," but that none of my brethren may misunderstand, Brother Moderator.

It is a pleasure to discuss any question about which brethren differ, when that question can be discussed according to the laws laid down by our moderators, and I assure you that it shall be my earnest effort to hold myself strictly to the rules of this debate.

It is not necessary that I should take any of your time making a speech of introduction. I am not so well known in this section of the country, and I have this in store for me—the delightful pleasure of meeting a host of people that otherwise I might never meet. And so let me say to you, my good brethren, whosoever you may be, whether you agree with me or not in this discussion, I sincerely trust that in your heart and in my heart there shall only be the kindliest feelings, such as should exist among brethren who love the same Lord Jesus Christ and who hold earnestly, faithfully, without one single doubt in any way, to the word of the living God.

I believe absolutely in the Bible, not as containing the word of God, but as being the word of God; and as much as any man of my generation, I am, I believe—and I say this by way of explanation—faithful to what we call the "Restoration Movement," that movement out of which this great people have come and which makes possible this, may I say, historic occasion.

Having met each other, I shall call attention to the particular thing for which we have met—that is, to find out the facts in the proposition we are to discuss. I take it that if we are discussing a thing, trying to find its meaning, we are supposed to be in an attitude in which we are ready to receive and to accept all evidence, regardless of the direction that evidence may point. In other words, if there be brought to my attention during this discussion, and to the attention of my brethren, evidence to convince us we are wrong, as honest men, as Christian men, we must accept that evidence. If, on the other hand, we shall bring evidence to show that we are right—not that you are wrong, but that we are right—then I take it that you also should accept and act upon that evidence. Otherwise I see no good that can come of such a discussion as this. I take it that my good brother has not the time, and I know I have not the time, to come here just to talk. We are here for business; and if I know my own heart, brethren, we are here on the King's business. If I did not believe with all my heart that I was here on the business of my Lord, I would not be here; it would not be right for me to be here.

Allow me to call your attention to the subject, which is: "Instrumental music in church worship is scriptural." I do not believe much discussion on this point is necessary; but I wish to read one short paragraph—scarcely a paragraph, just a sentence or two—that will, I think, give sufficient definition to the subject.

If I understand correctly—all arrangements were made while I was in Kentucky—if I understand, the only point at issue in arranging the discussion was in reference to worship; and that, I believe, has been interpreted by the committee. I shall read the understanding as I have it: "Instrumental music is in the worship only in the sense of being an item to the public service or ritual of worship." In other words, let me right here at the beginning say: I have not come down here to discuss any point that involves an instrument as being a part of the worship itself; in other words, to affirm that we worship with the instrument. I think that is clear. I think that is the understanding of the question. You cannot see this chart we have, but the affirmative position, the position which I occupy, the position which I am endeavoring to sustain, "To sing with or without instrumental music is scriptural," is printed on it.

Here I wish to introduce—I read it so that I may get it just right—a statement from a representative and leading brother on the other side of this question: "Now, this is the proper way to come at an argument, and the only way in which to settle the question as it should be settled, and we here say"—I am quoting from a leader who is opposing the affirmative of this proposition; not Brother Hardeman, but another leader among his brethren—"and we here say, with all frankness that we can command, that if Christ, by his word, to say nothing of his deeds and character, tells us in any way, shape, form, or fashion that we are permitted to use instrumental music in the worship, that will settle it at once and forever with us, and never another word of objection against the practice will we utter." I take it that this was uttered in the utmost frankness and without any moral or mental reservation whatsoever.

It was a custom, brethren, among the fathers in this movement, when they desired to discover a truth, just what the New Testament taught, to go to the words used by the inspired writers. We understand, all of us, that the New Testament was not written in the English language; that the New Testament which we read is a translation from the language used at the time of the apostles and the apostolic writers. This language was the language of the common people. It was the dialect of that day.

If you remember, time and time again you have heard our preachers say, among other things that constituted the fullness of time when Jesus came, there was a universal language—a language that was spoken all over the world at that time. Wherever a man would go, this language was spoken, and this language was understood; so that when an apostle spoke in Jerusalem, wherever his words went, the people of that day understood just what the apostle meant. And so if we wish to discover what the apostle meant when he used a certain word, we must go back to the time that word was used and find out what it meant; and whatever was the meaning at that time, that must be the meaning to us.

I think that is clear, and I am sure we all understand it. There is a certain word used by the apostle Paul. We have that word translated in the English version "sing" and "sing praises." Once it is translated "make melody." It is "psallo," and that is the word about which this discussion, if it comes to a discussion concerning a word, about which this discussion must be; and so we have gone to the care and trouble of preparing a chart, to which I call your attention.

Here we have the affirmative position: "To sing with or without instrumental music is scriptural." We have placed opposite the negative position. I merely read that. That is for the negative speaker to state for himself. The negative position: "To sing without instrumental music." That is the difference that exists between us, the difference that is keeping us separated to-day and yesterday, but I trust will not always keep us separated. Instrumental music, with or without, to sing with or without instrumental music, is the affirmative. The negative position is, to sing without instrumental music.

We have put proof here, and proof which we wish to offer; and the first proof that I desire to present to you tonight is the primary meaning of the word "psallo."

As far as my brother is concerned, I take it that it is not necessary to present the primary meaning of this word to arrive at a better conception of the word itself; but for the sake of getting before you more conclusively the idea in the word, I shall take up the primary meaning of "psallo."

Now, I believe I am safe in saying this: that while words

do change, they do not lose entirely their original or primary meaning; that meaning holds on, stays with it, throughout all of its life. I think I am safe in saying that. I shall risk it, anyway—that a word holds, in a way, whether it is used literally or figuratively, its primary meaning.

When we get the primary meaning of this word, we can understand better the meaning that the apostles had in mind when they used it in the New Testament. With this in mind, I present for your consideration a few authorities on the primary meaning of "psallo." These authorities, I take it, will not be disputed.

Wright: "Ψάλλω [psallo], I cause vibration, touch; discharge an arrow; scrape; pluck."

"Ψαλμός [psalmos], playing on a harp; air played on a harp, hymn; twang of the string."

Pickering: "Ψάλλω [psallo], to touch gently; to touch or play on a stringed instrument; to cause to vibrate; to play."

"Psalmos, the twang of a bowstring; striking the chords of a musical instrument; playing and singing to the psaltery."

Dunbar: "Ψάλλω [psallo], to touch gently; to touch or play on a stringed instrument; to sing; to celebrate with hymns."

"Ψαλμός [psalmos], the twang of a bowstring; a playing on a stringed instrument, singing to the psaltery."

Hamilton: "Ψάλλω [psallo], to touch, pull, pluck, cause to vibrate, play on a stringed instrument."

"Ψαλμός [psalmos], playing on a harp, twang of a string, strain of music."

Greek-English Vocabulary, Oxford Press: "Psallo, to touch, pull, twitch, to pluck, to twang; to play (i. e., a stringed instrument) with the finger (i. e., instead of with plectrum) ; to sing to a harp."

"Psalmos, a pulling or twanging with the fingers; the sound of the harp; any strain of music; a song sung to a stringed instrument, a psalm."

Prellwitz: "Psallo, I strike (the strings of the bow, the musical strings)."

"Psalmos, string-playing."

Maltby's Greek Gradus: "Ψάλλω [psallo], to strike gently; 2, to pull the strings of a bow, or of a harp; 3, to praise."

Zorell: "Psallo, I play on a stringed instrument, strike the cithara with the fingers; sing a hymn to the notes of the lyre."

"Psalmos, sound of the lyre; song to the sound of the strings, song to be sung to the strings, song to be sung to the sound of the lyre."

These are some of the lexicographers who give us the primary meaning of this word.

Now, I wish to get into your mind—and I am sure you have it—that these are not men who were particularly interested or interested at all in the discussion we have on hand to-night; they were men who were Greek scholars, simply looking to the meaning of the word, and have given us the meaning. There runs through this word the meaning which I have given to you, reading from these authorities.

We heard our moderator say that all authorities must be open for inspection, and that no authority should be presented that could not be so presented that any one who desires may see the authority that has been quoted here in this discussion.

Now, the thing that I have had in mind is simply this, brethren: to show you the primary meaning of "psallo." Understand, get me here. I am not saying that this is a New Testament meaning. This has to do with the meaning of the word in the New Testament only as this is the word used in the New Testament. I am reading to you the statements of the lexicons as to the primary meaning of the word. I have said that a word never loses its primary meaning entirely. I have good authority for that, and the authority will be produced at the proper time. I do not mean to say that the word has not changed; I do not mean to say that the word does not take on some meaning that it did not have before; I am simply saying that the primary meaning—that meaning which is in the word, that gives the word its meaning, that gives the word its loneliness, if you please, and yet at the same time reaches out and touches all other words in the language—that meaning continues and holds in the word; and what is it? It is to touch, to pluck; it may be a pulling out of the hair; it may be the pulling of a bow, the string of a bow; it may be the striking of the strings of a harp; it may be the plucking of the string the carpenter uses in his work. It means all these, and it means all these as we read about it to-night in these lexicons. It finally comes to mean to play upon a musical instrument.

I take it, friends, that you have that in mind; and I shall not tarry longer on the meaning, the primary meaning, of the word, but at once proceed to present to you the meaning of the word in the New Testament. Now, I want you to hold in mind—

MODERATOR: You have only six minutes.

MR. BOSWELL: Six minutes. I want you to hold in mind this—and it is well to keep these things in mind, because we are going to be here for several nights—that if we can find one word—and, brethren, we do not need that any one should say that if we can find in the holy word of God one single word that gives us the right to use instrumental music in the worship, in the church worship—if we can find one single word, it is scriptural, and our liberty cannot be overthrown.

God does not have to use all the words in his vocabulary to express a thing to us, to make it sure and steadfast. As far as I am concerned, one unequivocal statement from my Heavenly Father is sufficient for me; and I say that to you with all frankness; and I say to you that if that is true of my own heart, it must be true of every man and woman who loves the Lord Jesus Christ in all sincerity. Prejudice and pride and all such things should have no effect in preventing that word free access to our hearts.

Now, this word, we propose to show, is in the New Testament. I am not talking about "singing," I am not talking about "making melody;" I am talking about the word in the New Testament that has been translated "make melody," been translated "sing." I am not talking about the word that has come through translation, but the word itself. Here I wish to present to you some of the lexicographers who refer particularly and specifically to its use in the New Testament. Bearing in mind its primary use, listen to its new Testament use.

This is Bullinger: "A playing, music; in later usage, a song accompanied." I am talking about "psallo," the same word I discussed a few moments ago.

Trench says: "And, last of all, the song sung with this musical accompaniment."

Then we have Liddell & Scott, speaking of "psallo," verb, second definition: "Later, to sing to a harp." They give the New Testament meaning, "To sing to a harp," and refer to Eph. 5: 19; 1 Cor. 14: 15. "Singing and making melody." (Eph. 5: 19.) The two words, "making melody," are translated from "psallontes," from "psallo," the word we are discussing. "To sing to a harp." (Liddell & Scott.)

I do not need at this time to emphasize the standing of these lexicographers. Those who are acquainted with a subject like this know their standing in the world of scholarship.

Then we have Robinson, speaking of "psallo" in the New Testament: "To sing, accompanying stringed instrument." Of "psalmos," "in later usage," he says: "Song accompanying stringed instruments."

Then Donnegan: "By later writers, hymn, or ode, sung accompanied by harp."

All these are testifying concerning the meaning of the word in the New Testament—the word that you really have back, if you know the word, of your mind, every time you read the New Testament, where it is translated "sing" three times, "sing praises" once, and once it is translated "make melody." It is used five times in the New Testament.

There are certain authorities who are a little stronger than the ones just read, and I wish to read these, because I think it is wise to get the strongest. These are the lexicographers who use the word "absolutely." Now, when we are quoting lexicographers, we must say what they say. These say: "Absolutely to play on a stringed instrument, to sing to music." These are the lexicographers who testify that the word means "absolutely" and are defining the word used in the New Testament. They are Bagster, Green, Greenfield, Robinson, Liddell & Scott, Thayer. Webster says, defining "absolutely:" "Free from all limit, restriction, or qualification."

Now we will take some others that refer to its use in the New Testament.

Young: "To sing praise with musical instruments. (Rom. 15: 9; 1 Cor. 14: 15.)" These scriptures are all familiar to you.

Westcott & Hort: "To strike a musical instrument, to sing hymns. (James 5: 13; Eph. 5: 19; Rom. 15: 9; 1 Cor. 14: 15.)"

Thayer: "The leading idea of *psalmos* is a musical accompaniment. (1 Cor. 14: 26.)"

Yonge: "In the New Testament, to sing while touching the chords, while accompanying oneself on a stringed instrument, to sing psalms. (Rom. 15: 9.)" "*Psalmos*. 1. The music of stringed instruments. 2. A song sung to the accompaniment of music." "*Psallein*, from *psao*, *psallere*, properly to touch the strings of a bow, or of an instrument of music, to play on a stringed instrument."

Do you get the force of these statements? Do you hear what these scholars are saying? Not your speaker, for your speaker is not a scholar, and your speaker's word is not worth any more than any other man's word is worth concerning these things. These are scholars, and we have to listen to the words of scholarship when we are in their particular realm.

HARDEMAN'S FIRST SPEECH

(Thursday, May 31, 1923.)

Brethren, Moderators, Ladies, and Gentlemen: I congratulate myself especially to-night because, in the providence of God, we are privileged to meet the engagement made of our own accord, and I want to assure the people of Nashville that I am not unmindful of their high regard for things spiritual. I appreciate you because of your anxiety to investigate things that are sacred, because of your respect for the word of the Lord and your reverence for Jehovah. In coming to you to-night, ladies and gentlemen, I want also to congratulate you, as well as Brother Boswell, upon the spirit of the introductory remarks by him made. I trust that every person in this audience is well aware of the fact that we have met to deal with things that are not transient or ephemereal in their nature, but that are eternal in their everlasting issues—matters that do not appeal to the light, to the flippant, or to the frivolous, but to such as are to be characterized by the greatest solemnity and by that dignity and respect that dependent people ought to sustain to the God of their being.

I am glad that Brother Boswell has evidenced the characteristics that the subject demands, and I want to assure you, as well as him, that it shall be my chief purpose and whole intention to hold this discussion upon a high plane, and, if possible, to relieve and to remove the prejudice that sometimes exists in the minds of people with reference to religious discussions. Of all the means and avenues of finding out just what the truth is, it does seem to me that no better method has ever been suggested; but because sometimes the disputants forget themselves and in the heat of their argument lose self-control and say things that they ought not, many have lost respect for all kinds of religious controversy. Let me say again that it shall be my earnest endeavor to join Brother Boswell in having one discussion where all of such may be eliminated and the best of feeling may prevail from start to finish.

May I suggest to you, my friends, further, that I think Brother Boswell did not spend that time in defining all the terms of the debate that was due him as the affirmant of this proposition; and I submit to you that, in harmony with Rule No. 1 previously read, the terms in which the proposition for debate are presented and the precise point at issue shall be made so clear that there can be no dispute nor no possibility of failing to grasp the same.

Instrumental music was not defined. I take it that he assumed a clear understanding; but to help you to see the point, as I am sure he will agree thereto, he has reference to a *mechanical* instrument made by the hands of men. "Instrumental music in church worship is scriptural"—this is the proposition; and when he suggested a certain agreement with reference to what the term in the worship meant, I was at a loss to know what he meant; for with me and Brother Boswell no such agreement has ever been suggested or hinted at, in person, by correspondence, or otherwise. The proposition was sent to my home. I signed it, believing that it meant what it said—"*in the worship*." Brother Boswell is not clear in his statements as to how the instrument is connected with the worship. I simply call attention now to that fact, with the hope that he may enlarge and make positively clear what he means by the worship—just outline and distinguish to us in any way as he may see fit the association or the relation that the instrument may have in the act of worship.

The proposition suggests that it is in the worship, on the inside, within, and, from the formal statement of the matter, would necessarily constitute a part thereof; and, furthermore, the next words that need attention are "is" and "scriptural." The proposition is: "Instrumental music in church worship is scriptural." Not that it was, not that it shall be; but under the dispensation in which we now live, under the reign of Christ, in the New Testament, which both of us regard to be our rule of faith and practice, that, in the present age, it is scriptural. But he tells not what he meant by scriptural, and hence I must wait until the next address to get matters of that kind.

Just at this point I want to suggest to you this fact: I know that as a negative speaker the right to propound queries is granted. On the other hand, I am conscious of the fact that the negative speaker can load down the affirmant with a series of questions, which might be unfair, and I assure you that I have no disposition to do that. But that the matter may come squarely before us, that the precise point may be clearly understood, I have prepared in advance of to-night a few questions which I now read and want to hand to Brother Boswell, with ample opportunity afforded him to get an answer, that all may know exactly the thing for which we are striving and the position to be assumed by each.

1. Can Eph. 5: 19; 1 Cor. 14: 15; Rom. 15: 9; and James 5: 13 be obeyed and complied with without the use of the instrument?

2. Do you agree with Brother H. L. Calhoun, president of Bethany College, West Virginia, when he says: "It will be admitted that the New Testament nowhere mentions the use of an instrument in connection with the singing in the church. This fact settles, beyond all dispute, that the use of an instrument in connection with the singing in the church cannot be an act of acceptable worship; for it fails to fulfill one of the essential conditions of an act of acceptable worship, and that condition which it fails to fulfill is the thing that differentiates an act of acceptable worship from an act which is not acceptable. Worship by means of instruments to-day is not in truth, and, therefore, cannot be such as God seeks or accepts."

3. Do you believe that instrumental music is demanded, commanded, or authorized in Christian worship?

4. Is it authorized by God or by man?

5. (a) If by God, can the instrument be omitted with impunity? (b) If by man, is it, therefore, scriptural?

6. Is instrumental music a part of the worship?

7. Do you agree with your moderator, Brother John B.

Cowden, who says: "Instrumental music is in the church, but not in the worship?"

8. Do you agree with O. E. Payne, in whose compilations numbers of lexicons have been quoted, when Brother Payne says, "It is impossible to 'psallein' without a musical instrument," and that "if we forego musical instruments, we cannot conform to the divine injunction to 'psallein?' "

9. Was the *Christian Standard,* the paper representing Brother Boswell's side of the question, right when it said, regarding Payne's book, that it leads to the "overwhelming conviction that not only was instrumental music allowed in the worship of the primitive church, but that it was positively enjoined?"

10. Do you agree with Brother Briney, who says of Brother Payne: "The author intended and aims to prove that instrumental music in Christian worship is scriptural; and when I say his effort is a complete success, I state the case conservatively. He demonstrates (and I use the term advisedly) that when the New Testament was written 'psallo' carried with it the idea of the instrument of music." Was this as a "privilege" or as a "duty?"

11. Does the instrument inhere in "psallo?"

12. Is the use of the instrument in the worship to please God or man?

13. Please state your position so clearly and define it so accurately that there can be no dispute or possibility of misunderstanding.

Ladies and gentlemen, the Restoration Movement referred to by Brother Boswell began about the first of the nineteenth century. It was a movement to bring order out of chaos, an effort on the part of men who were disgusted with denominational rivalry and the general state of confusion that then existed, and who believed confidently that the prayer of the Savior ought to be considered, and professed Christians ought, to the very best of their ability, to bring about the answer thereto. They started out to find a basis upon which unity and oneness among God's people could be had, and that principle, incorporated in the fewest possible words that I may be able to express it, was that we find some ground that is common, some principle that is catholic in nature, that all can accept. With the Bible, and the Bible alone, as their guide, they accepted the statement that "we speak where the Bible speaks, and are silent where the Bible is silent." Adopting this as their motto and principle, they started out to find common ground on which all professed followers of the Lord could unite, and at the same time not sacrifice any matter of faith.

Now, to illustrate, they said that "baptizo" means to immerse; that immersion is common ground; that sprinkling and pouring are not universally accepted; that the whole world indorses immersion—all men could believe it and really did believe it. There is the ground for union. Immersion, therefore, was not in dispute, but the question for all these years has been whether or not sprinkling and pouring will suffice or can be accepted scripturally as a substitute.

Again, it was a question to find common ground on the *subject* of baptism, and they laid down the principle that penitent believers should be baptized. The entire world accepts that. The question that is in doubt and in dispute is, and has been, whether or not other than penitent believers were gospel subjects. But all men can accept the first statement; and, therefore, it is the catholic, or common, ground.

With reference to human names and human creeds, they laid down the name "Christian," and said that every follower of Christ on earth could adopt that and not sacrifice a matter of faith; with reference to discipline, the Bible, and the Bible alone; with reference to worship, it was to be governed and guided purely by that which is taught in the New Testament, and without authority therefor, or plain, express declaration in a form unquestioned, nothing was to be had.

Now, I submit to you to-night, ladies and gentlemen, Brother Boswell in principle has violated the very fundamental idea of the Restoration Movement, because publicly, orally, and on his chart he admits that the worship of God may be had without a musical instrument. Every professed follower of Christ on earth, so far as I know, accepts that statement. There is common ground. The thing that is in doubt, and the thing that divides the people of God and violates the very foundation principle of the Restoration Movement, is the injection into the worship, by Brother Boswell and by others who favor his side of the question, the use of mechanical instruments. The result is, a once happy, whole-hearted, concerted, and united brotherhood has been torn asunder. Strife, division, and bitterness have characterized the pathway of what ought to have been a united and harmonious movement, seeking to restore the primitive practice of apostolic days, which was carried on for a period after the days of Stone and of Campbell and of others for more than fifty years without mechanical instruments. There was a solid phalanx. Why? Because they were governed by the catholic principle, by common ground; they all said they could worship God without the instrument, and thus they did; and when it was first introduced into a church in the city of St. Louis, a committee was appointed to investigate the matter and to make recommendations; and that committee, occupying the principle of common ground still, reported that the instrument be removed, which was temporarily done, and the division was passed over. But the spirit developed and the demand grew, until by and by, over the protests, over the pleadings, and over the prayers of faithful, godly men, there were introduced into the churches instruments of music, which Brother Boswell himself has already admitted in his first speech are not essential to the worship of God. The result is the divided condition found in the city of Nashville and all over this land and country of ours to-day. In about 1858 there was a melodeon used in the church at Midway, Ky. ("Life of Benjamin Franklin," page 409.) Another was used in the church at Cleveland, Ohio, as early as 1867. But little attention was given at the first introduction, and they were usually removed, only to be brought in again as sentiment could be developed.

May I suggest to you, ladies and gentlemen, that it is but little short of a tragedy to the cause of Christ for such a state of affairs to exist to-night; and I would to God that this debate should result in striking hands with the restorers and the fathers of bygone days in accepting the declaration: "We will stand together and we will worship together on that which is common ground." You admit that the position that I occupy is a scriptural, safe, sound position. Let's unite, therefore, by discarding that which you yourself state to be a nonessential and not absolutely necessary. And may I insist, in harmony with the splendid speech Brother Boswell made and the fine spirit characteristic of it, if union is sought, peace is sought, and harmony is to prevail, Brother Boswell should give up that which divides and stand on common ground. Then heart to heart and hand to hand we will walk down the aisles as a solid phalanx against every evil, and may God hasten the day when the cause of the Restoration will sweep from center to circumference of this fair land of ours.

Ladies and gentlemen, the principle involved in this matter is broader than perhaps you know. It is a question to-night as to the respect you and I shall have for the word of God. Shall we be governed by what God says, or shall we be left every man to do after that which is in his own heart? Shall we go upon the principle of acting upon the silence of the Bible, or shall we be governed by God's word? Now, I may suggest to you, in review of some of the things Brother Boswell suggested, this idea further: He puts upon the chart, and states it for me, as the negative side of the question, that we contend to-night that the word "psallo" means the singing of praise without an instrument, and in that Brother Boswell misrepresents the negative side of the question—not intentionally so, but from a lack of understanding just what the negative believes.

Let me submit to you that in the study of the word to which attention was called and reference was made there are matters that you and I ought to get clearly before us; and if this discussion is to turn upon the word "psallo," I hope that you may get a clear understanding of the same. Words have etymological, primary, and original meanings; and then they have, as was suggested to you, an applied meaning, or a meaning according to the usage of the time in which the things are presented. The word "psallo" from the lexicons is defined to-night under two heads—first, with reference to its primary meaning, its classical use; and then its New Testament, or applied, use. The Greek word "psallo," from the best evidence that can be gathered—and he need not, neither need I, refer to a multiplicity of lexicons. One or two standard scholars of that type will suffice. Liddell & Scott stand at the very topmost round in classic Greek. I need not tell those who know to-night that Thayer's lexicon stands as the very highest authority in New Testament Greek. What is the meaning of this word as determined by them?

Etymologically and primarily "psallo" means to pull, or to pull out, as the hair. Brother Boswell does not think that is what it means in the New Testament; of course not. Second, it means to twang, with reference to the bowstring, as you pull the string back, let go the arrow. There is the idea of "psallo." Neither of us believes that it means that in the New Testament. Third, it means to twitch, as taking hold of a carpenter's line, chalked, and then letting it go. We do not think that it means that to-night as applied to the New Testament. Then, again, it means to touch the strings of the harp; and Brother Boswell even does not think that it means that, but he applies that meaning and makes the word "harp" a synonym or the representative of other musical instruments made by the hands of men. The word means to sing—to sing to the accompaniment of an instrument.

But the question to-night, and the only one for consideration, is: What, under the New Testament, is the instrument that accompanies the singing? The apostle Paul, in his peerless announcement, settled that once for all. He says we are to sing unto the Lord and "psallo" with the heart—not with the fingers, not with the plectron, but with the heart; and, therefore, the heart is the instrument that accompanies the singing.

But for the fact that Paul mentions specifically the heart as the instrument, there might be some ground for the furtherance of the discussion; and so, then, on the word "psallo," bear it in mind evermore that Paul said that the instrument upon which the "psalloing" is done is the human heart (Eph. 5: 19), and that without that there can be no "psalloing," and beyond that the New Testament gives no authority whatsoever.

But I suggest to you another matter just along in connection with that. The New Testament lexicons of the very highest type give the following statements: Bagster—"*Psallo,* to move by a touch, to twitch; to touch or strike the strings or chords of an instrument; to sing to music. In New Testament, to sing praises. (Rom. 15: 9; 1 Cor. 14: 15; Eph. 5: 19; James 5: 13.)"

Now, I call attention to this fact: Mr. Bagster very well said: "In the classic use, in the general use, it means to touch, as to touch a bowstring, or it means to pull, as a carpenter's line, or a hair." And then when he came to the New Testament, he said, "In the New Testament use of it, it means to sing praises," and quotes Eph. 5: 19. Accompanied by what? Accompanied by the heart as the instrument; and, therefore, the question is forever settled. But, again, he read from Thayer, who also stands at the very top of all New Testament Greek lexicographers, when he said it means to pull off, or a plucking out, as of the hair; it means to cause to vibrate by touch, and absolutely to play on a stringed instrument; absolutely means, without limitation, as Brother Boswell stated, positively and without any bearing, to play upon an instrument.

Now, the question between us is this, and can be reduced to a matter of the utmost simplicity: Brother Boswell, is the instrument the hair? That is one instrument in the word. Is the instrument the bowstring? Is the instrument the carpenter's line? Is the instrument the strings of a harp? If so, where would you ever get any wind instrument by any means? Or is the instrument the human heart? Let us let the Bible forever settle that. Paul, what do you say about that? It is not the plucking or the "psalloing" of the hair; it is not the "psalloing" of a bowstring; it is not the plucking or twitching of a cord or the plucking of the carpenter's line; it is not the twanging or the twitching of an instrument of artificial mechanism; but it is the touching or the twanging or "psalloing" of the heart, and that is the thing upon which the "psalloing" is done.

And it ought to be once for all conceded, in reference to the truth of the question before us to-night, that the word, as applied in the New Testament, carries with it the instrument mentioned by Paul; and that instrument is not the hair, not the bowstring, not the carpenter's line, nor that of a mechanical instrument, but the strings of the human heart.

And this is the testimony of the highest authority in the lexical field to-day, as well as substantiated and declared by Paul himself.

But may I submit to you this idea: In the five times used in the New Testament, the word "psallo" not one single, solitary time is ever translated by the King James or by the Revised Version "to play." These men, about one hundred and fifty in number, represented the scholarship of the world. They were selected and appointed because of their scholarship; and when they came to the rendition of the word "psallo" and to the translation thereof, without exception, without a dissenting voice, they rendered it "to sing, to make melody." Where? In the human heart.

I thank you.

BOSWELL'S SECOND SPEECH

(Thursday, May 31, 1923.)

Brother Moderator: I received with a good deal of pleasure the communication or letter handed me by Brother Hardeman, and shall give it my attention later. You would hardly expect me to get a lengthy letter and number of questions like that and answer them offhand, especially when I am going to answer every one of them before this debate or discussion is over. Every single question is involved in the discussion which we are to have. I am sorry that I did not make myself so thoroughly understood that Brother Hardeman could understand what I meant. I think he makes the statement that I did not state whether or not I believed the instruments could be left out. I believe if you will look up there [at the chart], you will see that is exactly what I stated. The affirmative position is: "To sing with or without instrumental music." There it is on the chart, and that is exactly what I said.

I know nothing about Brother Hardeman's communications with the brethren on his side of the question. I do know that I was given to understand—and that is a matter that will have to be left to the moderators—that this matter in reference to the terms of the question under discussion had been settled. I was very particular—he says I did not make myself understood—I was very particular to say, Brother Hardeman, that we do not—I do not use the instrument as a worshiping thing; that it is simply an accompaniment to the worship. I think I clearly made that statement, or made that statement very clearly.

I will answer all the other questions at the proper time, but I believe I ought to answer at this time some of the things in his splendid sermon which he has just delivered in reply to my argument.

A great deal of the movement with which we are now connected had its origin in and near Georgetown. I am preaching for perhaps the oldest church in our brotherhood in existence to-day, the old church that was established by Barton W. Stone. Raccoon John Smith, Thomas and Alexander Campbell, Walter Scott, John T. Johnson preached there; and all the hallowed memories of these and other mighty men still hang about that grand old church of Christ. I am in sympathy with the Restoration Movement. I think I understand it. I have been giving a great deal of time to the study of it there on the ground. I wish to ask Brother Hardeman, or, rather, I wish to state that I understood him to say—I am not sure that he did—that sprinkling and pouring were substitutions for baptism, and that after the same method we substitute the organ for singing. I do not know whether he intended to make it appear that we substituted the organ for singing or not. I am sure that if he did, he is mistaken; and I think that he will take our word when we say that we do not substitute the organ for the singing. I think I ought to know; but if it can be proved against me, of course I shall have to bear the burden. And when we say we do not substitute the organ for singing—there is no analogy between the two cases whatsoever—our affirmation must stand until the negative has been proved.

I do not intend to pay any attention whatsoever to much of his speech to-night, for the simple reason that all that he has said will be answered in course of time; but there is one thing that he said that has its appeal to me, and I feel that appeal. I am just as sincere in my desire for the union of God's people, if I know my heart, as any other man. He said: "Now, Brother Boswell, give up the organ and come on in and let us all go along together." Well, are you united? What about Brother Sommer and his position on the Bible school? What about our good friends of the *Firm Foundation,* who do not believe in the use of the organ, but who believe in rebaptism? What about our good brother, Robert Boll, and these various other divisions in your own ranks, brethren?

I would not have called attention to this; it was not in my heart to do so; but when you come to me and say, "Brother Boswell, come on in with us and we will all be together," I ask you: Are you together at this particular time? Are you not divided to-night by as many schisms as any other people? I have received, since this discussion was announced, letters from various parts of the country, with tracts showing that you brethren are not united, except on the one particular thing that is in controversy here, and that is the organ itself.

I think the question under discussion is so simple—and you are correct in that, Brother Hardeman—I think it is so simple that anybody can understand it. In fact, I think all the terms of this discussion are so simple that anybody can understand them. He asked me what I meant by instrumental music. Instrumental music is music made on an instrument, and you cannot make it on anything else.

Now, the purpose of the music is a vastly different thing. Let us draw a distinction. Instrumental music is made on an instrument, but the righteousness of the music or the evil of the music depends upon the purpose and the character of the music.

I wish to continue a while discussing matters concerning these lexicons and their value, and call your attention to the other things later on. But we do not wish to get away from the word we are discussing to-night—"psallo." I am very thankful to Brother Hardeman for admitting that "psallo" still has this meaning in the New Testament: "to strike the string." It still has this meaning, and I do not wish you to get away from his admission. I wish you to hold on to it.

And there is another thing I wish you to hold in your hearts; that is, if it can be proved that the instrument here is not the instrument he thinks it is—there is a great deal in our contention on this point to-night—if it can be proved to you that the words translated here "making melody in the heart" do not mean to play on the human heart—this point will be given especial attention before this discussion is over—if it can be proved that "making melody in the heart" does not mean playing on the human heart, that it is the instrument you "strike the strings of," and these are his own words, "You strike the strings of the harp, which is your heart, and that is the only harp"—if, then, it can be proved that the heart is not the harp, and there must be another musical instrument, I think my brother will have the opportunity to decide whether or not we will just lay the whole thing aside and come on in and all be united upon the word of the living God.

"Psallo." I was reading Yonge in my first speech, "a playing on stringed instrument." This refers to classical usage. I am reading all, whether it seems to be just what I want or not. I cannot change it, brethren. And here let me say that the word "psallo" came to mean—and proof will be produced at the proper time—to mean instrumental music. I will prove by authority that you cannot deny without going back upon some of the very best of your own leaders that it came to mean instrumental music.

Yonge: "*Psallein,* from *psao, psallere,* properly to touch the strings of a bow or of an instrument of music; to play on a stringed instrument. In the New Testament, to sing while touching the chords, while accompanying oneself on a stringed instrument, to sing psalms. (Rom. 15: 9.)"

I am not disturbed over what this word means. If a word in the New Testament means whatever it may mean, then it is my duty to-day to do that, regardless of the consequences. The word "baptism" means a certain thing, and we are commanded to do what that word requires, regardless of the consequences; and whatever may have been our opinion has nothing to do with it. We must find out what this word means in the New Testament, brethren; and whatever it means in the New Testament, it means to every one of us, and we cannot get around it. That is our position, Brother Srygley; that is our decision. Whatever it means in the New Testament, that is what it means to you and to me; and if I have to play on a harp to measure up to the full meaning of the New Testament statement, I would have to play on a harp. That is all there is to it. Now, get that. That is how far I go in my loyalty to the New Testament. But I do not have to play on the harp. "Psallo" is not limited to the music of stringed instruments. Now, listen: "To sing, sing to the accompaniment of music." It does not say "stringed music."

Robinson: "*Psallo,* to touch, to twitch, to pluck the hair of the head or beard." Now, of course, brethren, we know it is not a religious exercise to pull your hair out; and I admit frankly to-night that if pulling out the hair was in the New Testament, we would have to pull out our hair; but there are some people who would soon get out of the New Testament, because they could not pull very long. So we will just say we know it does not mean that. It means playing on a musical instrument, in the New Testament. "Also to strike, to twang—e. g., the string of a bow; especially of a stringed instrument of music; to touch or strike the chord. Hence, oftenest, absolutely, *psallein,* to touch the lyre or other stringed instrument. In Septuagint and New Testament, to sing, to chant, properly as accompanying stringed instruments." That is Robinson.

Liddell & Scott: "The noun, *psalmos* (Ψαλμός), a touching, sharply, a pulling, twitching, or twanging with the fingers. Later, a song sung to the harp, a psalm. LXX., N. T."

I do not deny the standing of Thayer; I do not for one moment deny it. The only thing I deny is that Thayer does not belong right over along where we have him. I am going to prove that Thayer belongs in the column where we have him placed. He does not belong in his column.

Brother Hardeman, as I turn to introduce this—I pause just a moment—says that I do not correctly state him. I think he took the position that to sing without instrumental music was scriptural—to sing without it. If that is not his position, I misunderstood him; and maybe we believe the same thing, after all, because if Brother Hardeman believes you can worship without it, and I believe you can worship with or without it, and he believes we can worship with or without it, then all we shall have to do is to get together and arrange the terms. That is all. Then, why this debate or discussion? Where is the difference, brethren?

Now, let us take Parkhurst: "*Psallo.* 1. To touch, to touch lightly, or perhaps to cause to quaver by touching. 2. To touch the strings of a musical instrument with the finger or plectron, and so cause them to sound or quaver. So musicians who play upon an instrument are said to *psallein,* to touch the strings, or simply *psallein,* and because stringed instruments were commonly used both by believers and heathen in singing praises to their respective gods, hence to sing, sing praises or psalms to God, whether with or without instruments. (Rom. 15: 9; 1 Cor. 14: 15; Eph. 5: 19; James 5: 13.)"

Now I ask a question. He asked me a question. I have the same right. If in the New Testament I find the authority to worship without the organ, what right have you to say I shall not worship that way? If, according to the New Testament, I have the right to use the organ in the service of the church, in the worship of the church—you and I understand what we mean by "worship," so far as we usually define it—to come into the church building and have our service—I am willing to take that for the definition; we come into the church and worship and use the organ as an accompaniment to the worship—if the New Testament gives me this right, by what authority does Brother Hardeman, or any other brother, say I must not exercise that right?

If, after all, Brother Hardeman says we can sing without it or sing with it—I do not say he says that; I am saying that he says I did not correctly represent him when I read from the chart, "to sing without the instrument"—if it be that we can sing with or without it; I say he can sing without it, and I will fellowship him as a brother; why say I cannot sing with it and refuse to fellowship me as a brother? That is the difference between us to-night, and the thing I want you to get. It is a question of liberty in Christ.

Coming back to Parkhurst: "*Psalmos.* 1. A touching or playing upon a musical instrument. 2. A psalm, a sacred song or poem, properly such an one as is sung to stringed instruments. (See Luke 20: 42; 1 Cor. 14: 26.)"

Fortunately for the truth, there is an up-to-date lexicon (1922) that gives decisive testimony upon this question. Its author is G. Abbott Smith, D.D., D.C.L., "Professor of New Testament Literature in the Montreal Diocesan Theological College and Assistant Professor in the Oriental Department in McGill University." This lexicon is especially devoted to New Testament Greek, and in defining "psalmos," a New Testament word, it says: "And hence in later writers, (2) a sacred song sung to musical accompaniment, a psalm (LXX.). (1 Cor. 14: 26; Eph. 5: 19; Col. 3: 16.)" Thus this very latest authority directly refutes the unlearned claim of unscholarly men that this word repudiated the idea that there is no mechanical instrument in the word.

Now, then, I wish to read again from this Greek lexicon of the New Testament by G. Abbott Smith—I have it right handy here—under "psallo:" "To pull, touch, twang, as a bowstring, to play a stringed instrument with the fingers; later, to sing to the harp; sing songs; sing a hymn; sound praises, psalms, chiefly striking or twitching with the finger; hence a striking of musical strings, and hence in later writings a *sacred song sung to musical accompaniment,* a psalm." Giving Eph. 5: 19; Col. 3: 16; Acts 13: 33, in the New Testament, and Ps. 44: 24, in the Old Testament, as references.

Brother Hardeman asked me if I agreed with J. B. Briney, with Calhoun, with John Cowden, and with brethren scattered all up and down this country. Brethren, I do not know. I did not come here to affirm my belief in the position of these men. I did not come here to defend the position of any of these men. I ask Brother Hardeman if he believes these Greek scholars whom I have quoted when they say what the word means. That is the question I ask him. These men whom he has mentioned here to-night are able men, but are not in the class with the men I have quoted as Greek scholars. I ask him to-night if he believes what the Greek lexicons say, the New Testament lexicons—the same lexicons from which he gets the meaning of "baptizo"—if he believes them when it comes to "psallo."

But let me read another quotation, from the Standard Lexicon of New Testament Greek (Souter). I read here: "*Psallo,* I play on the harp or other stringed instrument." "*Psallo,* to sing thanks and praise to God with an accompaniment on the harp." This is a little lexicon recently gotten out, and has taken up the special study of the language of New Testament times—an especial and particular study of the Greek language used by the apostles and the people of their day; and this little lexicon is here for investigation.

Now, brethren, we cannot get away from this word. I am going to insist, I am going to state, as the affirmative of this debate, that this word should be attended to by the one who is on the opposite side of the discussion. I am going to ask him to take these lexicographers; I am going to ask him to discover whether or not they are wrong in their statements, whether or not they are reputable Greek scholars, whether or not they understand the language they are talking about, and whether or not they are authoritative when it comes to the Greek language of the classical period or of the New Testament period. These are questions that pertain to his particular part of this debate; and I feel that it is but just to the negative, it is but just to you people out there, it is but just to you people to-night who believe in and love Brother Hardeman, that he answer these questions. I am glad you do love him. I have no complaint to make of that, for it would certainly disturb my heart if I should come into a community to discuss a question with a man that did not have the love of the people before whom he stood and whom he represents; and so I am glad to-night he has your love and your confidence, and I say with all due kindness, and yet with Christian frankness, Brother Hardeman owes it to you, as well as to himself and to the discussion that we are having now, to enter into and discuss this word; and after we have gotten rid of this part of the discussion, we can take up all the other things that we may discuss in the four other nights we have at our disposal; and so I ask of him to-night that he pay particular attention in his next speech to these lexicographers.

I promise you and I promise him that every question that my brother shall ask me that is germane to the proposition under discussion—that every question he shall ask me that bears exactly upon the thing we are discussing, if not answered in the regular series of speeches, will be answered before this discussion closes. I have absolutely no desire to in any way evade any question, any proposition; but my desire is to come before you and present to you what I believe.

And now, as Brother Hardeman has made the statement that I failed to define my position, I think that he is in the same boat, for this is in our proposition [pointing to the chart]. If this is in my proposition and this is in his proposition, then he has not defined his position and I have not defined mine. But I thought I was very particular to define my position; and if this is not Brother Hardeman's proposition, if he does not take the negative of the affirmative position, that to sing with or without instrumental music is scriptural—in other words, that it is scriptural to use the organ in the worship—if that [pointing to the chart] is not our position and that [pointing to the chart] is not his position, then what are we discussing? I say that is our position, and I believe all of us can understand that. If not, I will be glad, if I can, to throw any further light in my power upon it. And I sincerely trust that he will either affirm or deny. Now, I am not asking him to take the affirmative side of this question, but he said I did not correctly represent him in his position. Now, I can ask him this, I think, and stay within my rights. I can ask him to state whether or not the negative position, as stated on the chart, is his position. I have a right to do this, and so I am asking him to make that very clear and very distinct to us tonight, and I want you now to get the force of this. I am contending on this because I do not want to notice other matters at this time. I think you have had just as much along this line as you can carry.

I realize this, my friends: that the great majority of those who are in this house to-night do not understand these words, do not speak in the language of the Greeks, do not fully understand just what these Greek words may mean when they are first brought to you—words of a foreign language. I want you to think about now, that Brother Hardeman admits there is no necessity of discussion, that the word "psallo" in the New Testament means to strike the strings of an instrument. You get that? He admits that it means to strike the strings of an instrument. It meant to play upon a musical instrument. He admits that. But he says that the musical instrument is the heart. So, then, there is no difference between Brother Hardeman and me as to the meaning of this word—that it does mean to make music on a musical instrument. I am not saying that Brother Hardeman said that it means to make music upon any musical instrument, but I am saying that he and the lexicographers say musical instrument, and that coming up through its use are these meanings, and it still has all these meanings, every one of them.

"I take it that if a carpenter, during the days of the apostle Paul, desired to stretch his string that he might make a chalk line, he would have used the word 'psallo.' I take it that if he had drawn his bow, he could have used the word 'psallo.' I take it that he could have pulled his hair out and said that he was 'psalloing.' I take it that all these meanings inhere and continue in the word, because 'baptizo' means to dip, to immerse, regardless of the particular element in which the immersion takes place, and the word 'psallo' means to touch or strike, regardless of the particular object twitched or struck. These are the inherent ideas in these words, running through all their varied uses; and they are the key to the meaning in every instance, whether the word be used literally or metaphorically."

These are the words of Brother M. C. Kurfees. I said in my first speech that I would prove to you by an eminent leader—I did not intend to call his name unless I had been forced to do so; but when the names of these other men were called, I felt at perfect liberty to introduce Brother Kurfees, and I here introduce Brother Kurfees to sustain my point that that word still has its meaning, and did have its meaning, notwithstanding the fact that in another place he said it had lost its meaning.

HARDEMAN'S SECOND SPEECH

(Thursday, May 31, 1923.)

Brethren, Moderators, Ladies, and Gentlemen: I appreciate the patience of this splendid company throughout these addresses thus far, three in number, and hope that the last thirty minutes may be pleasant and profitable to all. Just as earnestly and candidly and correctly as I may, I want to follow the address to which you have listened, noticing the points therein made.

Brother Boswell has placed himself in the attitude, as viewed by me, of one position contradictory to another—so much so that I am anxious for the morrow's night to come, and subsequent ones, to see how he may be able to extricate himself therefrom. He suggests at the first that the instrument can be left off, and that it is perfectly legitimate and in harmony with God's will to worship him in all the demands of high heaven and leave the instrument out; and then before he closes that address, with force and vigor and power he says to you that the instrument inheres in the word "psallo," and it must be done. It seems to me that Brother Boswell is in this kind of a predicament: First, God demands it. The word means it, and you cannot do what "psallo" means without the use of the musical instrument. That is Brother Boswell's contention, as from the lexicons to which he has referred; and then the next part is, notwithstanding the word means that and notwithstanding that idea inheres in it, yet I can leave it out. In the name of high heaven, Brother Boswell, if the word means an accompaniment of a mechanical instrument, and that is a command of God, how can you do God's will and omit the very thing demanded? Now, it was such an unfortunate statement for him when he said it was like the Greek word "baptizo"—that it means immerse. It means to dip. And he further said I cannot do what God said by the word "baptize" unless I immerse or dip. I think he was right in that statement. Why? Because the idea of dip and immerse and plunge inheres in the Greek word "baptizo." Now, said he, so it is with "psallo;" the accompaniment or the use of the musical instrument inheres therein. I cannot obey God, I cannot do what God suggests I do, therefore, unless I use the instrument. Why? Because that is what the word means.

Now, ladies and gentlemen, if the word means that and you cannot obey God without doing that, how can a man say that I can worship either with or without the instrument? I want to ask you, Brother Boswell, in all candor, can you immerse either with or without water? Can you immerse either with or without burial? Can you baptize either with or without a dipping? Can you "psallo" either with or without an instrument? You said that "baptizo" means to immerse; that "psallo" means the instrument. How, then, can you leave off one and yet tenaciously cling to the other? Consistency demands that he take the position, the only sensible position.

MR. BOSWELL: Just a point of order, Brother Hardeman; I read from Brother Kurfees.

MR. HARDEMAN: And you said repeatedly, Brother Boswell, that it means to use the instrument.

MR. BOSWELL: But Brother Kurfees, in there [pointing to Kurfees' book], he said that.

MR. HARDEMAN: You are the man that is debating now, Brother Boswell. Brother Kurfees suggests the truth, as presented in my first speech—namely, that the word "psallo," like the word "baptizo," carries with it always the idea of pluck or twang an instrument. No question about that. The point at issue with us is: What is the instrument as used in the New Testament? The word "baptizo" doesn't carry the precise instrument with it. It might be a baptism of the Holy Ghost; it might be immersion of suffering; it might be a baptism of fire. The precise element used in baptizing must be learned from the context. Just so with reference to "psallo." The idea of pluck or twang the instrument is in the word, but the precise instrument that is necessary to the fulfillment of it in each case depends upon the context. If you refer to the hair, the hair becomes the instrument; if you refer to the bowstring, the bowstring is the instrument. But in the New Testament, when you refer to singing, God said the heart is the instrument; and that is the position, if you please, that the word demands to-night.

Now, he suggested to me that the opposite of the term stated on the chart was without an instrument. Why, Brother Boswell, the negative of your proposition, as you put it yonder, "to sing with or without instrumental music," would be "not to sing with or without the instrument." [Applause.]

I believe, ladies and gentlemen, that I want to take the liberty, with the concurrence of Brother Boswell and the moderators, to ask of you not to applaud. I am sure that he appreciates your hearty approval, as well as do I; but we are in the midst of a *religious* discussion, and I believe I will ask that all demonstrations be omitted, lest there be a levity and a lighter strain than ought to characterize our effort to-night. So, then, if that meets with the approval of the audience, it has my hearty concurrence. What say you, brethren, regarding this? [Replies of "Amen."]

Then may I ask the audience to-night to refrain from all sorts of demonstration, lest we be led astray from the soberness and seriousness of the matter before us.

Let us get it again. Brother Boswell says "psallo" means to sing with or without the instrument. He can do it either round or flat. He can either fulfill what "psallo" means by using the instrument or by leaving it off. Now, the negative of that proposition would be to add the word "not" in front of it and make it read, "not to sing or not to play;" and hence when you knock out one of them with the negative stroke, you knock out both of them.

Now, I am in the negative, and am under no obligation to assume any position. My practice is not in question, but I will not hesitate to state just what I believe, because truth, and not victory, is the professed object of all honorable controversy. I believe, ladies and gentlemen, that God Almighty wants us to sing his praise, and, in so doing, that he wants us to accompany that singing with an instrument.

But the question is: Is it a mechanical instrument made by the device of men? That is Brother Boswell's idea. My contention is, based upon God's declaration, that we are to sing, and accompany that with an instrument, but the instrument is mentioned in the Bible. Paul says, "Speaking to yourselves in psalms and hymns," singing and "psalloing" in the heart, or with the heart, and thereby mentions the definite, precise, and specific instrument that shall accompany the same.

As a matter of fact, there have been vocal strains poured forth from the lips of many a singer that were not worship. Why wasn't it worship? Many times has "Jesus, Lover of My Soul," been sung, and yet no worship in it. Why? Because it was lacking in one of the elements necessary thereto—namely, that vocal expression was not accompanied with the instrument, which is the human heart, the spirit with which a man must sing, and, therefore, weighed in the balance and found wanting. Just as in the Lord's Supper, by the way, there are two elements—the bread and the fruit of the vine; the man who partakes of the bread and leaves off the wine has not obeyed God; but I must partake of both of them, and until this is done correct worship has not been rendered. Just so in presenting psalms and hymns unto God, there must be, to fulfill heaven's demand, the singing; and, in addition to that, there is the word "psallo" that carries the idea of accompaniment, of the instrument. But, Paul, what is the instrument? Paul says: "With your heart." And that settles the question, ladies and gentlemen, beyond the shadow of a doubt. When we sing, therefore, let us sing with the spirit, let us sing with the heart, the understanding. Let us not only sing by vocal expression, but let us accompany that, not, as did the heathen, upon mechanical instruments, but let us accompany that singing with melody, striking the strings—metaphorically, if you please—of the heart. That is the idea, as taught in the book of God. And, furthermore, just as you cannot baptize without immersion, neither can you "psallo" without that instrument that God calls the "heart." Therefore, when Brother Boswell says you can either worship "with or without," he stands in opposition to the peerless apostle to the Gentile world. When he suggests to you that the word means "to accompany with a mechanical instrument," he says that which no living man can prove, and it is not recorded that any dead one ever did.

It is strange that all of the apostles, who knew the Greek language in its primitive use, failed to learn, as Brother Boswell has discovered, that "psallo" means an accompaniment of a mechanical instrument; for be it remembered that no man can show where they, as Christians in the worship of the church of God, ever used a mechanical instrument wrought by the hand of man's device. The Greek Catholic Church, which has continued to speak the Greek language, excludes from its service and from its worship mechanical instruments such as those for which Brother Boswell is contending, and it fulfills in that one respect the idea of making melody upon the instrument announced by God Almighty.

So, then, Brother Boswell, the difference between us is this: What is the instrument upon which "psalloing" is done? You contend that it is a mechanical device made by man's hand; I say the instrument is the human heart, and God says that in Eph. 5: 19. Question: Which shall we take regarding it? Shall we take Brother Boswell's idea, or shall we take God's word, plainly put?

That is the issue, ladies and gentlemen, as to what the instrument is. As for me and mine, in harmony with apostolic practice, in perfect accord with God's declaration, we sing the praise of God and accompany that praise by the instrument ordained of God, which is the human heart, and without that no service acceptable to God can be rendered.

But he suggests, again, that the instrument is not a worshipful thing, that we do not use it as such; and I think, my friends, that I speak your sentiment by saying Brother Boswell is still not clear on what he means by that. But he did go so far as to state: "Brother Hardeman, I use the instrument as an accompaniment to the singing." Let me ask you: When you play the instrument in your church service without the singing, what does it accompany then?

You play the instrument when they do not sing. If it is an accompaniment, what does it accompany? Because that is the only thing going on, and hence that position is absolutely wrested from the man on that particular remark.

But he said, speaking of the grounds of union, but touched it very, very lightly, that he failed to get the point that I made, but sought to answer it by suggesting that there were divisions in the ranks of Brother Hardeman's crowd, or company, which is a lamentable fact. But, Brother Boswell, the division on other matters, be they great or small, just or unjust, does not constitute any answer to the division over instrumental music. Let the brotherhood be divided by other things or many things, such would give no ground for the division between Brother Boswell and myself on instrumental music. But let me say that the company with whom I affiliate are no worse divided than the company with whom Brother Boswell is allied. In a recent convention held in the church where he preaches resolutions were passed condemning some of his brethren for their deeds, and warning went out against them. If he wants to go into that field, I am ready to show division upon top of division, bitterness, rancor, and strife in his own ranks. But instead to-night of heralding that fact, I am asking again that on this one point we get together.

You have laid down the proposition that you can worship God without the instrument; my brethren suggest as a matter of conscience that we cannot worship with it. Now, then, if the position that we occupy is safe and secure and you can adopt it in all good conscience, why won't you do it? Is it because you want to perpetuate the strife? If you can, therefore, accept the worship of God without the mechanical instrument and do not do it, this audience will interpret, Brother Boswell, that you long not for that unity for which Christ prayed. But the old Georgetown Church, of Kentucky, in which he has an instrument to-night, was visited by the pioneers of the Restoration Movement, he says. Let me say to you, Brother Boswell, not one of them practiced what you do in Georgetown to-night. They were against the very thing that you have injected, which things have divided asunder the body of Christ; and hence the cause of that division and the responsibility for it lies at the door of the man who practices that for which there is not the slightest authority in all the book of God.

If these brethren — Morgan, Cowden, Gorsuch, and Walker—indorse the statement that you have made—viz., that you can worship God acceptably without the organ—and still will not give it up, I must charge you with the responsibility of perpetuating division and strife against the pleadings and prayer of our Lord. But if the word "psallo" means to accompany with a man-made instrument, you sin against God when you omit it.

So, then, my friends, I charge to-night legitimately that these brethren stand as a barrier in the city of Nashville to the harmony, peace, and oneness of the people of God. For what? Over a thing that they come, by their representative, and say is nonessential. "We can worship, Brother Hardeman, just as well without it as with it." Then why have it, unless you love your instrument and division more than you do the peace and harmony of the people of God?

But from that I pass to this idea, as it comes next to mind. I want to repeat that Brother Boswell has not defined what he means by things being scriptural, and to help him get the matter before you I suggest the following: A thing can be scriptural only upon three grounds. First, if God commands it or demands it, it is scriptural and must be complied with; second, if it can be shown to be approved by apostolic example, even in the absence of the commandment, it is then binding upon us and must be accepted; third, if there is drawn from the matter presented a necessary inference, I accept that as a scriptural ground. I want Brother Boswell, openly and candidly, as he has evidenced a spirit thus far, to come out plainly. Brother Boswell, do you claim the instrument on the ground that God commanded it or the apostles practiced it? If not, number three and last, do you claim it on the ground that necessary inference demands it? And if that covers not the ground of scriptural approvedness, then I beg of you to suggest other grounds that may elucidate the matter and bring it clearly before us.

I want, my friends, Brother Boswell to-night, as representative, to lead out and tell this audience in clear-cut words exactly on what grounds he proposes to stand for the instrument.

He cannot take the position on the ground that the word means that, because he has repudiated the meaning and said: "I can worship *with it* or *without it*." It was unfortunate, Brother Boswell, that you made these two statements. Consistency would have been either, "The word means it, and, therefore, I must do it, like 'baptizo' means immerse, and I have no other choice in the matter," or, "It does not mean it, and, therefore, I can eliminate it."

And so you leave to-night, ladies and gentlemen, with this thought: Where is the scripture, where is the authority, where is the proof that instrumental music, such as is made upon a mechanical device wrought by the hands of men, is scriptural?

Let me suggest to you, further, that the term "worship" has been touched very lightly. It remains undefined.

There is such a thing in the Bible as ignorant worship. (Acts 17: 22.) There is also such a thing as a vain worship. (Matt. 15: 9.) And then there is such a thing as true worship. (John 4.)

There are many things that are right within themselves and yet wrong when brought into the worship or service of God, be it as an accompaniment or as an integral part thereof. In that class comes the washing of hands, an act harmless *per se*, but when used in worship to God becomes vain worship. Further, the eating of meat is an innocent act in and of itself, but when put in the service of God is against scriptural authority.

In all candor, the playing upon an instrument is a harmless exercise or enjoyment; but when brought into the service of God, because of its lack of heavenly authority, it becomes an act similar to the eating of meat, like the washing of hands, that I fancy the Savior would describe as a vain worship, holding as it does to the doctrine of men rather than following after what God commands.

But, last of all, let me suggest to you this, a point untouched: Those scholars selected especially because of their genuine scholarship, when they came to translate the Bible, in the first (the King James) version—there were forty-seven of them, representing the cream of the scholarship of the entire world, coming from different religious bodies, many of which used instrumental music in their worship—yet when they came to translate the word "psallo," about which so much has been said, these forty-seven scholars of King James, without a single exception, in every place translated it, "sing and make melody in your hearts unto the Lord." Not one time did they translate it play or accompany with a mechanical instrument made by men's hands.

Then in 1881, when a committee of one hundred and one of the world's best scholars was appointed, especially selected, peculiarly fitted because of their great scholarship, they gave us what is considered the best version of our English Bible. Most of these belonged to churches which use mechanical instruments; and yet when they rely upon their scholarship, they translate "psallo" "to sing, to make melody in our hearts." To this there is not an exception, not a dissenting voice.

So if Brother Boswell sustains himself and follows the deductions of his own suggestions, he must, and I predict that he will, join Brother Payne, from whom he has quoted or collected his authority, and be forced to repudiate all the revised translators, as well as King James. But our English Bible has stood the test of time, and men of the type of O. E. Payne and his satellites will never be able to shake your faith in it in order to prove their unscriptural—and, therefore, impossible—proposition.

What does "psallo" mean? These one hundred and fifty scholars say it means to sing God's praise, to make melody in the heart, to sing with the spirit and with the understanding. I repeat, therefore, let Brother Boswell find where God demands it, or where Christ authorized it, or where the apostles practiced it in the church of the living

God, or where a necessary inference may be drawn, and then I am ready to investigate the reference made; and if correct, I pledge you my word and honor that I am ready to close and to indorse the position therein mentioned.

I am pleading to-night, as I have in your splendid presence time and again, for the Bible, and the Bible alone; for us to speak as the oracles of God speak; not to add unto the declarations of Holy Writ, but to lay down that which is common ground upon which all God's people may stand. I plead with Brother Boswell not to come to me, but to remove that which he himself says can be done, and let us go to him with open conscience, and we will all worship as we did previous to the injection into the churches of Nashville this human instrument that has divided the body of Christ and torn asunder professed Christians all over our fair land. I pray God that the time may come and the day may speedily dawn when there will be that disposition on the part of my brethren here who admit that it is unnecessary, and admit that they can do without it, to say: "Brethren Hardeman and others, we have removed the barriers, and we can worship God on common ground. Come on, therefore, with us." And you will not have to make a second invitation. Brother Boswell, take out that which you yourself say is unnecessary, and we are already there; we would have come yesterday if it were possible thus to do. And when that time shall have come and those barriers removed for which Brother Boswell and those who sympathize with him are responsible, the condition will be brought to pass in Nashville that prevailed previous to the unfortunate matter over in Woodland Street just a few decades ago.

Ladies and gentlemen, as we come to the conclusion of the session to-night, let me thank you for your patience and splendid attention.

BOSWELL'S THIRD SPEECH

(Friday, June 1, 1923.)

Brother Moderator and Brethren: I was taken to task somewhat last night because of my seeming failure to define the word "scriptural." I did not define it because I was of the opinion that a body of people who took the Bible to be the word of God and who appealed to the Scriptures upon every occasion would hardly need such a definition. I believe in the New Testament, as much so as Brother Hardeman, and am willing to abide by its teaching; but I am not willing that he, or any other man, shall have the right to place his interpretation upon the Scriptures, and, without offering any proof as to the correctness of that interpretation, say that his voice is the voice of God, and call upon you either to believe God or Brother Boswell. Such dramatic appeals lose their force when confronted by the facts. What are the facts? He takes "sing" or "make melody," and with no support, other than his "I say so," tells us that this is the word Paul used, the word that God inspired him to use. He knows, and all of us know, that the Holy Spirit led Paul to use "psallo," and that it is the meaning of this word that is under discussion. The word "sing" is not under discussion. It is the word "psallo."

I call special attention to the fact at this time that I heartily indorse the eloquent sermon he preached last night on Christian unity, but it was not a discussion. It was an assertion to insinuate that those who introduce the organ are destroyers of unity. To show you that he might possibly be mistaken in what the New Testament says, or rather means, let me call your attention to a mistake made by him last night on this very subject. He said that the Woodland Street Church was divided by the introduction of the organ. I wish to introduce a witness on the other side of the question. I read to you from a book entitled "Gospel Lessons and Life History," by Brother E. G. Sewell. On page 292 I find the following words:

"When the reading was ended, I said: 'Yes, that is all very nice; and you very well know we have dwelt together in unity from the very beginning of this congregation until now, and you also know that it is the effort to introduce something into the congregation that never was in it before, that is causing the disturbance now; and you know, moreover, that the something you all are trying to introduce is not found in the Bible, and that is the foundation of the whole trouble. So now cease to push this matter, and trouble will cease at once.' This brought silence. He knew that what I had said was true, and saw very plainly that if he would put a stop to the untaught society matter, we could be in unity again."

And then on another page, page 296:

"No man that knows the truth and loves the truth can be content to remain where the truth is trampled upon. If he does, he is encouraging the error and is himself a partaker of their sins. We gave them every chance possible to treat us as the gospel requires, but all to no effect. They showed in every way that they loved their man-made society more than their brethren and sisters that opposed them. So there was nothing left us but to walk out, or stay there and violate our conscientious convictions of truth and duty. So several of us ceased to meet with them any more, or to recognize them as in any way entitled to the appellation, 'a church of Christ.' "

This has reference to the trouble that took place in the Woodland Street Church, which Brother Hardeman said was caused by the organ.

And, my brethren, may I call attention to his statement again in reference to his desiring that we should come in and worship with you and be at one with you in this unity? If I am not incorrectly informed, it has not been long since you were holding a great and very successful revival in this building. You sent out invitations to the several churches. One of them came to the Vine Street Church; and when the Vine Street Church met your invitation in the way that invitation seemed to intend, you refused to accept their proffered help, and in that way shut them out from full participation in the union meeting, when they were willing to come and worship without an organ.

I admit divisions in our ranks; I do not try to hide them; but these divisions—I am speaking of the divisions among the people with whom I am identified, that body of people who love to fellowship in every way possible without the sacrifice of liberty in Jesus Christ—I make no effort to hide these divisions; they are over certain missionary work and infidel teachings by some professors in some of our colleges.

I am glad Brother Hardeman called attention last night to the congress in Georgetown; but I wish you might know just what action was taken in that congress, that you might see that the congress—and I had much to do with that congress—was directing all of its efforts along these two things I have mentioned.

Now, he desires to mention splits among us. I can more than duplicate all that he may present upon my side, or our side, of this question. Last night he made a very profound and eloquent plea for the union of God's people; and I am ready to do all I can, in a proper way, to bring about the union, not only among us, but among all the people of God upon this earth; for I believe, and you believe, that we cannot possibly fulfill the prayer of our Master until all God's people are one. And—O!—what a magnificent thing it would be, brethren, if you and I and all God's people, with hearts loyal to the Lord Jesus Christ, faithful to attend to the word which he has given us, should unite all of our force against all the evils that confront us in this land! And may I say to-night that I believe that we shall never have peace—peace among brethren, peace between capital and labor, peace between nations—until Jesus Christ has been enthroned in our hearts, in the hearts of his people, as the "Lord of lords, and King of kings;" and when that time comes, we will not need ships, we will not need guns, we will not need great world police power; for Jesus, the Prince of Peace, will govern and control and guide his people. So tonight I am with him in every plea he can make for Christian unity, and will agree with him as far as I can without surrendering my liberty in Christ Jesus.

The same appeal that he made last night—that we give up the organ—could have been made by the Judaizing teachers to the apostle Paul: "Come and accept circumcision, and we will be with you. Fasten circumcision on the church, and we will stand by you." But this grand old soldier of the cross resisted them and said that he would not give way.

And so the apostle Paul has given us apostolic example, scriptural precedent, for resisting encroachment upon that liberty which is ours in Christ Jesus; and we do not wish to be entangled in a yoke of bondage. We stand with Paul.

The same appeal Brother Hardeman made on "sing" can be made with equal force on baptism. Remember, my friends, that "baptism" is not translated, "baptizo" is not translated; it is simply brought over from the Greek. And I say to every man to-night that if I stand and appeal to you and say, "Take the English word 'sing' and let us see what that word means, and eliminate from it everything that that word can mean and does mean, for every one of you knows that the word can and does mean with or without musical instruments," another man could stand and say: "Come and take the word 'baptism;' we do not believe in immersion; your word is 'baptism.' " But immediately, my friends, we go to the original word, immediately we go to the Greek, immediately we go to "baptizo," and we stand there and say the scholarship of the world says the word means "immerse," and we demand that we follow what his word meant when used by the apostle Paul, inspired by the Holy Spirit. Let me say to you to-night that when I speak of this New Testament I speak of it as the inspired word of Almighty God.

Brother Hardeman asserts that Jesus would have withstood such a thing as a musical instrument in the worship. Brethren, walk in the footsteps of the Master. See him as he goes to the temple yonder in Jerusalem. He associates with these people; he worships with them in the temple where they had musical instruments, and worshiped with those musical instruments. Go with him, if you please, and hear him as he condemns them scathingly, bitterly, with a tongue that was the tongue of Almighty God, rebukes them for their traditions and evil practices. Now go with him into the temple, go with him as he drives out those who sold oxen and sheep, and had those who sold the doves to leave the temple and overturned the money changers' table; and yet not one single word did he say or one single thing did he do against those who were using the instruments in the temple. Had they been wrong, he would have driven out the musicians with their instruments.

Now, do not be led astray. I know the Bible too well and I know our own position too well for one moment to be led into having you believe that I am saying to-night that because instrumental music was in the temple it ought to be in the church. I know that the law was nailed to the cross; I know that we are not under Moses, but under Christ; I know that we are not living under Moses, under the law, but under Christ. I know these things, and in saying what I have just said I am simply saying that when Jesus was here he did as I have said, and you will find it in the New Testament, the book that is inspired by the Holy Spirit of God, the book out of which I am quoting to you to-night.

The same appeal made by him last night can be made by the *Apostolic Review*, of Indianapolis, on Sunday-school literature, Bible colleges, paid ministers, settled pastors, and evangelistic authority. Are you willing to give up your liberty in Christ and give up all these things? But I can multiply them.

And the same principle, identically the same principle, that you are bringing to bear on me, on us, to-night, to exclude the musical instrument from church worship, is identically the same principle that these brethren are bringing to bear upon you to force you to give up your Bible colleges; and I ask you this question to-night: As I traveled your city, I saw that you were exceedingly religious, and I found on one of your principal streets a building with this sign: "Church of Christ Community House." I want chapter and verse for the community house of the church of Christ in the city of Nashville. I do not condemn the community house; I indorse it; but I call for the chapter and verse that authorize it.

Brethren, I said last night I was going to answer Brother Hardeman's questions as far as they were germane. I try always to fulfill all my promises.

The first question is this, and involves the whole discussion. Asking questions is an easy thing, and a thing that can throw a smoke screen over the entire discussion. But I meet the issue to-night. He says:

1. "Can Eph. 5: 19; 1 Cor. 14: 15; Rom. 15: 9; and James 5: 13 be obeyed and complied with without the use of the instrument?"

He must have written that question before he heard me speak or saw the chart. The affirmative position is: "To sing with or without instrumental music."

That question is useless, as far as this debate is concerned, except that I may show you something in it, and I appreciate the opportunity.

It is not my answer that I am going to give, but the answer of the scholarship of the world. I accept this answer, the answer of scholarship, and make it my own. In Brother Hardeman's question there are a number of references. In Eph. 5: 19 the word translated "make melody" is "psallontes," from "psallo." In 1 Cor. 14: 15 the word is "psallo." "I will sing ["psalo"] with the spirit, and I will sing ["psalo"] with the understanding also." In James 5: 13 the word is "psalleto," from "psallo." The scholarship of the world has already answered by saying that "psallo" means "to sing with or without the instrument." Rom. 15: 9 has a different history entirely, and I am calling attention to the peculiarity of this reference. It is a quotation made by the apostle Paul, and is from the Greek translation of the Old Testament. This translation is called the "Septuagint." The Old Testament was written in Hebrew; and whatever meaning the word translated in the Septuagint by "psalo" had, "psalo" must have that same meaning. And whatever meaning "psalo" had in the Septuagint, it must have that same meaning in Rom. 15: 9, unless we accuse the translators of the Septuagint, or Paul, or both, of mistranslation. That would be a misquotation on the part of one or both.

What is the word used in the Hebrew Bible? It is "azammera." I do not know whether I get that accent just right or not; I am not a Hebrew scholar. It is from "zamar." The scholarship of the world has given us its meaning. They say: "It means to play an instrument or to sing with instrumental accompaniment." If that is the meaning of the Hebrew word and the translators of the Hebrew used "psallo," then "psallo" has to mean the same or they were not honest in their translation. Brother Kurfees quotes Prof. Clinton Lockhart as follows: "In the following passages 'psallo' is the translation of 'zamar,' which means to play an instrument or to sing with instrumental accompaniment." Then he gives a number of references, among which is Ps. 18: 49, which is the quotation made by Paul. He also gives a definition of "nagan" and "shir." Continuing, he says: "'Zamar' means to touch the chords of an instrument, to play, to sing with the instrument, and, when done in honor of some person, to celebrate." On this Brother Kurfees says: "Thus he tells us that 'zamar' means to sing with instrumental accompaniment, and that 'to play' is a translation of 'nagan,' which means to strike strings, to play an instrument, but does not mean to sing. And we accept both these statements as correct." He also quotes Gesenius on "zamar" as follows: "To touch or strike the chords of an instrument, to play; Greek, 'psallein;' and hence to sing, to chant, as accompanying an instrument."

And I suppose Brother Kurfees was speaking for his brethren when he said: "We accept both these statements [that "zamar" means to sing with instrumental accompaniment, and that "nagan" means to play an instrument, but does not mean to sing] as correct." And "zamar" is the word translated from the Hebrew into the Greek Old Testament in the quotation made by Paul. If to-night any man—any man—says that when Paul wrote "psallo" into the New Testament it did not have the meaning "zamar" had in the Old Testament, he is either denying the inspiration of the Scriptures or is saying that the apostle Paul violated God's own effort to inspire. I answer again. I read again from Brother Kurfees' book: "To touch or strike the chords of an instrument, to play; Greek, 'psallein;' and hence to sing, to chant as accompanying an instrument." I answer as the scholarship of the world answers. How do you answer, Brother Hardeman? I stand with the scholarship of the world; I stand on this word "zamar" with Brother M. C. Kurfees, but not with what he says about the change in the meaning of "psallo." I do not quote that. If you wish to see it, you can get it. I do not wish to quote it. You can quote it if you wish to. I shall not be hurt if you do.

2. The second question concerns the statement of H. L. Calhoun. And I ask him when this statement was made. Here is a statement made by H. L. Calhoun. When was it made? What is the date of it? Was it before or after Brother Calhoun gave up his contention concerning instrumental music in the worship? Now, brethren, there is something in this. The date here means much. I do not know when he wrote it. I do not know anything about it. I do not have to. I do not agree with him. I do not see why Brother Hardeman asked the question. I would not be here discussing this question if I agreed with him as to the meaning of "psallo."

3. "Do you believe instrumental music is demanded, commanded, or authorized in Christian worship?" Why put so many words in there? Do all these words mean the same thing? Do "demand," "command," and "authorize" mean the same thing? If so, why use so much ink? I can answer this question in a very simple way. "Do you believe instrumental music is demanded, commanded, or authorized in Christian worship?" I believe that it is scriptural. This question is the question under discussion. Do not get away from that.

4. The same as No. 3, and answered in No. 3. No. 5 is answered in No. 3.

6. Answered in my definition at the beginning of the discussion—that is, "instrumental music is in the worship only in the sense of being an item to the public service or ritual

of worship." I will try to be clear. I never had the reputation of speaking so people could not understand me.

Nos. 7, 8, 9, and 10. Regarding my agreement with John B. Cowden, O. E. Payne, the *Christian Standard,* and J. B. Briney. It is not germane to this discussion whether I agree with them or not. They have nothing to do with this discussion, except as I may quote them or be drawn into their defense. They are old enough to defend themselves. They are of age; ask them.

11. "Does the instrument inhere in 'psallo?'" Now, let me answer that, or, rather, let Brother Kurfees answer this question. He says: "'Baptizo' means to dip, to immerse, regardless of the particular element in which the action takes place; and the word 'psallo' means to touch or strike, regardless of the particular object touched or struck. These are the inherent ideas in these words, running through all their varied uses, and are the key to their meaning in every instance, whether the word be used literally or metaphorically."

12. "Is the use of an instrument in the worship pleasing to God or man?" It depends upon the attitude of the worshiper.

13. My position is stated on the chart. What is written can be easily read.

Brother Hardeman said last night: "You admit the position that I occupy is scriptural and a safe and sound policy." I do not admit any such thing. I did not admit it last night. Your position is that it is unscriptural to use the instrument. I deny this. There is more involved in your position than the use of an instrument. Your position robs me of my liberty to use the instrument. He quoted me last night as admitting his position. Here is what I said last night: "I ask this question right now, brethren—I am quoting from my speech as given in this morning's paper—I ask this question right now, brethren: If in the New Testament I have the right to worship without the organ, what right have you to say that I shall not worship that way? If in the New Testament I have the right to use the organ, by what authority has Brother Hardeman, or any other brother, the right to say I must not exercise that right?" I believe in the New Testament, and have no desire to do other than what that inspired book directs.

Brother Hardeman makes the bold claim that the New Testament says such and such a thing, and makes no attempt to prove his assertions. The things which he asserts are the very things we are discussing. I wish to drive this into your hearts to-night, my brethren. The assertions he made last night in all of his appeals and in all of his eloquent sermon are the things at issue between us. I frankly confess that I love to hear him preach, but I would like to hear him discuss now the questions we are discussing. I would like to have him come to the point at issue between us—the meaning of the word "psallo" as given by the Holy Spirit and the apostle Paul. This is the issue, not "sing" as translated in any version.

HARDEMAN'S THIRD SPEECH

(Friday, June 1, 1923.)

Brethren, Moderators, Ladies, and Gentlemen [removing the box on which Boswell's notes lay—applause]: I beg of you, friends, while I appreciate your applause, to respect the request of last evening and the moderators to-night as well. If Brother Boswell prefers the box, he may have it; but since I do not read my manuscripts, I think I do not need it.

I want to say to you that I like Brother Boswell; I like the splendid spirit manifested by him; but when I say to you in his presence I am disappointed in his reputation, as it came to me, as a disputant and debater, I only express an honest sentiment. I want to return the compliment in regard to preaching, inasmuch as Brother Boswell seems to be afraid of his proposition and unable to stand up squarely in defense of it. I would be very glad, indeed, to hear him preach a sermon.

May I suggest to you, ladies and gentlemen, that the terms of this proposition, as demanded in Rule 1 of the book that we have indorsed, have never been defined; and he makes the puerile excuse that he assumed the audience understood what "scriptural" means, and still refuses to give attention to it. I tried to take the initiative last night in order to help him to get some matters before you. Brother Boswell, there are three terms to which you owe it to yourself to direct attention. They are the words "scriptural," "unscriptural," and "antiscriptural." Those three things before an audience, on the part of a man assuming the laboring oar of affirmation, ought to be defined. Just what do you mean when a thing is scriptural? Until this hour this audience doesn't know what you think about it. But I think I understand that there is something back of it of which Brother Boswell seems to be just a little suspicious, and, therefore, refrains—intentionally so—by suggesting that I take it for granted that all of you know respecting it.

Now, let me call your attention to the one word "psallo," on which Brother Boswell seems to let the whole of this discussion suspend. He seems unable absolutely to state my position, though three times he has tried publicly to do so, and misrepresented it again to-night. It seems to be a matter that he is unable to get. Why, he says Hardeman's position is that the instrument doesn't cling to, is not allowed in, the worship of God. Ladies and gentlemen, that is exactly the opposite of my position. I want to state to you candidly, I believe that it is impossible to worship God in this act acceptably unless there be the accompaniment of the vocal expression with that instrument described in God's book—namely, the making of melody or the striking on the strings or playing upon the cords of *the human heart.* And there is the man that says you can worship God without the instrument, because yonder is his declaration. Brother Boswell, I accept the first of it. You cannot worship God without the instrument. It is there. You are the man that says you can do without it; and you teach it either round or flat. You say that God demands it, and yet you can render obedience to God and refuse to do it.

Does the God of the universe command us to "psallein," meaning thereby to use an instrument, and then, in the next utterance, suggest that we do not have to do what it means? Such is Brother Boswell's idea. It means it, and the instrument is implied in it, and all the lexicographers so declare. You have brought to bear a great array of lexicons on that subject, proving that the word means the instrument, and then upon the chart deliberately and with consideration of it beforehand say that I do not believe my own lexicographers, for they say "absolutely" with the instrument, and yet you slap all of them in the face and say you can do it without the instrument.

Brother Boswell, honestly, do you believe your own lexicons? I accept all of them on the chart; and if you have any more, I believe them, too. Get out all of them. There is not a Greek lexicon on the earth of standard recognition but accepts the meaning to play, to twitch, to twang, to play an instrument, and I believe that. And what is the instrument? That is what I have not been able to get him up to as yet, though the Bible speaks it and names it.

Let me call attention to the parallel of the two words with the hope that this audience will understand some things regarding it. There is the Greek word "baptizo," which means to dip, to plunge, to submerge or immerse, without respect to the object in which it is done or the instrument through which or by which the end is accomplished. When you speak of being baptized, you cannot tell from that word in what it is to be done. The classic use is baptized in sorrow, baptized in suffering. In such a case suffering is the instrument. Baptized in drowsiness, baptized in drunkenness, overwhelmed; but when you come to the New Testament, there is our same word "baptize," which meant or means to immerse. What is the element, what is the instrument? Why, Brother Boswell, nor I, nor you, either, would know unless God says, and in the New Testament he says, baptized in water; and the very fact that he says baptized in water forbids baptizing in buttermilk or any other kind of liquid. So when God Almighty said "baptizo," and then told the element in which it was to be done, that settles the question, and it is not a matter of you can or cannot. The fact is, you cannot fulfill the demands of the word "baptizo," ladies and gentlemen, without being immersed; and it is not a question of liberty, it is not a question of expediency; it is a question of whether or not you propose to do what God says, and that is all. Either obey God or not obey him.

Now, let us try the Greek word "psallo." What does it mean? It means to pull, to pluck, to twitch, or to play upon an instrument. Now, then, in the New Testament what is the significance of it? Back in the classics it was to pull the hair, to pluck the strings, to twang a bowstring, or pull it out and let it go, as a carpenter's line to be twitched. But in the Bible there is the word "psallo." What does it mean? It means to pull, to touch, or to twang. Does it mean to touch the hair in the New Testament? No! Does it mean to touch a bowstring? No! Does it mean to touch the carpenter's line? No! Does it mean upon a mechanical instrument? No! What is the instrument? God has said, and he said the instrument with which you "psallo" is the human heart. The very fact that he said it was the heart forbids its being any other thing. Just as God says be baptized in water forbids all other liquids, even so to "psallo" upon the heart forbids all other instruments. Brethren, I want you to put it down in capitals. You cannot "psallo" without the instrument. To-night when we were singing the splendid song, "All Hail the Power of Jesus' Name," I noticed all the brethren singing, my Brother Boswell and others of his company or sympathizers. What were they doing? Were you making a mockery of it? If you just had the very expression of the words only, it was not worship. Unless you sang with the spirit and the heart, and played upon the chords thereof, metaphorically speaking, and used that as the instrument, you did not worship God.

Now, note further. There is this difference between "baptizo" and "psallo:" The word "baptizo" has never been translated in the Bible; it has been Anglicized; and the only change on the earth in it was to drop the final "o" and to put on the English letter "e," which, instead of making it "baptizo," makes it "baptize," and that stands as a pure Greek word in the Bible to-night. Hence when we come to find out its meaning, we have to go to the lexicons, for the Bible does not define the word.

Not so with "psallo." When that same company of scholars came to the word "psallo," instead of Anglicizing it and making it an English word, they translated it. Of the King James committee, there were forty-seven of the greatest and ripest scholars of the entire world, selected men, who belonged to churches favorable to instrumental music; yet when they rose to the heights of their scholarship, those forty-seven men came forward and said: "We will translate 'psallo.' " And what did they give us? They gave us the word "sing," which implies not only giving expression to vocal sentiment, but accompaniment by striking the chords of the heart; and then in the year 1881, when the Revised Version committee was selected, it was made up of the cream of the scholarship of the world—one hundred and one rich in scholarship. Were they prejudiced against instrumental music? No! The majority of them belonged to churches that used it. But when they came to give us the Revised Version, they translated the word "psallo;" and what did they do? They put it down in the Bible as "sing and make melody in your hearts to the Lord."

Now, ladies and gentlemen, there is but one position that can be taken with consistency, or even a show of logic, and that is to say, as did O. E. Payne (and I am ready to tip my hat to him for his courage), after bringing an array of scholarship before the world, a wonderfully large collection: "Gentlemen, from the foregoing it becomes evident that we cannot 'psallo' without the instrument; and if we forego the instrument, we cannot comply with the divine command." Now, I believe that statement. The difference between Brother Payne and myself would be this: He thinks it is a mechanical instrument; I know that it is the human heart, for God so said. But when these brethren here indorsed Payne's book so heartily as they did, counting it the last word to be said, unconsciously those who gave it their indorsement, among whom was Brother Boswell's moderator, they sawed off the limb between themselves and the tree to which they clung. You walked into the trap this fixed. That is the only consistent position that has ever been taken. It means to sing with the instrument, and you cannot "psallo" without the instrument. But the instrument is laid down in the Bible.

Ladies and gentlemen, it is a question of which you will have—Brother Boswell's *ipse dixit* or the faithful translation of the word of God.

Now, I call your attention to Col. 3: 16; 1 Cor. 14: 15; Eph. 5: 19. In this connection I want to read to you some statements and some commentaries upon these passages. This is taken from Conybeare & Howson, two great English commentators of the New Testament: "There is a contrast employed between the heathen and the Christian practices—namely, when you meet, let your enjoyment consist"—now note—"when you Christians meet, let your enjoyment consist not in the fullness of wine, but in the fullness of the Spirit; let your songs be not the drinking songs of the heathen feasts, but songs and hymns; and let your accompaniment be not the music of the lyre, but the melody of the heart while you sing the praise, not of Bacchus or Venus, but of the Lord Jesus Christ." What was the consideration of the song of the heathen? It was to sing the songs of Bacchus and Venus, to be filled with wine, and to play upon the mechanical instrument. In contrast with that, Christians are to sing spiritual songs and make melody, not upon the lyre, but upon the cords of the heart, as thus described by them.

But let me call attention to others right along the same line. I read from Jameison, Fausset & Brown, in their commentary, respecting the same word, in which they have this to say: "Eph. 5: 19. Make melody; Greek, playing and singing. Make melody in your heart, not merely with the tongue, but the serious feelings of the heart accompanying the singing of the lips." And then they quote Conybeare & Howson, making it the same thing as did they.

But the next I am calling your attention to is Robert Milligan, at one time president of the College of the Bible, in which he said: "The word 'sing' is from the Greek noun 'psalmos,' to touch, to play upon a stringed instrument with the fingers, and, finally, to make music or melody in the heart, as in Eph. 5: 19. The meaning of the noun conforms with that of the verb, and means touch or play on a stringed instrument; and hence it is evident that the word 'sing' may or may not refer to instrumental music. Its proper meaning, however, in any case, must be determined by the context; and, according to this fundamental law of interpretation, it is pretty evident in Ephesians and Colossians the term has no reference to instrumental music, for in both instances it is the strings of the heart upon which the melody and the music is made."

These might be multiplied, one scholar after another, regarding matters of this sort.

But let me call attention now, ladies and gentlemen, to some other things. The good old church at Georgetown, Ky., planted in the early part of the nineteenth century, was characterized by the preaching of the veterans of the Restoration Movement. It is the church where Barton W.

Stone, of Kentucky, first met Alexander Campbell, of Virginia, in 1824; it is the church wherein Raccoon John Smith, Jacob Creath, Moses E. Lard, and others who were devoted to the Restoration Movement, sounded out the gospel time after time. In those days there was no organ or mechanical musical instrument in the church at Georgetown. I want to ask Brother Boswell to listen to what some of these brethren think of him. I read from some of the scholars of the nineteenth century.

First, I read from Thomas Campbell when he laid down certain principles: "Our differences, at most, are about things in which the kingdom of God does not consist—that is, about matters of private opinion or human inventions. Who would not be the first among us to give up human inventions in the worship of God and cease from imposing his opinion upon the brethren that our breaches might be healed?" Not only that, but he said whatsoever is not expressly taught or directly commanded is not to be introduced as a part of the practice of the Restoration Movement. One thing, however, a man may do. He says he may have his opinions, but let him hold them as his private property; let him not impose those opinions upon others and make them indorse the same by continually having them present in their midst.

Not only he, but his son, Alexander Campbell, the great scholar and reformer, who justly stands at the head of the list, says: "To those who have no real devotion or spirituality in them"—now note the kind—"whose animal nature flags under the operation of church service, I think that instrumental music would not only be a thing desired, but an essential prerequisite to fire up their souls to animal devotion; but I presume to all spiritually minded Christians such aids as the organ would be as a cowbell in a concert."

That is the type of men that preached at old Georgetown, Ky.; yet Brother Boswell claims to be true to the Restoration Movement. Why, Brother Boswell, Alexander Campbell says it is to fire up your animal nature, and to the spiritually minded it would be as a cowbell in a concert!

But Brother Boswell was educated under Brother McGarvey, and I want to read what he says regarding it. He stands as one whose scholarship is beyond question. Brother McGarvey has this to say (this is Brother Boswell's old teacher; he left Memphis, Tenn., as a boy, and went to Lexington, Ky., and sat at the feet of J. W. McGarvey, the superior of whom in Bible knowledge and biblical lore, I think, has not lived in the generations that have gone by) : "Any man who says that the apostle teaches the use of instrumental music in the church by enjoining the singing of songs is one of those smatterers in Greek who can believe anything he wants to believe." And, again: "No scholar has ever taken the position that in singing the songs the use of instrumental music inheres. It would be just as easy to say that the Greek word 'baptizo' means to sprinkle or to pour as to say that 'psallo' means an accompaniment by a musical instrument. Not only so; it is universally admitted by those that are competent to judge that there is not the slightest indication in the New Testament of divine authority for the use of instrumental music in the worship."

Now, Brother Boswell suggests to-night an argument that his brethren and those who sympathize with them have used all over this land. I want to put the matter to the test. He has, with a bold assertion, said that Christ entered into the temple and participated in the affairs connected therewith, among which there were instruments of music, and yet he never opened his mouth against such. If that statement were true, it would be no semblance of authority; it would as well prove that we ought by the same authority to burn animal sacrifices and incense. But, Brother Boswell, the temple built by Solomon 1050 B.C. was destroyed by old Nebuchadnezzar 587 B.C. Fifty-one years thereafter Zerubbabel came back and rebuilded the temple. About twenty years before Christ was born old Herod the Great became the ruler of the land of Palestine; and after the death of his beloved wife, Mariamne, the last of the Maccabean line, Herod tore down the temple built by Zerubbabel, enlarged it, and built the temple in which Christ and the apostles worshiped; and I want you, sir, to show, either from the Bible or from standard history, where there was ever an instrument of music in the temple built by Herod the Great. Brother Boswell, you have paraded that all over this country. Bring forth the proof where Christ or the apostles, in the temple of their day, ever heard one strain of instrumental music.

An amusing thing, if it were not serious, is the fulfillment of the promise to answer the questions. "I have answered that, as I said I would." Friends, I failed to get last night the "as I said I would." "Can the five passages in the New Testament wherein 'psallo' is found be complied with without the use of an instrument?" meaning a mechanical instrument, of course, as he represents. He answers: "With or without." Yes and no! I must say that I am surprised at that kind of an answer, and the duplicity on the question does not measure up to my conception of Brother Boswell as a high-toned gentleman and debater. But I can appreciate the situation in which he has placed himself.

That thing, ladies and gentlemen, cannot be answered by Brother Boswell and maintain his consistency. But he said that in Rom. 15: 9 the very same word was used as was spoken of back in the Septuagint version. Correct. What did the word mean back there? It meant an instrument. What does it mean? Everywhere the same thing. Question: What is the instrument? And I have not been able yet, Brother Boswell, to get you to tell what the instrument is. Was it a banjo, a Jew's harp, a fiddle, or a cornet? What is it? You say it is an instrument. Name it! And yet all over this land and country those brethren introduce the organ and divide the churches, when they would not have the organ in their own homes. They would say the thing is "tacky," and no one wants an organ in his home! And yet a thing that they will not have in their private homes, as an organ, they will put into the house of God, and thereby prefer it to the fellowship and to the membership of a large number, notwithstanding they say: "It is all right with us either way."

Gentlemen, show me your faith without your works; I

will show you mine by my works. If you are consistent and can worship God without it and want peace, harmony, and union, why not give it up?

I knew the history of the trouble at Woodland Street. Whether the split came over the organ or the society, the principle involved is the same—that of human innovations. Vine Street, of which Dr. Morgan is pastor, had its trouble directly over the organ. The controversy is the same.

Brethren, I want this committee on unity here, composed of Dr. Morgan, Cowden, et al.—this great commission, this self-made machine—to begin to function. It has been running on two cylinders all this time. It is a six-cylinder machine. I beg you, brethren, to get together to-morrow and oil her up. Let us put that commission on unity to work. If you will take out the barrier, which you say you can do, you and I will worship together next Sunday morning, and we will strike hands and march down the aisle together, and there will be nothing in the way. It is your position that makes the barrier to-night and hinders my worshiping with you next Sunday.

I thank you.

BOSWELL'S FOURTH SPEECH

(Friday, June 1, 1923.)

Brother Moderator and Brethren: Just a few questions. But, first, I am sorry Brother Hardeman is disappointed—very sorry. However, I sincerely hope that before the discussion is over, after I have had a little more instruction from him, I will be better prepared to meet him. I want to do the best I can, and I appreciate his patience and loving tenderness toward me; but I do not feel that the title, "high-toned gentleman," can mean all it seems to mean with the word "duplicity" attached to it as a tail to a kite. I think he has charged me here with duplicity. In "appreciation of the situation, as pertaining thereunto," I ask this question, Brother Hardeman: When you preached at Alamo, Tenn., and the piano was used, did you worship? Was the worship acceptable when you worshiped?

In reference to Alexander Campbell, no one has a higher admiration for Mr. Campbell than I when it comes to scholarship; but when Mr. Campbell is expressing a matter of taste, and he does not know the difference between music and a cowbell, he certainly does not qualify; and I wish to say, furthermore, Mr. Campbell does not say, in either of the quotations made—I am not saying what Mr. Campbell says; I am simply saying that he does not make any statement as to whether or not instrumental music in the service, in church worship, is sinful. He admits that people who have not quite reached the high spiritual plane of my good brother need it; and if I need it, brother, why not let me have it, and maybe after a while I can reach higher realms of holiness.

I did go to school to Brother McGarvey, a man of sainted memory. I do not know that I am even a smatterer in Greek; I make no pretensions to being a Greek scholar; and there was no necessity for that gratuitous fling toward me of my being a smatterer in Greek. Brother McGarvey was in a service with me in Crab Orchard, Ky.; and when I said to him, "Brother McGarvey, shall we remove the organ because you are here with us to-day?" Brother McGarvey, with that sweet smile of his and with that great, big, saintly heart of his, said: "Brother Boswell, use your organ; *that is a matter for the local congregation.*"

I am delighted when the brother introduces witnesses upon this platform. He made the statement that the lexicons give the meaning to play upon the heart. I now offer him one hundred dollars for the lexicon that says that. Now, I want them to speak. The "heart" is not in the lexicons; it was just slipped in. I do not say that he intended to slip it in; but in a number of definitions he gave he said "to play on the heart," or words to that effect. He used the "heart" as given by the lexicon, and I now offer one hundred dollars for that lexicon.

A few more things. I am glad Brother Hardeman is improving. I think this debate or discussion has already helped him. He has moved up some. Heretofore they have held to the position that the word had lost its meaning entirely as far as musical instruments were concerned, and Brother Kurfees makes the statement in his book, "Instrumental Music in the Worship," that before the year 146 B.C. it had entirely lost the meaning it had in the classical Greek. Not only so; he quotes Sophocles and Thayer as sustaining this. To-night I ask my good brother if he stands with Brother Kurfees in his statement concerning Sophocles and Thayer. And Abbott Smith gives almost identically the same definition that Thayer gives, and I ask him to examine that lexicon, and if he will take the same position on Smith that Kurfees does on Thayer.

I shall let pass, for the time being, that wonderful statement concerning Herod's temple. I want you to think about that for a while. He said I walked into the trap. He admits he set a trap; and so he understands some of the rules of debate, though many of them he does not seem to understand. There is one he understands; and now that I am in the trap, he will grant me the privilege of walking around a little while that I may eat a little of the cheese; and when the proper time comes, I will come out of the trap.

He said he did not catch what I said last night about answering his questions, but he caught it to-night all right, and I want him, if he can, to put the human heart in Rom. 15: 9. I want him to put the human heart in "psallo" in that reference. I ask him another question. He speaks of "baptizo" being brought over by the change of a letter, and gives us some Greek. I wish to ask him this question: Will you stand on "baptizo" as it is in the King James Version, without going back to the original? If so, then stand on "sing." But if you won't stand on "baptism," why stand on "sing?"

He asked me: "What instrument?" The tuning fork! That is the instrument; and if that thing "zooms" the least bit before you commence singing or you commence singing before it quits "zooming," you are singing to the musical instrument. If you are going to split hairs, let us split them.

But he spoke about the beautiful situation at Georgetown years ago, and particularly he was speaking about Alexander Campbell. Then he went on to say what a miserable come-down it seems, after having such men as that—to have had Campbell and Smith and all those other men there in that pulpit—to have a smatterer in Greek to preach in the pulpit of such men. Brethren, I am not Alexander Campbell, and I do not even think I am. I am just a plain, ordinary preacher in a town of about four or five thousand people. They are satisfied with their minister. I have one member there who heard Raccoon John Smith, and he is still worshiping in that church. He worshiped there when Raccoon John Smith preached there, and he says I can preach as well as Raccoon John Smith. He says I can preach as well as any man that ever preached there. He said the other day, said before my wife: "You can preach as well as any man I ever knew when you want to, but you don't always want to." Now, that is just my way of showing you that the church has not completely "petered" out. There is a little left; and if I can ever get out of the trap he set, I am going back up there.

Now, I wish to continue just where I left off, because I say this to you, brethren, and I say it most kindly; but it is a fact that if you will take out his discussion on Greek and smatterers and take out his discussion of the committee on unity—his "six cylinders running on two"—and his splendid historical discourse about the temple, he is giving you the same speech to-night that he did last night. No wonder he does not have to look at his manuscript! And not only so, brethren; when he did get to something new, he had to take his book up just as I do.

Now, I wish to start right back where I was, and I am going to continue right along the same lines on which I began this debate or discussion; also I am going to continue answering his questions.

Now, I was talking about misrepresentation last night. He called attention to some misrepresentations, and they will be answered in this very speech I am making if I just have time to finish it.

He quoted me last night as saying the word "inheres." Now, listen: "The word inheres, or the instrument inheres, therein—the idea of it—and it must be done." He quoted me as saying that last night. I rose to my feet to correct it. I made most emphatic denial. I called upon him to make good his statement. I did this last night, and told him what I did say, mentioning the fact that I had quoted from Brother Kurfees. Here is what I said, as reported by the reporters: "I believe I am safe in saying this: that while words do change, they do not lose entirely their original or primitive meaning. That meaning holds on, stays with it throughout all of its life. I think I am safe in saying that. I shall risk it, anyhow, that the word shall hold, in a way, whether it is used literally or figuratively, its primary meaning." That is a vastly different thing from saying: *"It must be done."* I certainly know my own proposition too well to make such a statement. Again, I said: "I have said that the word never loses its primary meaning entirely. I have good authority for that, and the authority will be produced at the proper time. I do not mean to say that the word does not change." I am reading what I said last night. "I do not mean to say that the word does not take on some meaning that it did not have before. I am simply saying that the primary meaning—that meaning which is in the word, and that meaning which gives the word its loneliness, if you please, and yet at the same time reaches out and touches every other word in the language—that meaning accompanies and holds in the word." The authority which I promised to quote, and did quote, was M. C. Kurfees. He says: " 'Baptizo' means to dip, to immerse, regardless of the particular element in which the action takes place; and the word 'psallo' means to touch or strike, regardless of the particular object touched or struck. These are the inherent ideas in these words, running through all their varied uses, and are the key to their meaning in every instance, whether the word be used literally or metaphorically." Brother Hardeman has stated the same fact. Here are his words: "Brother Cowden suggests the truth, as presented in my first speech—namely, that the word 'psallo,' like the word 'baptizo,' carries with it evermore the idea of pluck or twang of the instrument. No question about that."

To read again: "The point at issue with us is . . . as to the difference between Dr. Boswell and myself. It is this: What is the instrument as used in the New Testament?" There is the record as I get it from the paper today. Brother Hardeman further said: "I believe, ladies and gentlemen, that God Almighty wants us to sing his praises, and, in so doing, that he wants us to accompany that singing with an instrument. But the question is: Is it a mechanical instrument, made by the device of men?" At the proper time that will be discussed. I want to see if he has another speech. The matter of the instrument will be attended to later. We are now discussing the primary and New Testament meaning of the word "psallo." He says it is pronounced "sallo" and not "p-sallo." I understand him to admit or affirm that the word in the New Testament means to play on a musical instrument. Did you so admit or affirm? This question is germane to the subject, and I think I have a right to call for his answer. I think he is coming up to it. He has almost answered that. He said: "Brother Boswell's position is to sing with or without the instrument. . . . Now, the negative of that proposition would be to add the word 'not' in front of it, and the negative position would be, from that statement, 'not to sing, or not to play;' and hence when you knock out one of them with a negative stroke, you knock out both of them." No, sir! Answer: In this statement he failed to use my verbal statement and to correctly read the chart. The matter of dispute is not "sing or play," but whether we can "sing with or without an instrument," or whether we "must sing without the instrument." My position is that we can "sing with or without the instrument." He made a play on this, seemingly forgetting that we are not discussing the main proposition, or the word "sing," but the primary meaning of the word "psallo," the word in our original New Testament, the New Testament from which we get all our English versions—King James, the Revised, and all the rest. The discussion was on the meaning of the word, regardless of the instrument. Before I am through with this I am going to show you, friends, that we translate it just as I am asserting to-night; but I am not through yet. The discussion as to the instrument will come later. We will discuss that all right, brethren. I am ready to discuss that question when the time comes for me to discuss it.

I now demand that he address himself to the specific subject before us—not the English translation, but the original word as revealed by the Holy Spirit. I ask him: Was that word "sing" or "psallo?" I also call upon him to give me book, chapter, and verse where Paul said "sing." And I respectfully call the attention of the moderator to this point. The two positions must be clearly and correctly stated and acknowledged before the issue can be known and arguments made either for or against. The affirmation has made the third statement on the two positions and the issue of the same. The only statement the negative has made on the two positions and the issue is that he puts "not" before to "sing with or without instrumental music." That means one of five things. The position of the negative is, first, that "psallo" in the New Testament does not mean to sing at all; second, that "psallo" means to sing; third, that "psallo" means to sing with musical accompaniment; fourth, that "psallo" means to sing both with and without instrumental music; fifth, that "psallo" means to sing without instrumental accompaniment. The conclusion is reached by elimination. If he takes the first, he must stop singing in the church worship; but if he takes the second, there is no issue between us, as both take the same position; or if he takes the third, he must put an instrument in the church building and use it whenever he sings; the fourth is impossible, because he cannot sing with and without the instrument at the same time; if he takes the fifth and last, he takes the position stated on that chart—that is, "to sing without instrumental music." If he refuses to take this position, he denies the practice of his churches. They sing without instrumental accompaniment.

Now, as he has admitted the primary meaning of the word, I will take up its New Testament meaning, the word as used in the New Testament—the New Testament from which they translate our English version, the Revised, and all the others. And I shall have something to say about these revisers, as to why they translated it "sing," and something about what the scholars themselves say about it, and many other things along that line, when the proper time comes for that. But the thing that we are discussing now is the meaning of the word in the New Testament—the New Testament from which you get your English version; and so I read some of the authorities I read last night that you may get it again.

Bullinger: "A playing, music; in later usage, a song accompanied." "New Testament Synonyms" (Trench): "Last of all, the song sung with this musical accompaniment." Liddell & Scott: "Later, to sing to a harp. (Eph. 5: 19; 1 Cor. 14: 15.)" And then I read from Yonge: "*Psallo* (only of playing on stringed instruments)." "In the New Testament, to sing while touching the chords, while accompanying oneself on a stringed instrument, to sing psalms. (Rom. 15: 9.)" "*Psalmos*, a song sung to the accompaniment of music." Then we had Robinson last night, then Parkhurst, and then we came to the New Testament Greek lexicon of Zorell: *"Psallo,* I play on a stringed instrument, strike the cithara with the fingers, sing a hymn to the notes of the lyre." *"Psalmos,* sound of the lyre; song to the sound of the strings, song to be sung to the strings, song to be sung to the sound of the lyre, to be sung in honor of God." And then Ebeling Greek-German Lexicon to the New Testament: *"Psallo,* to play on the cithara and to sing thereto." And then from Souter's Standard Lexicon of New Testament Greek: *"Psallo,* I play on the harp or other stringed instrument."

I read you these last night, calling attention to the fact that they say "psallo" means to sing with musical accompaniment, an instrumental accompaniment. That is the meaning of the word, and the questions I wish you to answer are: Are these lexicons correct? Do these New Testament scholars speak the truth when they say that the word means to play on an instrument, and that instrument is not the heart? O, friends, to-night, do you think, does Brother Hardeman think, that I believe, that any Christian man believes, you can do anything pleasing to God without the heart responding? Does any one here to-night believe that any man who believes in Jesus Christ as the great heart of God, bleeding, broken upon the cross, and stretching out his nail-pierced hands as though he would enfold in his loving arms the great, seething, sinful world outside—do you believe, does any man believe, that your speaker now, or any man who believes in such a God, ever, for one moment, thought it would be pleasing to God to worship him and leave the heart out? It is impossible, my brother, to do that.

Now, some more references to the word used in the New Testament. I come now to contemporaneous writers. I must hurry on. We have had the lexicographers, and I am quoting contemporary writers to show that "psallo" had not lost its meaning in New Testament times.

Septuagint, 135 B.C.: "David played with his hands. (1 Sam. 16: 16.)" Strabo, 24 B.C.: "Nay, even the professors of music, who give lessons (*psallein*) on the harp, lyre, and pipe, lay claims to our consideration. Plutarch, 85 A.D.: "And King Philip, to the same purpose, told his son, Alexander, who once on a merry meeting played (*psallanto*) a piece of music charmingly and skillfully: Are you not ashamed to (*psallon*) play so well?" Josephus, 85 A.D.: "The Levites stood round about them with their musical instruments and sang hymns to God and played (*epsallon*) on their psalteries as they were instructed by David to do." This is Josephus, A.D. 85, long before 160 A.D., the date of Lucian. He is speaking about something that took place in the days of King Hezekiah. He uses the same word, "psallo," that Lucian uses. Lucian, 160 A.D.: "And the other arts cannot serve their possessor without instruments; for it is impossible to play the flute without a flute, or to play the lyre (*psallein*) without a lyre, or to ride horseback without a horse." Again: "You cannot play (*psallein*) the flute if you have not one to play; lyrical music requires lyre." Clement of Alexandria, 190 A.D.: "And even if you wish to sing (*odein*) and play (*psallein*) to the harp or lyre, there is no blame."

All these books can be reached. Every one of these authorities I have quoted is accessible. They are in the Vanderbilt Library. Any one in this audience can see whether these things are correct or not. And I am showing you here now that not only do the writers of the Bible use "psallo" with the meaning to play with an instrument, but other writers contemporaneous with Bible writers use it in the same way.

And now, in closing the six minutes of my last speech for to-night, I wish to make this statement, which I made at the beginning: In the beginning our people appealed to the Bible, to the word of God, to the New Testament, as our rule of faith and practice. We are doing that same thing now. When we desired to know what the book said, we went to the English version. When there was any dispute about the meaning of a word, we went back to the Greek—that is, the original New Testament. We went back to the Greek, and we settled it by the Greek. We settled that way concerning "baptize," and we will settle it the same way concerning "sing." And that is the only way it can be properly settled. "To the law and to the testimony"—to the word of the living God—we must go.

[Moderator notifies that time is nearly out.]

Thank you. I want you to go away to-night with this in your hearts: I do not for one moment doubt your faith in the word of God. I trust you do not doubt my faith in his word. If I did not believe that you believed in God's word, I would not appeal to you upon the ground of his word; and if I did not believe in God's word as the revelation of his will to me and to you and the New Testament as our one rule of faith and practice, I would be unworthy of your consideration if I stood before you to-night and made such a plea.

I call to your attention to-night that I am "anathema" among some people; that the hands of many are raised against me to-night because I dare defend that book, because I dare attack men who attempt to tear it to pieces. And you ask me, Brother Hardeman, to get a little more backbone, a little more courage, and rush in and accept what you say about the matter. If there is anything "on the face of God's green earth," to use a Hardeman expression, that I believe I have, it is that thing called "backbone;" and if I believed it to be my duty to-night to accept the leadership of my brother, it would not take long to do that. But, brother, before I follow you in anything—I am perfectly willing to follow you—but before I follow you in this matter I want you to get a little bit closer to the New Testament. I want you to get back to the book and find out just what "psallo" means; and when we meet on that word and on all the other propositions we shall discuss, we will then come to the proposition as to whether or not this heart is the instrument.

Go away to-night with this in your hearts, my friends: If I should attempt to sing in my home, even with a "tacky little organ," it would be scriptural. He said that those of us who believe we have scriptural right to use an organ will put a "tacky little organ" in the church that we would not have in our homes, and thus divide churches. That is the flimsiest argument I ever heard. Bless your heart, we have "tacky" little windows in our churches we would not have in our homes; we have "tacky" carpets in our churches we would not have in our homes; we have a lot of "tacky" things in our churches we would not have in our homes. I am sorry for it, but it is a fact.

I thank you.

HARDEMAN'S FOURTH SPEECH

(Friday, June 1, 1923.)

Brethren, Moderators, Ladies, and Gentlemen [applause upon rising to speak]: I would like to insist, my friends, that you respect the wishes of both Brother Boswell and myself and the moderators on the point of applause or demonstration, lest we go from bad to worse, and thereby incur the censure on the part of the citizenship of the city regarding the levity that characterized this discussion. You will do me a favor if you will refrain from that during the time that I shall address you.

Now, it is pleasant to refer to the address just made and to speak of some things that were entered into. It was suggested at the first that in the heat of the discussion things might be said that would be better left off. I am certain that when Brother Boswell suggested he had not quite "petered out" he would rather not have made a statement of that kind.

Friends, I used the word "duplicity" not in the sense that was ascribed to it, but in connection with the statement on the board, which says "with or without," and that carries the sense of the word as I thus intended.

I call attention to the questions, some of which were answered and some were not. Brother H. L. Calhoun said that "worship to-day by means of instruments is not in truth, and, therefore, cannot be such as God accepts or seeks or approves." The only answer that Brother Boswell attempts to make is to ask the date of it, which is equivalent to no answer at all. Suffice it to say that is Brother Calhoun's sentiment of the matter to-day, as I have a comparatively recent letter from him indorsing and incorporating the same statement.

Now, No. 3: "Do you believe instrumental music is demanded, commanded, or authorized in Christian worship?" And watch the evasion and sidestepping and the lack of that courage that he spoke of at the last hour. Why, he said: "Brother Hardeman, it is scriptural." What is the answer?

Is it demanded, is it commanded, or is it authorized? He refuses positively to answer, but with another word altogether he says "it is scriptural." And I ask: What do you mean by "scriptural?" Distinguish and discriminate between "scriptural" and "unscriptural" and "antiscriptural." And then it comes with poor grace to talk about a man having courage to walk out and meet the issues as they are presented. Then in No. 3: "Is it authorized by God or by man?" He says: "I have answered that in No. 3 in the other one." I beg to say he did not answer No. 3. And No. 4: "Do you believe Brother Cowden's statement about Payne's book? Was Brother Briney right? Was the *Christian Standard* right? Do you believe Brother Payne expressed the truth on it?" Now, watch the puerile, childish answer. He seems to say: "Brother Hardeman, I haven't the courage to state an idea on it. My knees trembleth, my courage faileth, my backbone shaketh." He did say: "Ask them; they are of age." Ladies and gentlemen, the ridiculousness of it! A man boasting of his courage and then refusing to answer! "There is the answer, Brother Hardeman. I cannot answer it. Ask them." You should do better than that. The truth, ladies and gentlemen, is that the answer to these questions, as I apprehend them, would involve him in contradictions from which it would be absolutely and positively impossible for him to escape or maintain any ground of consistency in the light of what has been said; and, therefore, he took the course of prudence, and virtually said: "I will not answer that. If you want that answered, ask them; don't be asking me. Although I am in the lead and I am obligated to answer everything asked, yet I just throw up the white flag and say: 'Brother Hardeman, ask them; don't be asking me.' " In the name of all that is sacred and calm and in harmony with debates to-night, ladies and gentlemen, that is about the climax after the boasting that has been characteristic of the speaker.

Now, then, does the instrument inhere in "psallo?" He answered that by saying: "Yes." That is the kind of an answer a man ought to give. Now, if the instrument inheres in the word "psallo," then you cannot do the "psallo" act without the instrument; and, therefore, the statement of the chart that says we can "psallo" without it is contradictory to the answer. If the instrument is within the word—and that is his position—then you cannot do the thing that the word says without the instrument.

Then, on the other hand, he says: "While I said 'yes' up yonder, I meant 'no.'" And there stands the gentleman to-night in that dubious position. One time it is, and then, on the other hand, it is not. If I ask Brother Boswell this, "Does the word 'baptizo' mean to immerse?" he says, "Yes;" and I cannot fulfill that word unless I be immersed. No two ways about it. Now, then, does the instrument inhere in "psallo?" "Yes." To be consistent, you cannot do what "psallo" requests without the instrument. But he has said that I can; and, therefore, his statements are contradictory, as printed upon the chart.

And next: "Please state your position so clearly that there can be no misunderstanding regarding it." That question was passed absolutely; and the audience to-night, I have an idea, does not really understand what Brother Boswell's position is regarding this matter. But he says: "Hardeman is making the same speech." Well, Hardeman is following him; I am just answering him; and if he covers the same ground, why, of course, I will make the same speech. You are in the lead. I am following in your footsteps. Again, he says: "I am answering what you ask." Yet in his remarks he said I preached a commencement sermon at Alamo in the Methodist meetinghouse, and in that service they had the piano and some other instruments. He asked: "Did you worship?" No, not in the singing, for I did not sing. I hope you understand that.

He next, ladies and gentlemen, proposed to reflect upon Alexander Campbell by saying that it is not his comment upon the instrument, but his mere statement regarding it and his lack of appreciation for it.

It comes as the voice of the reformers, as the voice of the restorers, with Campbell, with Stone, with Scott, with Smith, and with others—men who stood as a unit against the instrument. My point was not reflecting upon Brother Boswell as the minister at Georgetown, but in harmony with what they preached back there; the custom has changed, and the procedure has changed; and if Alexander Campbell were back on earth to-day, and Barton W. Stone, they could not enter into the Georgetown Church, of which he is a minister, and feel at home or worship God conscientiously. Why? Because there has been injected into the service that for which there is not a particle of authority under heaven in the New Testament Scriptures. Still, he says, by way of implication, Hardeman reflects upon him as a smatterer of Greek and wants to make capital out of it. It is your "dear, old, sweet-spirited" Brother McGarvey, and not Hardeman at all; and hence, ladies and gentlemen, let no such things as that be palmed off as the sentiment of his opponent. Brother McGarvey said that "when any man who poses as a preacher thinks that there is authority in the word 'psallo' for the use of musical instruments in the service of God, he is one of those smatterers in Greek that can believe anything that he wants to." That is what your beloved teacher said about you, and not what your opponent had to say about you, by any means.

Well, he said: "Brother Hardeman, I will give you one hundred dollars for any lexicon that says play upon the heart." Brother Hardeman never suggested a thing of that kind. Here is what the lexicon suggests: that the word "psallo" means to play or strike or touch. Brother Boswell, Paul said "in the heart," and there is the man—not the lexicon, but Paul—that put the heart into it. And isn't it strange that out of four speeches the man has never yet quoted Eph. 5: 19—never has turned his attention to that? Yet he promised me last night to answer the questions; and he is a very promising young fellow to-night, and suggests that on to-morrow night he will tell you regarding it, and I begin to get shy of his promises. Last night: "I promise you, Hardeman, to answer all the questions put to me." And yet to-night you see he skips over five or six of them and says: "They are old enough to defend themselves. They are of age; ask them." If that is the way his promises are met, there is not much in store for us to-morrow night.

"O," he says, "Brother Hardeman, do you agree with Brother Kurfees?" Let me say, candidly, I have never pledged my faith to any man uninspired; but on the point you ask, Brother Boswell, yes, I agree with Brother Kurfees when he said, on page 44 of his book, that the word loses its meaning. What did he say it was? To pull the hair. It no longer means pull a hair. It lost this meaning.

And he has a right to tell what he means, and I read from the "Review of Payne," page 15: "And let the reader never forget that from the very earliest time, the earliest usage of the word, while it continued to carry through all its subsequent mutations the original meaning—namely, to touch or to strike some object—yet no particular object inhered in the word to the exclusion of the others. Neither the hair, nor the bowstring, nor the carpenter's line, nor the stringed instrument inheres in the word." But what is there? The idea of touch is there. It lost, Brother Kurfees said, pulling the hair, it lost touching the bowstrings, it lost twitching the carpenter's line; but it did not lose the pulling. It lost the hair, the bowstring, the carpenter's line, the mechanical instrument; but did not lose the original idea of pluck or pull or touch or twitch or twang; and the instrument has to be supplied in the context where it is found.

So, then, in the New Testament, Paul uses the word "psallo," and uses it with its original meaning. What is it? To touch, to pluck, or to twang. What is the instrument? God says it is the heart; and beyond that no answer, no attempt whatsoever, has been made in refutation. Hence, the principle must forever stand.

But he says Brother Hardeman claims that he set a trap. No, I never said any such thing. I said that Brother Payne set the trap, and all you gentlemen walked in, and in so doing you sawed off the limb between yourselves and the tree. Can't you get me right?

But, in regard to Herod's temple, I want to put the matter to a test. Brother Boswell, I want you to show, either by the Bible or profane history, where Christ or the apostles ever heard instruments of music in Herod's temple. That is the declaration made. I want you to defend it; I want you to demonstrate a statement that has been made by your sympathizers all over the land—that in the temple in Christ's time and the apostles' day there were ever instruments of music, and that Christ and the apostles ever heard the same. And I state, in addition, even if you could do that, it would force upon you the irresistible conclusion that you must offer animal sacrifices and burn incense, if these things that happened in Herod's temple are to be our precedent for instrumental music. You must accept all or none.

Now, I pass from that statement; and here he asks me about the harp in Rom. 15: 9. Let us just turn and read a minute. There is something in the Bible, ladies and gentlemen, that always precludes the possibility of doubt. Commencing with verse 6: "That ye may with one mind [or with one heart] and one mouth"—in verse 6 Paul uses both the "heart" and the "mouth," showing the thing about which he is talking—with one heart and with one mouth as the instruments, if you please, about which he is talking. What will I do in verse 9? "For this cause I will confess to thee among the Gentiles, and sing unto thy name." What do you mean, Paul? "I will confess Christ's name among the Gentiles, where I will sing God's praises; and in that 'psalloing ' I will sing with the spirit and with the understanding. The heart shall be in it." And Brother Boswell made a fine statement when he said here: "Brethren, I think that you cannot do any act acceptable to God Almighty without the heart." Brother Boswell, I am not impugning your motives, but listen: When we join in the singing of "All Hail the Power of Jesus' Name," and pronounce those words with the lips, and then accompany that with the heart, have we fulfilled God's demand in the word "psallo?" Have we, or have we not? is the question. Your chart says "yes" in one statement and "no" in another, and hence it is either way—just to suit the situation, anything, a matter of pleasure purely to men and not to God Almighty. Hence,

I state in all kindness, Brother Boswell, you are gone on the proposition. Come up to the Bible. Is it scriptural? Show direct command; show apostolic example; show necessary inference. O, we are going to do that at a subsequent time, and hence for to-night not use any one passage of scripture.

In Eph. 5: 18 Paul said: "Be ye filled [be "ye"—plural] with the Spirit." Who? Every one of you. "Be filled with the Spirit." "Speaking to yourselves." Who? You do it. Just one? O, no; but all of you. "Speaking to yourselves in psalms and hymns and spiritual songs, singing"—that word is plural also—each one of you singing. And what else? "Psallontes"—making melody. Who? Plural—every one of you. If it means mechanical instrument, Brother Boswell, it cannot be fulfilled until each member has an organ himself and each one plays on it. Every member—hear it—every member of the church is admonished by Paul to sing; every member of the church—plural—is admonished by Paul to "psallontes." If that means a mechanical instrument, then you cannot worship God by proxy, like they vote in a Democratic caucus or convention. Every man must "psallontes." What does it mean? According to the gentleman's declaration, it means a mechanical instrument. Then you cannot have just one fellow doing the "psallontes-ing" and the other doing the singing, but every one of them. Who? All of them. And hence it is an instrument for every one; and thus we contend that the Lord Jesus Christ has provided that every child of his, whether an artist on the mechanical instrument or not, can go on his journey to the eternal realm by singing and striking the strings of his own heart; and when he does that, he has worshiped God in spirit and in truth, without the aid of a mechanical device or invention of man.

I was amused, just a little bit, when he said: "Brother Hardeman, you asked me for the instrument. It is the tuning fork." Why, Brother Boswell, the tuning fork is not a musical instrument! Don't you know that? A musical instrument is that which is capable of producing a succession of melodious sounds—plural. A tuning fork has but one. It cannot, therefore, and does not come under the head of a musical instrument at all, and I beg you search Mr. Webster and find out what a musical instrument is. A thing that makes but one tone is not a musical instrument. You can touch a pitchfork as well as a tuning fork, but it is not a musical instrument. Why? There can be but one sound produced upon it.

Now, let me call attention to another thing. I mentioned last night that the Greek Catholic Church, which has spoken the Greek language all these years, reared in it, taught in it, brought up and educated—the Greek Catholic Church uses the word "psallo" to-night, and they understand thoroughly its meaning. What do they say about it? In the Greek Catholic Church there has never been a human instrument of music introduced. Why? They understand what the word "psallo" means—that it has reference to an instrument, but that it is an instrument described by Paul, the human heart, and not a mechanical device.

And that is not all; but Sophocles, to whose lexicon reference was but slightly made, stands to-night as the peer of all with reference to New Testament Greek; and when the great Greek, himself a native of Greece, a graduate of the various schools of his own country, a man who occupied the distinguished position of professor of Greek in Harvard College for a period of thirty-eight long years, wrote his lexicon, he said the word "psallo" meant—not the singing with artificial accompaniment, but to sing God's praises, to chant.

My opponent made the argument that David used the word "psallo" or its equivalent and designated the instrument, which was the cithara or harp. This is all true; but it is clearly against Brother Boswell, and yet he seems wholly unable to see it. "Psallo" means to touch, pull, twang, etc.; but the instrument thus touched does not inhere in the word. That must be determined from the context. In David's day the instrument was the harp, and is specifically mentioned. Now, the word "psallo" means the same thing in the New Testament, and the instrument is especially mentioned. What is the instrument? Paul says it is the heart, and that forever settles that matter.

But he suggests, again, that David played with his hands. Yes, that is the difference between David and Paul. David played with his hands, and that is what Brother Boswell wants to do. God says Christians play with the hearts, and hence the difference between Brother Boswell and the Bible on that proposition. He wants to worship God with the hand, because his proposition is that instrumental music, of the mechanical kind, is in the worship. And if it is in it, it is in it. It is not like the Dutchman's statement—near by—but it is in the worship. He wants to worship God with the hands, when Paul specifically says: "Worship God with the heart." The worship under the law in David's day was physical and outward. Under Christ it must be spiritual and inward.

But what did he do with the illustration I made when I said: "Go, baptize with water?" I made the point that when God named water, that excluded every other element. What did he do with it? O, nothing at all, but continued to read from his manuscript!

What further point? In like manner, when God said "psallo" with the heart, that forbids "psalloing" with any other instrument, by the law of exclusion. And what is his answer? With the four speeches made, not one word said regarding that. But he said, "Brother Hardeman, I believe the Bible with all of my heart;" and then he made a splendid appeal to the audience, which I trust you received. But now I want to ask Brother Boswell in your presence: Brother Boswell, do you believe the English translation of the Bible as we have it to-night? Do you believe that when, in the King James Version, forty-seven men translated "psallo" to sing, and the one hundred and one revisers translated it to sing and play upon the heart, they translated it correctly? I said that Mr. Payne's position forced him to reject the entire English version of the Bible. Brother Boswell is in the same fix, for he says: "I propose to read other versions." What does that signify, ladies and gentlemen? "I pass by King James, which translated the word; I pass by the Revised Version, which translated the same word. I am going to ignore them, and I am going to bring some that translate it otherwise." But I predict this: he will not bring a single translation—mark the prediction—he will not bring to you a single translation of any recognition whatsoever but that puts it with the heart as the instrument described by Paul in Eph. 5: 19.

Brother Boswell suggests that he is noted for his courage in preaching. I want to say, if that be true, he is an exception to the brotherhood with whom he stands. It is commonly understood in this country, Brother Boswell, that your preachers are weak-kneed in declaring the principles of the Restoration; that they will not, in the presence of the denominational world, come out and condemn sectarianism; that they will not draw the line of distinction between the church of God and human denominations; that they will not preach baptism for the remission of sins; and it has been suggested in the city of Nashville that the preachers who are weak-kneed and compromising on these very foundation principles should cut loose from the shackles of denominational affiliations and associations with men who are not in line with the Restoration Movement. Then you can stand for the principles once for all delivered unto the saints. And your beloved Peter Ainsley, the chairman of the Commission on Unity, up in Maryland, said: "I will accept the Presbyterians and Methodists on their sprinkling and their pouring; I will not think that they are not as good as I am, although I have been immersed. I will fellowship them." That is the sweet spirit; but when that is done, the faith has been compromised. Ainsley further said, in substance: "Brethren, I am big enough and broad enough to do that. Presbyterians, Methodists, all of you, come in; we will accept your sprinkling and pouring, and we will all be good fellows together." And that is the kind of preaching that characterizes the man who sidesteps from the foundation principles and accepts a practice for which there is no direct authority in all the book of God.

I submit to you, ladies and gentlemen, that it is possible for the brotherhood to stand together in Nashville. What is the barrier? The organ is one of the leading hindrances. With that eliminated—and my brother says he can worship

God conscientiously without it—with that out of the way, our other difficulties, I fancy, would be eliminated.

I thank you very kindly.

MODERATOR: At the conclusion of these four speeches, possibly four of the most brilliant speeches that we have ever heard in the city, it is requested that this audience stand and join in singing, under the leadership of Brother Pullias, "Praise God, from Whom All Blessings Flow."

BOSWELL'S FIFTH SPEECH

(Saturday, June 2, 1923.)

Brother Moderator, Brother Hardeman, Brothers, and Sisters: It has been my purpose to conduct, as far as possible, this discussion in the best possible spirit. I made up my mind, if it were possible, that I should say or do nothing during this discussion that would call for any apology upon my part, or feeling in my heart that I had in any way transgressed the rules of discussion; and I am very sorry, indeed, that I am under the necessity to-night of calling attention to some things that have been said by Brother Hardeman. These expressions of his are the earmarks of one who is driven into a corner and finds difficulty in extricating himself by sticking to the proposition. What I shall say is said in the spirit of utmost kindness, but in clear frankness. He took it upon himself last night to reprove me for drifting into slang. I can only offset that by saying that the seeming slang of mine was not comparable to his reference to "baptism in buttermilk." The next thing to which I wish to call your attention is that he has referred to my arguments as "puerile" arguments, and has expressed himself as greatly disappointed in the ability of the one who is discussing the affirmative of this position. And then, last of all along this line, he used an expression last night to which I called his attention and which he tried to pass over by giving some sort of a definition and very kindly suggesting that I get a dictionary, Webster, and look up the meaning of the word.

I refer to the charge of "duplicity" as attached to my answer to his question; and that you may understand why I took exception to it and why his explanation is worse than the offense, I shall read to you just what he said, as recorded in the paper. "Let me suggest," he said, "an amusing thing, if it were not serious, is the fulfillment of the promise to answer the question. 'I have answered that, as I said I would.' I failed to get last night the 'as I said I would'—just how he meant to answer that. But let me suggest to you, when I suggested the question, 'Can the five points in the New Testament wherein "psallo" is found be complied with without the use of an instrument?' meaning a mechanical instrument, of course, as he represents, he answers: 'With or without'—'yes or no.' I must say that I am surprised at that kind of an answer, and his duplicity on the question does not measure up to my high conception of Brother Boswell as a high-toned gentleman in other respects. But I can appreciate the situation as pertaining thereto."

This followed the charge that I did not have the courage to state my position. This whole statement was made to break the crushing force of my answer to this question. It was not "with or without"—"yes or no;" it was answered fully. He suggested I take up the word in Webster, and then gave a definition which has to do with the technical meaning of the word and could not apply in this case. The general definition holds good here, the meaning which usually goes with its use. It is this, and this definition is the one that fits his statement, my friends: "Doubleness of heart or speech; deception by pretending to entertain one state of feeling, but acting under the influence of another."

Again, I call attention to the concluding remarks of his address last night—an attack upon the speaker of the affirmative and an attack upon those who are associated with me, among those people with whom I am associated rather, and an attack upon the ministers of this city in whose congregations they have instruments. Brother Hardeman had every reason in the world to know that I have withstood with all the power that is within me the position of Peter Ainslie. Everything I have ever written—every public expression, every writing—is an emphatic condemnation of Peter Ainslie's position; and everything I have written, everything I have said, is an emphatic contradiction of the position taken by the United Christian Missionary Society and by infidel teachers in some of our colleges. With these facts known to him, he charged me with indorsing these false teachings, turning to me and saying "your beloved Peter Ainslie." I think he should produce the witnesses or retract the statement.

He has charged the other ministers of this city with the same sort of action. I am here to say that I believe that John B. Cowden, J. J. Walker, and Carey Morgan, the ones with whom I have been most intimately associated, are as true to this book, as true to the principles of the Restoration Movement, as ever Brother Hardeman dared to be.

My friends, I love personally Peter Ainslie. I do not destroy the personal love in my heart for men with whom I differ. Ask Peter Ainslie how we stand; ask any of these men how we stand. I am saying to you to-night that if there is anything that Jesus denounced with most scathing rebuke, it was that pharisaism which causes men to draw the robes of self-righteousness about them, thus keeping themselves from coming in contact with men who had not come under the influence of Jesus himself or who teach and practice false doctrines. One of the most stinging, scathing denunciations that Jesus ever uttered was given by him when it was said he associated with publicans and sinners; and in the story of the prodigal son Jesus told us not to hold ourselves aloof from men, but to bring ourselves in heart contact with them; and if we are growing more and more in the image of our Father, we will come in contact with the men who need us most. My friends, I am sorry I had to call attention to this, but I felt impelled to do it. My self-respect, my respect for the position I occupy, and my respect for the men with whom I am associated, compelled me to do it.

Now, I wish to address myself to the question at issue. Brother Hardeman said a few nights ago, or rather asked the question, and has continued to ask: "What do you mean by 'scriptural?' " I replied that I did not think it necessary to define such a term to a people who had always appealed to the Scriptures. I thought they would understand the term as always used by us. He then gave the definition which has always been current among us, and I did not see the necessity of further discussing that term. Everything that I have brought to this discussion has been predicated upon all three of the elements of his definition—terms found in the Scriptures, apostolic precedent, and necessary inference. I have followed that definition from the beginning until now. I have never shied from it, nor has there been anything in my heart of fear, that I could not afford, as was insinuated, to stand for it. I now ask him to give a scriptural definition of "heart."

In his first rejoinder on Thursday night Brother Hardeman said: "Now, the question to-night, and the only one, for consideration, is: What, under the New Testament, is the instrument that accompanies the singing? And, ladies and gentlemen, the apostle Paul, in his peerless announcement, said, once for all, that we are to sing unto the Lord and 'psallo' with the heart—not with the fingers, not with the plectrum, but with the heart; and, therefore, the heart to-night accompanies the singing, or, as I expect to sound forth the vocal praises thereof, since that expression of the lips is accompanied by the human heart's power being in it, back of it, and prompting the utterance thereof, it is not the worship described in the New Testament." This statement is reported in the paper, but I am sure that "not" should be eliminated. I am certain of that, or the sentence would have to be changed. It would make it say that all these things are not, when I think it means that they are, acceptable worship. With the elimination of the statement that the "apostle Paul said, once for all, that we are to 'sing unto the Lord ("psallo") with the heart—not with fingers, not with the plectrum, but with the heart,' " I accept the statement as correct.

What Paul did say was: "Singing ["adontes"] and making melody ["psallontes"] with your heart unto the Lord." "Psallontes," from "psallo," is the word under dispute. It is translated in the other places three times, "sing;" once, "sing praise." Brethren, the statement that Brother Hardeman accredits to Paul is Brother Hardeman's statement of what Paul meant. But I am going to grant that for a moment and propound some questions. Grant that Paul meant the heart as the instrument in Eph. 5: 19, where he says, "Speaking one to another in psalms and hymns and spiritual songs, singing and making melody in your heart to the Lord," how would those to whom James wrote when he said, "Is any among you suffering, let him pray; is any cheerful, let him sing praise," know that the instrument is limited to the heart? Note, James was written 44-60; Ephesians, 62-63. If James was written and the word was being used before Paul wrote what Brother Hardeman says he wrote to the Ephesians, how would those in Corinth know when Paul wrote them, "I will sing with the spirit, and I will sing with the understanding also," when his First Corinthian letter was in 57 and Ephesians in 62-63? When the Corinthian brethren were reading the statement of Paul, with that same word "psallo" in it, he had never written his letter to the Ephesians with "psalloing in the heart." How would the Roman Christians know when Paul wrote them, therefore, "I will give praise unto thee among the Gentiles, and sing unto thy name," when Romans was written in 58-59 and Ephesians in 62-63? These are things that demand attention. Years before the apostle Paul had ever given the definition or explanation that Brother Hardeman says he gave, these other admonitions or commands were being read by the Corinthians, by the Romans, and by those to whom James wrote. They had to wait, then, until Paul wrote to the Ephesians before they could find out, before they knew any better than that the word carried with it the use of a mechanical instrument.

I cannot understand why Brother Hardeman has been so disturbed over my not using the word "mechanical" in connection with "instrument." The very proposition I am discussing carries that with it. And when I said the other night that the tuning fork was the instrument, he took it seriously. They always do when you mention tuning fork. It is a sort of a fork that forks some things out of the way. It sticks them.

Now, the question at issue between us is—but I want to ask another question right here. In Romans—and don't forget this—in Romans the word "psallo" is taken from the Septuagint, and the Septuagint is taken from the Hebrew, and the word in the Hebrew is "zamar." That word does not mean to sing without an instrument; it means to sing with an instrument. And how did they know what Brother Hardeman was trying to make it appear that Paul told them without Paul's being there? The Romans had Paul's epistle before they had a visit from him. I will have more to say about "zamar" later on.

The question at issue between us is: What is the instrument that accompanies the playing? I trust I state Brother Hardeman's contention correctly. Brother Hardeman's contention is that there is no mechanical instrument in the meaning of "psallo;" but the instrument must be specified, and that instrument is the heart. I accept all Brother Hardeman says as to the heart's being in all our worship. I did that at the beginning, and have done so from the beginning. I now wish to submit proof that the word "psallo" includes the use of a mechanical instrument.

The lexicons which I read from as to the primary meaning of the word, and which I offer in evidence, show that the meaning carried with it the idea of playing upon a musical instrument. And right here let me say that I have already said, quoting from Brother Kurfees, that "psallo" at one time carried with it playing upon a musical instrument. Brother Kurfees says that "psallo" had lost this meaning before the beginning of the New Testament times, and is never used in the New Testament nor in contemporaneous writers in this sense.

Brother Hardeman has forsaken the contention that it lost that meaning, and has agreed with the meaning of these lexicons, only he wants to have Paul say what he says Paul said—that is, the heart is the instrument. Pickering: "To touch gently, to touch or play on a stringed instrument; to cause to vibrate; to play." I only quote a few of these to show you that the ones I have already quoted indicate this idea.

I want to come over, then, to the New Testament use, getting away from the primary meaning. Reading from Robinson: "In Septuagint and New Testament, to sing, chant, properly as accompanying stringed instruments." "Later usage, song, properly as accompanying stringed instruments." That is "psalmos." Yonge: "In the New Testament, to sing while touching the chords, while accompanying oneself on a stringed instrument, to sing psalms. (Rom. 15: 9.)" Liddell & Scott give practically the same definition, and so do the others.

I come now to some that speak directly. The first is the Interpreter of Aristophanes, 200 B.C.: "*Psallo*, the sounding of the cithara."

The Scholiast, 250 B.C., defining the word "psalmos" (used about a century and a half earlier): "*Psalmos*, properly the sound of the cithara."

St. Augustine, 396 A.D.: "*Psalmos* is produced by a visible instrument, while *canticum* is produced by the mouth."

Lexicon by Cyril of Alexander, 435 A.D.: "*Psalmos*, a musical utterance, while the instrument is played rhythmically according to harmonic notes."

Donnegan: "The touching of the chords of a musical instrument, the playing on a harp or similar instrument."

Handworterbuch der Griechischen Sprache, 1823 A.D.—I am not a German—says: "*Psallo*, to play a stringed instrument." "*Psalmos*, the playing of the cithara or of any other stringed instrument; the song sung to the playing of a stringed instrument."

Lexicon Manuale, Bretschneider, 1824 A.D.: "*Psallo*, to touch strings, strike the lyre, play the lyre, to produce music either to musical instruments or with the voice alone, and only of a joyful music, hence to glorify in song."

Thesaurus Græcæ Linguæ: "*Psallo*, musicians are said to *psallein* their own strings, or simply to *psallein*. Paul, in Epistle to Ephesians (5: 19): 'Speaking to yourselves in psalms and hymns and spiritual songs.' *Adontes* (singing) and *psallontes* (making melody)—i. e., striking the cithara or lyre, playing; for it is properly used of touching the lyre."

Harper's Dictionary: "*Psallo*, to play on a stringed instrument, especially on a lyre or cithara, to sing to the cithara or lyre."

Andrews: "*Psallo*, to play upon a stringed instrument, especially to play upon the cithara, to sing to the cithara."

Sophocles: "*Psallo,* to chant, sing religious hymns." "*Psalmos,* psalm." "*Psaltes,* one who plays on a stringed instrument, harper." "Classical, chanter, church singer." "*Psaltoideo,* to sing to the harp." The latter part of that word is the singing; the first part is the harp. "*Psaltos,* played upon the psaltery, sung."

I wish to bring to you now some scholars. These scholars will not only testify to the meaning as I have been quoting all along, but they will also testify, as most of them have already testified, that the word carries with it the use of an instrument made by the hand of man. "I know of no instance"—this has reference to the loss of the word before the year 146, and I will not read that, as Brother Hardeman has given up the contention that the word had lost its meaning.

Prof. A. T. Robertson, of the Southern Baptist Seminary, speaking, quoting Gregory, 370 A.D., says: "The psalm ["psalmos"] is the melody produced on the musical instrument [the "organon"]." "The song [ode] is the utterance of the melody ["melos"] through the mouth with words." "Hymn ["humnos"] is the praise offered to God for the good things that we possess." "The psaltery ["psalterion"] is a musical instrument which emits the sound from the upper parts of the structure. The music made by this instrument is called 'psalm' ["psalmos"]—i. e., the music made by this instrument is the kind Paul repeatedly bids Christians employ in worship."

Robertson, commenting on this, says: "This threefold definition by Gregory, so exactly to the point and so conclusive, is as as good as you could wish."

He says: "*Psallo* originally meant to strike an instrument like a harp, and then to sing to the music of the instrument. This was its common use, and the psalms were sung with musical accompaniment. The early Christians seem to have followed Jewish usage in the use of musical instruments in praising God."

Prof. Richard Gottheil (Chief of Oriental Division, New York Public Library): "*Psallein* in classical Greek always means to play a stringed instrument with the fingers, as opposed to *krekein,* to play on such instrument with the plectron. I think your contention that *psallo,* in the New Testament, indicates the instrument, is correct."

Prof. Maurice Hutton (University College, Toronto): "This general truth is certain: *Psallein* does not only not preclude a musical instrument, but it necessarily implies one, and most naturally a harp, though the word might cover less naturally a flute, or even a modern organ or piano, since it means to strike with the fingers."

He is talking about the classical and Christian use of the word as accompaniment to the stringed instrument. He says: "The Christian use of the word is singing with the accompaniment of a stringed instrument. St. Paul's Epistle to the Ephesians (5: 19) is the authority for this use, given by Liddell & Scott; in addition, Rom. 15: 9 and 1 Cor. 14: 15. In all these cases I assume the meaning to be, properly, sing to the accompaniment of the harp. There cannot be the shadow of a doubt about the proper meaning of the Greek word 'psallo' and of its original use in the apostolic age; no doubt (as Dean Alford says) it came to be used carelessly, and generally of 'songs of praise;' but it properly means, rather, melodies—tunes of praise, played on an instrument, and, naturally, upon the harp in particular, since that was the instrument which the Greeks used most, and which was played by the tips of the fingers striking its chords."

HARDEMAN'S FIFTH SPEECH

(Saturday, June 2, 1923.)

Brethren, Moderators, Ladies, and Gentlemen: I appreciate the fine spirit that prevails to-night, and I would not have my friends to fail to recognize the fact that I am quite appreciative also of your interest and your respect, as you are disposed to evidence it; but let me suggest to you that these are matters that pertain to our eternal destiny, which we have to answer after the things of time shall have passed. I do not want that criticism to be justly made that this discussion has drifted into a lighter vein, lest there be a prejudice engendered against religious discussions that would some time prevent their recurrence. I trust, therefore, that you will most heartily acquiesce in the suggestions made at the very beginning with reference to demonstrations in any form.

There are some things to which I want to call attention, though they be not logically arranged; but as a negative speaker, following the affirmative, they have to come just as they are presented and as attention is called thereto.

The proposition is that "Instrumental music in the worship is scriptural," meaning by that, as defined by my opponent, instruments of a mechanical nature. Some evenings ago I asked him to be specific, and he said, "I mean they are in the worship;" and yet by some kind of an expression that was not at all clear to me he said: "They are not in the worship." Finally he suggested that they were matters of accompaniment to the singing. Then I asked him the direct question: "What do they accompany when you don't sing, since I have heard the organ used when there wasn't a song being sung?" Although the evenings have passed and speech after speech has been made, not one solitary reference has been made thereto, and so I ask again to-night. During the Lord's Supper, Brother Boswell's people sometimes play the mechanical instrument. Does it accompany the Lord's Supper? Sometimes they play it when they are taking up the contribution. Does it accompany the quarters and the half dollars or the pennies and sometimes dollars? They play it when there is not anything else going on; and hence he owes it to himself, as an affirmant whose position is in question, and he owes it to that position, to explain these matters. I want also to keep before you this fact, further: the faith and practice of your humble servant is not in doubt, is not in dispute, is not in question. There is not a single thing that I preach or practice but that Brother Boswell will indorse. And I will pledge him this now: if he will call my attention to anything that I do preach or practice that is not in harmony with that which he says is scriptural, I shall be exceedingly glad, as far as conscience will permit, to drop that thing in order that I may come to you and give you no occasion for offense whatsoever. Name one item, therefore, in the acts of worship presented to-night, and if there be not a "Thus saith the Lord" for that act of public worship of the church of God, I want to drop it. I want to occupy no ground that all my brethren cannot stand upon.

One-half of this debate with Brother Boswell is over—fifty per cent of it gone. In looking over my notes to-day I have this to suggest, not positively, but from any remembrance that I could have since its beginning: I could not recall one single scriptural quotation that Brother Boswell has ever offered in support of his proposition. If that man to-night in each of his five addresses has quoted one solitary passage of scripture, from first to last, and said. "Brother Hardeman, upon this I make my claim," I do not remember it. I really think that you have had "psalloing" to your heart's content. But to-night it is the same old story over and over, reading from Mr. Payne's book, which he dare not indorse, though some of his number have previously. He has recounted over and over and over again the same old things, and not one of which adds an iota of additional proof.

Now, I want Brother Boswell to understand one thing and not to grow serious and take the matter personally when I suggest to the gentleman that he has absolutely failed to measure up to his proposition. Brother Boswell, it is no reflection on you; you have done as well as any living man on earth can do.

MR. BOSWELL: A point of order. I dislike very much to interrupt, but I just ask you the point of whether he says he made the statement that I did not measure up to the proposition. My recollection is, I did not measure up to his estimation as a high-toned gentleman in other respects.

MR. HARDEMAN: All right; have it either way you want it.

Ladies and gentlemen, let me suggest this: Brother Boswell is a man, I take it, of splendid ability. I never saw him until this discussion; I am very glad to meet him. But the weakness of the affair and the failure to come with a direct scripture and to measure up as an affirmant ought to, is due not to the man, but to the weakness of the proposition, which no man on earth can prove to-night, either in the Bible or out of the Bible. There is the trouble and there is the weakness, as is evidenced on every hand.

Now, I thought when Brother Boswell reviewed some of the hard sayings of Hardeman there would be some things that I certainly had overlooked; but when he touched the keynote, it was the word "duplicity." Then as I listened carefully to the definition of the meaning from Webster, which he read, one of those meanings was "doubleness of speech." In all kindness, Brother Boswell, accepting your own declaration, I must say to you: I think you are guilty of "doubleness of speech." Look up yonder at the chart—the New Testament word of "psallo." Now note: It says: "The word of God for instrumental music." That is one statement. Look at the next word: "Sing *with* or *without* instrumental music." At the top part of the chart it is, "God's word for it;" in the next line you say, "with or without." If that is not crossing the question, then, as the boys sometimes say, "search me."

But, again, that is not all. Look at the next statement: "The negative position is to sing without instrumental music." Brother Boswell, the reason that is not so is that it is exactly the opposite of the truth. The negative position is that you cannot "psallo" without the instrument. Your chart is wrong and deceptive.

Now, no man, ladies and gentlemen, appreciates a high-toned discussion more than I do, and I say to you candidly that I allow no man to be more kindly disposed toward his fellows or further from that which would wound or offend. I speak plainly, but kindly, in all matters.

Now, Brother Boswell mistook the point entirely last night in reference to his beloved brother, Peter Ainslie. I did say his "beloved;" but if he does not care to fellowship him, I'm sure I have no objections. I did not care whether Brother Boswell indorsed Peter Ainslie or not; I don't care whether or not the *Standard* does. The principle I wanted to get before you is this: Whenever a man departs from the gospel of Christ and "Thus saith the Lord" for acts of worship, the end of it is to drift toward infidelity and skepticism of various kinds. While Peter Ainslie once stood as a faithful gospel preacher, one departure prepared the ground for another; and so he has drifted until by and by, growing weak-kneed on the principles of the Restoration Movement, losing courage to stand in the presence of the denominational world and preach the gospel, his faith has been weakened and he has become so large that he accepts Methodists and Presbyterians upon their sprinkling. I want to say this to the Methodists and Presbyterians, as I have said repeatedly: You are a consistent body of people. I don't think you are right, but you are consistent in that you believe the church is but an organization nonessential to the salvation of men. But Peter Ainslie and his type have once believed that immersion is baptism, and that alone—that baptism is for the remission of sins; and the point I make is that he has given up the plea of the fathers and sacrificed the truth of God. Brother Boswell will not deny but that a number of his preachers have thus sacrificed the truth and have become rank infidels.

Let me just say this: that while the preachers with whom I stand are divided on many points, I will tell you what you can do, Brother Boswell. You can take a fine-toothed comb and rake the entire number, and there is not an infidel, there is not a destructive critic, in the entire list—not one. They ring true to the fundamentals of the gospel of Christ.

And now may I offer, because I have a right to speak as one having authority, my good Brother Boswell just a word of advice without being out of order? I suggest to you, Brother Boswell, when you go to build your new school, that you put the "creed in the deed," lest they steal it from you like they did Lexington some years ago. You know that it was built with the money of men that believed the gospel. Faithful men put their hard-earned dollars into Transylvania University for the teaching of the Bible under McGarvey and others. What happened? Some of their own would-be brethren, under the camouflage of genuine Christians, crept into the board of trustees, gained possession thereof, and the result was that they wrested Transylvania from you, and your once happy institution, in which you were a student, is now an infidel school. I think you are right now when you advise your brethren not to put their money in it. Now, then, lest when you collect money from your brethren and build your new school—how do you know that twenty-five years hence they will not come and take it from you? Protect your property, lest they take it from you, even though they had not builded it with their own means.

When Brother Boswell comes to the idea of scriptural, he says: "I accept Brother Hardeman's definition. It is by direct command, apostolic example, and necessary inference." All right, Brother Boswell, I want to ask you: Where did God command the instrument? Where do you find apostolic practice for it?

Was it in the temple? I want Brother Boswell to find the proof positive where instruments were in Herod's temple, and that Christ and the apostles ever heard one strain of music. I have emphasized this with the hope of his giving special attention to it. Did the apostles burn incense and offer sacrifices? Such were in the temple. Must we have them now? Why do you leave out these? You will not accept the temple practice. Why use it, then?

Now, he asked: "Brother Hardeman, please tell me what the heart is." Well, if I were to do like Brother Boswell, I would say: Why, we have talked about that so much and we preach about it so much that I just guess everybody understands that, and pass on. That is about what I would say. But I want to be specific. My obligation when I come to engage in a debate is to take nothing for granted—I think that is out of order—but to examine everything with fairness and with candor. That is what one of the rules suggests, and it comes with poor grace for him to intimate that the rules have been violated by the other side of the question, when the first rule says the question should be so well defined that there can be no doubt regarding it, and that whatever argument is presented should be weighed with candor and fairness. It is not sufficient to say: "I thought everybody knew it, and hence no use to define it."

The heart is that part of man, as used in this connection, responsible, accountable, and amenable unto God. It is that which differentiates between man and the animal and that which rises to heights sublime in its opportunity and privilege of worshiping the God of heaven. It is called in the Bible sometimes the "heart," it is called the "mind," and it is sometimes called the "eyes," alluding not to the physical eye, but to the mind's eye or spirit's eye. To open their hearts was the purpose of the gospel.

When Paul preached to Lydia and her household, the Lord opened their hearts—their understanding, their minds, their spiritual responsibility—by bringing to bear upon them facts and truths and evidences from the gospel of Christ; and hence with God's word as the means Paul opened the thing with which Christian people are to make melody unto God.

My attention is called to James 5: 13. James says: "Is any merry? let him sing psalms." Suppose that a brother be out in the field hoeing cotton or plowing corn, and he becomes merry and wants to sing psalms. According to Brother Boswell's idea, he would have to take out the mule, ride to town, and hunt up a musical instrument and carry it back to the cornfield before he could do what God said.

Now, note again. On that point I think the exact idea Brother Boswell had in his mind was that James was written before Paul said to the Ephesians: "Make melody in your heart." Also the Corinthian letter was written before Ephesians, and Paul had not as yet told them how to make melody. But Paul said in 1 Cor. 14: 15: "Let him sing." How? "With the spirit. Let him sing with the understanding." That is the "how." But it becomes next to impossible to suggest that the inspired apostles had failed to teach all along the line other Christians just as Paul did those Ephesians. I want to ask Brother Boswell if Ephesians and all the Bible were written during the first century, how could they know anything about the organ, since it was not introduced until the seventh century? The Restoration began in 1801-1804, and it was 1869 before the brethren ever learned to use the organ. Where did they find that out?

The plain facts are these: Brother Boswell and his brethren learned the use of the organ and instruments, mechanical, from the denominational world. The denominations learned it from the Catholics, who introduced it about the middle of the seventh century, and, according to the histories and the encyclopedias, the Catholics got it from the heathen; and since that time the practice has been perpetuated on down the line. That is not the only thing you borrowed from the denominational world, but, to be like the nations around about, you have gone into various affairs unheard of by the apostolic church. Well, he said in that declaration: "I will stand on Hardeman's declaration and statement of 'psallo.'" Brother Boswell, if you will, the matter is ended and unity on that point, at least, will prevail. If I occupy safe ground with reference to this proposition, that you can sing without a mechanical instrument (and you admit it), I beg of you to remove the barrier and let us go to meeting together at once. What say you? There is the hindrance. Is it on my part? No, sir, I have not anything to keep you from going with me. I could honestly invite you to go with me into any congregation and not feel that I was imposing upon your conscience. Put yourself in the same attitude, and I will go with you right now. What is in the way of Brother Boswell's and my standing together? What is it? That which he himself says can be dispensed with. Had you rather have the organ or the fellowship and union of the people of Nashville? Here we are, perhaps ten thousand strong in this city, and we would worship together with you if the organ were removed, believing confidently, as I do, that other differences could be ironed out and all would be happily joined together. Why not make the start? And that start could be made by the removal of that which he himself says would be all right and no violation of God's word.

But on the word "psallo" I want to ask Brother Boswell three or four questions, together with others that are directly related, and it will bring up this same statement that has been gone over heretofore. Brother Boswell, can you baptize with or without an element? What is the element? Can you circumcise with or without an instrument? What is the instrument? Can you "psallo" with or without an instrument? What is the instrument? In King James and the Revised Version is "psallo" correctly translated? Next, what lexicon says you can "psallo" without an instrument? You said it, and you are wonderful on lexicons. Now, you have been trying to give the lexicons that said you could "psallo" with it. Now, let us have some that say you can "psallo" without it; and I pass you those with the hope that you can get to them immediately rather than postpone it until next week.

Ladies and gentlemen, one other point that I want to call attention to and get it in the record with reference to the meeting of last year and the refusal, as it was put, of a contribution to the meeting held here. I just give the facts without comment thereon.

Previous to that meeting, as I have been told, there was a letter sent out by my brethren to every congregation in Nashville, not one excepted, not one denomination but that received a letter. Vine Street Church acted upon it and sent to the committee a check of three hundred dollars. Now, that committee discussed the disposition of that act in a very fine spirit, to my certain knowledge; and upon consideration of some matters, they returned that check, and here is the letter they sent, and I want to get the letter in the record:

"NASHVILLE, TENN., March 28, 1922.

"*The Elders, Vine Street Christian Church, Nashville, Tenn.*

"DEAR BRETHREN: We appreciate your very friendly offer to assist us in financing the Hardeman-Pullias meeting, also the brotherly spirit which you have shown in discontinuing your night services while the revival is in progress. It is our intention during this meeting to declare the whole counsel of God. In so doing we may preach against some things which you are practicing that have caused a division which we greatly deplore. We feel that to accept financial aid from you would be unjust to you, and also would create the impression that we indorsed those things."

Now note:

"We are accordingly returning your check for your further consideration."

Now, the point was simply this: We are going to preach, perhaps, in that meeting things that Vine Street does not believe, and we want to be perfectly frank and free about it, and we would not be in the attitude of accepting their check without stating that in advance; and upon informing these brethren that we may do that, we returned it for their further consideration, and the matter then was turned over to them for their further disposal. Now note the next thought:

"Though we do not see our way clear to accept your financial aid, please understand that we desire your attendance and personal interest in the meeting. We wish further to say that should our differences be discussed it will be done in a spirit of brotherly love and with regard for your convictions on these questions.

"In conclusion, will you not join us in the earnest prayer that the time may soon come when all God's people will be united as they were in the days of the apostles? And we want you to know that we are willing to make any sacrifice consistent with our honest, conscientious convictions reaching that end; and may God and his richest benedictions rest upon us in order that union, which once existed, may be brought about."

Now, that is the much-talked-of letter and the kindly spirit that was exhibited in the same.

But so much for that. Now, ladies and gentlemen, I have called Brother Boswell's attention to this fact, which he has not answered: That the Greek Catholic Church, which has always spoken the Greek language, which knows its mother tongue, has never, and does not to-night, use a mechanical instrument. I want to ask: Is it not a fact that the native Greeks ought to know what the word "psallo" means; that it means to accompany with an instrument not made by hands, but the instrument described by God when he said: "Make melody in your hearts unto the Lord?" And, then, Professor Sophocles, a native Greek himself, of high standing, defines the word as it is used in the New Testament, and suggests that it means "to sing the praise of God, to chant the songs thereof." And I ask again to-night, when fifty per cent of the debate is over, what passage has Brother Boswell recited upon which you can rely?

I thank you very kindly.

BOSWELL'S SIXTH SPEECH

(Saturday, June 2, 1923.)

Brother Moderator and Brethren: I just wish to say that I have said nothing about the applause, because you might have misunderstood me, thinking perhaps because there were more people here that know Brother Hardeman you might misconstrue me; but so far as I am concerned, the applause does not make any particular difference with me.

MR. SRYGLEY: I think we had better not have it.

MR. BOSWELL: I think it would be better not to have it.

I am sorry I cannot please Brother Hardeman. He kept after me for several nights to discuss "in the heart," or "the instrument—what is the instrument?" But as soon as I got to it he went off on something else and presented me with more questions. Every question that he has presented is answered in the speeches that have been made. It is not my fault that he cannot remember; it is not my fault that he does not know a great many things; it is not my fault that he does not read the reports that are printed in the papers. I am not his tutor. I do not have to tell him about that temple until I get ready to tell him about it. I told him last night that I was going to stay in that temple until I found out all about it. I can tell him to-night, but I don't want to tell him. I want to keep him in painful ignorance a little bit longer. It is a fine thing for some men not to know some things. I see that my arrows are reaching some. Now, friends, that hissing does not worry me a particle; it only hurts you.

I wish to give Brother Hardeman an address where he can get some information concerning Sophocles and the practice of the Greek Church. I shall handle that myself when the time comes. But I desire to refer him to the priest, Charlontes—something like that; the writing is such that I cannot read it, and the name is unfamiliar to me; but he is the Greek priest in charge of the Greek Church here in this city, and he will tell you something about the Greek

Church, and then I will tell you what he says later on, and then I will tell you some other things.

Now, brethren, Brother Hardeman thinks his assertions are arguments. He says I have not quoted scripture. Is there no scripture except in the English? Have we not been talking about particular scriptures? We are not talking about the garden of Eden to-night; I am not discussing Revelation, the book of Revelation; we are talking about the meaning of a certain word—the word which he says means to sing, the word which I say means to sing with or without an instrument. I have said that constantly. That is the thing I am affirming. That is the meaning the lexicons have indicated; any number that I have read have indicated that. What difference does it make whether I quote Mr. Payne or any one else? Doesn't he quote some people? Are things wrong for me to do that are perfectly right for him to do? Has he answered all questions that I have asked him? The right to use the instrument is the thing we are discussing. He says I have said that there is no difference between us, and that he is standing on scriptural grounds. I have never said that. To the contrary, I denied that emphatically, and can show it in the written record. I am saying that I am standing on my liberty in Christ Jesus; that I have the right to use the instrument; that I have the right not to use it. He says I have not the right to use it at all, and he disfellowships me because I want to exercise my right, against which he has not brought one single argument, but mere assertions.

I am here to show you that this word "psallo" gives me the right to do it. He says I haven't quoted authority. I shall read one that is before my eyes at this moment—Prof. L. R. Higgins, Department of Greek, Ottawa University: "*Psallo*, in Greek, meant (1) to play a harp, or (2) to sing to the accompaniment of some such instrument. Possibly it may sometimes have been used to sing without a musical accompaniment. I should say that an instrumental (harp) accompaniment is naturally included in Rom. 15: 9 and in 1 Cor. 14: 15."

He says: "What is it that keeps me from fellowshiping

him if he is right, and I admit that he is right?" The very fact, my brother, that you make the organ a test of fellowship. The next thing is that you put the "creed in the deed." The following is a sample of the "creed in the deed:"

It is the object of those building this house to encourage and build up churches that will in all work and worship use only what is ordered and required by the New Testament, rejecting all the inventions and devices of man, such as the use of the organ and other instruments of music in connection with the worship, and of any society other than the church of Christ in carrying out the work of God.

"In the event of any division arising over these or other questions that may come up, the title of this property inheres to those, whether a majority or a minority, who most rigidly adhere to the requirements of the New Testament.

"If at any time there should be *no dissenting voice* [Italics mine] to the use of the instruments and devices herein mentioned, and should they be used as a part of the worship in the building or on said lot, then said building or said lot shall go to the control of the churches of Christ in--------------------, State of Tennessee, worshiping according to the requirements herein approved, to be used and controlled by churches for the work approved by them in said County, --------------------, State of Tennessee."

He has had much to say about Carey Morgan and these other brethren driving him and his brethren out of the church by introducing the organ. When did the Vine Street Church put it in the deed that you could not worship in that church without the organ, provided the majority of the church wishes to do so? When did they or any of our congregations put it in the deed that you could not put the instrument out of the building, and if you did you would forfeit the building? Brethren, the "creed in the deed" is a most flagrant violation of the New Testament and of the Restoration Movement. Instead of putting in your deed that you must not deny the resurrection, the bodily resurrection, of Jesus, that you must not deny the deity of Christ, that you must not deny that immersion is baptism, they leave all that out, so that they can do that if they see fit after a while; but do not let them put in a musical instrument, the use of which is not condemned in the word of God! And they will not fellowship those who use the organ. In replying to my statement that when the Vine Street Church accepted the invitation to have part in the meeting held in this building, and the proffered help was refused, Brother Hardeman read a letter written to the Vine Street Church in which the proffered help was returned. But the fact remains that the Vine Street Church was refused fellowship because something might be preached that would be contrary to what the members of Vine Street believed. Regardless of what the letter means, they injected that, and have it to go to when they want to go to it. They say that we cannot accept your aid for fear that we may insult you or hurt your feelings.

Now, let's be perfectly frank, brethren; let's meet this thing face to face; and I insist upon this thing being done: that instead of discussing me, instead of discussing my brethren, and instead of discussing things that have gone wrong among our people, he address himself to the arguments that I have presented. I have a right to do that, and now I demand it. What difference does it make? We are not discussing Peter Ainslie; we are not discussing infidel churches; we are not discussing these other things; and all in the world these things are brought in here for is to prejudice your mind, because he cannot meet the arguments that have been presented. Now, if that is not so, if I have not made a statement of fact, let him meet the arguments and let these other things alone for a while.

I am coming down to an issue now, and I propose to continue reading along this line. I have questions that he has asked me. I have them written down. They will not be missed, and there are other things. But I must get rid of the thing he has been begging me, he says, to talk about—that is, "What is the instrument?" He says it is the heart only, and then he gives two or three definitions of the heart. So you are "psalloing" with your understanding; you "psallo" with the mind's eye; you "psallo" with all these other things. I could dwell on this if I wanted to get into the same sort of argument he makes. But I do not make that as an argument. I am just showing you how we can drift into such things as that.

I read from Prof. Benjamin W. Bacon, Professor of New Testament Criticism and Exegesis, of Yale: "Of the meaning of the word 'psallein' at the time [when the New Testament was written] there can be no question. The meaning, 'play a stringed instrument,' is primary; the application to 'sing,' secondary. If the revisers knew Greek, they must have known the word in New Testament times did allow the use of an instrument. If not, their opinion is valueless."

Professor Bacon, the scholar, makes the statement that singing is secondary, and says: "If the revisers knew Greek, they must have known the word in New Testament times did allow the use of the instrument"—fitting exactly "with or without." "If not, their opinion is valueless."

Prof. Walter C. Summers, University of Sheffield, England: "The responsibility for assuming that 'psallo' can be used to denote singing without musical accompaniment may fairly be thrown on those who put the view forward." "There is a passage in Sextus Empiricus, a writer of the third century of our era, in which he speaks of the fingers of the flute player and 'psaltes,' showing that, to him, 'psallein' meant a harp playing. The word is common in Latin, and Latin dictionaries are far superior to Greek lexicons. Thence I cull:

"Gell. 19: 9: 'Persons of either sex who sing with the voice and who "psallerent" (play on the lyre).'

"Suet. Tit. 2 (second century A.D.): 'The emperor was not unmusical; he sang and played ("psalleret") on the cithara pleasantly and skillfully.' "

Prof. George Dahl—that has reference to another proposition, and so I will not quote him; nor Professor Hodge.

I read now from Prof. John H. C. Fritz, Dean of Concordia Seminary, in St. Louis, Mo.: "The word 'psallo' in Greek originally means to play on a stringed instrument, and then it has also the meaning to sing, especially to sing praises to the Lord. It can, therefore, mean to sing with or without musical accompaniment. We know that in the Old Testament service musical instruments were used. It is, therefore, likely that he who used the word 'psallo' rather had in mind singing with musical accompaniment."

Dean Alford, whose scholarship is beyond question, says: "The word ["psalmos"] properly signified those sacred songs which were performed with musical accompaniment. 'Hymn' is the word for a song without accompaniment. James 5: 13: 'Psalleto,' let him sing praise; literally, let him play on an instrument; but used in Romans, First Corinthians, and elsewhere of singing praises generally."

Brethren, if a man is out on the desert and he wants to be baptized and there is not a drop of water anywhere on the face of the earth, what is Brother Hardeman going to do? If God commands a thing, it must be done. Whether a man is plowing with a mule between the plow handles or not, that has nothing to do with it. And I even yesterday affirmed that a man could praise God without a musical instrument. I have granted him that right. But the thing that I am saying is that no man has the right to make the use of the instrument a test of fellowship. That is the thing that I am presenting to you.

Again: "Word Studies in the New Testament" (Vincent): "James 5: 13: 'Psalleto.' The word means primarily to pluck or twitch. Hence, of the sharp twang of a bowstring or harp string, and so 'to play upon a stringed instrument.' Our word 'psalm,' derived from this, is, properly, a tune played upon a stringed instrument. The verb, however, is used in the New Testament of singing praise generally."

Matthew Henry's Commentary, Vol. VI., 1136: "By 'psalms' (Eph. 5: 19) may be meant David's Psalms, or such composures as were fitly sung with musical instruments. By 'hymns' may be meant such others as were confined to matter of praise."

Next I present to you "Critical Doctrinal and Homiletical Commentary" (Schaff): "1 Cor. 14: 15: 'I will sing with the spirit, and I will sing with the understanding also'—a proof that the prayer was accompanied with song and harp also."

Again: "Word Studies in New Testament" (Vincent):

"1 Cor. 14: 15: 'I will sing' ["psallo"] (see note on James 5: 13). The verb 'ado' is also used for 'sing' (Eph. 5: 19; Apoc. 5: 9; 14: 3; 15: 3). In the last two passages it is combined with playing on harps. In Eph. 5: 19 we have both verbs. Some think that the verb has here its original signification of singing with an instrument. This is its dominant sense in the Septuagint, and both Basil and Gregory of Nyssa define a 'psalm' as implying instrumental accompaniment, and Clement of Alexandria, while forbidding the use of the flute in the agapæ, permitted the harp."

"James 5: 13: It seems almost certain that at the time of the establishment of the church tunes or melodies were unknown." What does that mean?

My friends, can you find any congregational singing in the New Testament? Do not Ephesians and Colossians refer to the social circle rather than to the church? At least there is a question there. I am not affirming, at this particular time, where it belongs; but I am saying that at least it is ambiguous, if no more.

Again, Meyer, who ranks with the world's greatest and fairest exegetes, comments thus on Eph. 5: 19: "Properly, 'psalmos' (which originally means the making of the cithara sound) is a song in general, and that, indeed, as sung to a stringed instrument; but in the New Testament the character of the psalm is determined by the psalms of the Old Testament."

Again, C. F. Kling, Doctor of Theology, Marbach, renowned scholar and expositor, commenting on 1 Cor. 14: 15, concludes thus: "A proof that the prayer was accompanied with song and harp also."

I wish to read from a more recent one at this time. I haven't time to read them all, but I wish to read you this from the "Expositor's Greek Testament" (Nicoll): "*Psalmos* is a religious song, especially one sung to a musical accompaniment, and par excellence an Old Testament psalm. *Psallontes,* singing especially to the instrument. (Rom. 15: 9; 1 Cor. 14: 15; James 5: 13.)"

Cambridge Bible (Moule): "*Psallontes,* playing instruments. This seems to assume the use of lute or flute on such occasions." "In your heart"—listen, brethren: Moule, this commentary of Moule, says: *"In your heart"*—both voice and instrument were *literal* and *external,* but the use of them both was to be spiritual, and so in the heart."

There is where I stand. There is where I have been standing all the time, and there is the thing I have been saying from the beginning.

T. K. Cheyne (Encyclopedia Biblica): "Let the words which tell of Christ (ὁ λόγος του Χριστου) dwell in your midst abundantly, while in wisdom ye teach and instruct yourselves, while with psalms, hymns, and spiritual songs ye sing pleasantly with your (whole) heart to God, giving thanks to God the Father. (Col. 3: 16.)" "Be filled with spiritual influence, while you speak to yourselves in psalms and hymns and Spirit-given songs, singing songs and chanting psalms with your whole heart to the Lord, while you give thanks always for all things. (Eph. 5: 19.)"

"The hymns are described by these terms, the first of which ('psalms') may imply the influence of Old Testament models, though it need not do more than express the suitableness of songs spoken of to be accompanied by music."

Westcott: "In the heart," the outward music was to be accompanied by the inward music of the heart.

Who has ever denied that? Where is the man that loves the Lord Jesus Christ, where is the man that is familiar with the word of God, that does not know that every prayer, that every word, that every sermon, that every song, that every psalm—everything that he says and does—must come from the heart? Obey that form of doctrine from the heart. Without the heart's being in it there is nothing to it worthy of acceptance at the hands of your Heavenly Father. But, brethren, the thing that I am contending for is that though we play in the heart and everything is done in the heart, it does not exclude the use of a musical instrument. What wrong thing is there in a mechanical instrument? What is there in the thing that makes it bad? I ask any man to disclose to me the inherent evil in any musical instrument.

So to-night as I bring to a close my last address, I again

call attention to the fact that we are not discussing the shortcomings of my brethren, that we are not discussing the division among us; we are discussing whether or not you or any other man has the right to say to another man: "I will not fellowship you, because you believe in the God-given liberty in Christ Jesus our Lord, and, believing in that liberty, you believe you have a right to use an instrument of music made by the hands of man." What right has any man to say that? What right have I to say to you that if you do not believe in the use of an instrument I will not fellowship you?

We have no right, brethren. When we have the word of the living God, we must follow that; and while Brother Hardeman has constantly told you what Paul says, what God says, at no time has he made any effort to prove that his interpretation is correct. He simply turns to me and makes appeal after appeal, and appeals to your prejudice, because of the shortcomings of some of my brethren.

Grant that everything he says concerning the mistakes of these men is true, grant that all such things he has brought into this discussion are true, that would not prove that the word in the Greek New Testament does not mean what the scholars say it means. And not only so; he asked me a question in reference to the organ playing during the communion, during the time when there is no singing being done. I did not answer that question, because that does not bear upon this subject. Grant that it is wrong, grant that it is sinful, grant whatever you please about it, that would not prove that the New Testament does not give us the right to use the instrument in the worship. I am not pleading that everything I say and do is right; I am not pleading that everything my brethren say and do is right. I am simply here to defend the proposition that instrumental music in the church worship is scriptural, and that is all I am contending for. If it is scriptural, then you can use it or not use it; and when I accepted his definition of "scriptural," he does not seem to be satisfied. Any one could see by what I was saying, who was studying the question, that I was measuring up to it. But he has confessed to you that he has not been paying much attention, and it had slipped his mind—so many of these things.

So I ask you, brethren, to think of this to-morrow, which is the Lord's day, when you come around the Lord's table and meet at that supper of emblems. Jesus says: "Do this in remembrance of me." See, if you please, back of that table where the bread is and where the wine is, see back of that table the cross of Jesus Christ, see him upon that cross, hear him as he says: "Father, forgive them; for they know not what they do." Look into his face, the face that has upon it the picture of the sweetest agony the world has ever known—the agony that comes from a heart that is breaking in love for sinful men. And—O!—my brethren, if I make an appeal to you at all, I make an appeal to you that we get out of our heart all of this prejudice and come to this question fairly and squarely, as children of the living God who want to know what God would have us do; and we can do this by coming to his word and studying that word carefully without appealing in any way to the prejudice of our brethren. That is not argument, brethren—to appeal to your prejudice and mine. I have not attempted it. You know as well as you know anything that I have not attempted to do so at any time—not attempted to appeal to the prejudice of my own brethren here; not one time. Nor have I at any time, so far as I recall, said anything disrespectful or made any statement concerning him, except this one thing. When he asked me to come and join with him, that we might unite if we got rid of the organ, I called attention to the fact that the very principle on which he stood was constantly keeping them divided, and was dividing them more and more, and would constantly do it. I talked as pleasantly as I knew how. I came to you a stranger; I came to you with a reputation to sustain, and that reputation is the reputation of one who wants to be only a Christian—a Christian who wants to stand for the ordinances of God's word as written in the book, one who wants to hold up Christ crucified for the sins of the world, one who wants to be used by the Master in his service and take his message to the ends of the earth; and I want to leave this message with you as the thing for you to think on to-morrow. I call upon the brother to meet the statements and arguments which I have been making.

I misunderstood a few moments ago. I understood I had only five minutes, and, therefore, I was drawing to a close. I am glad I have a few minutes more, and I will go back and call attention to a few of his statements made in reference to the heart.

Now, bear in mind, brethren, that the discussion between us is this, not a discussion concerning anything else in the world. What did he say? Now listen to what he said: "The only thing that is keeping us apart is the organ. Get that out of the way, and all of these other difficulties can be ironed out." O, brother, I think the difficulties that are sweeping through the church are much more than that! And let me read you a thing that came to me accidentally the other day in a letter. Brother Hardeman keeps talking about this division that came up and saying: "We did not have any division much until the organ question came up." The organ question wasn't anything much in this country with anybody during that time. The Campbells were antiorgan before they ever left Scotland. It is only recently that organs have gone into the churches in Scotland. Here is a letter written by Alexander Campbell that was found the other day. It was written to Col. James Mason, of Mount Sterling, Ky., and is dated April 4, 1828; and I wish to make the sentiment of this letter my sentiments to your heart and to show you our sailing has not always been very calm and peaceful. It says: "I have just time to thank you for your recent favor and to rejoice with you in the progress and power of light. It appears from all quarters of the country that the ancient gospel is beginning to be understood, and that the superstition and tradition flee before it. A letter from Walter Scott informs me that in the northeast part of Ohio, where he has been laboring for some months, he has within four weeks immersed two hundred people. I trust the time will soon arrive when the demon of discord will be firmly bound in the bottomless pit. I am sorry to hear of the divisions and bickerings in Lexington.

They do harm and cannot do any good. What a pity that they who profess to serve the same Lord and have the best opportunities of doing much good should be contending about trifles, while thoughtless multitudes are hardened in their mad career and posting on to ruin! Wishing you much joy and fruitfulness in your work, I remain, your affectionate brother in the glorious hope, A. Campbell."

Lest you misunderstand me, the use of the word "trifles" here, I do not apply it to the organ question. As for those of you who believe it is against the Scriptures to use it, I would not insult your faith. I would not insult your conscientiousness by insinuating any such thing. I am not that kind of a man. But this I say: I believe that you are conscientious; but if you are conscientious, you should study the word.

HARDEMAN'S SIXTH SPEECH

(Saturday, June 2, 1923.)

Brethren, Moderators, Ladies, and Gentlemen: I trust that this last thirty minutes may be just as pleasant to you as possible for me to make it. I would that Brother Boswell had put in that part of his speech in which he made a dramatic appeal to-night in giving himself to the question, since there are so many things asked him and so completely and kindly postponed by him until it may die out of your memory and you lose the connection in which it is put. I wish to say to you that were I in the affirmative and he to ask me a list of questions so simple, I would not postpone them two nights hence and keep you in suspense as to my conception and idea regarding the same; and I wish to say to you again that it evidences weakness on the part of the proposition that the man is trying to sustain. It is always lamentable to see good men get in things unaware. Brother Boswell had something to say last night about being caught in a trap, and to-night, ladies and gentlemen, it does look like the thing was fixed and he walked in in spite of all that could be done.

I have referred to the Greek Church time and again, and as a grand-stand play to offset it, they kindly refer me to the name of a priest in Nashville from whom I can get the information. I am much obliged to you, but I got the information to-day, Brother Boswell, in advance.

But, ladies and gentlemen, they had no idea what the Greek priest would say; but the idea was to stand Hardeman off by giving him the address and thus postpone the matter until Monday night. Now, I want to read you a letter received to-day from a member of the Greek Church who was this morning in conference with his priest with respect to matters pertaining thereto.

"Nashville, Tenn., June 2, 1923.—To Whom it May Concern: This is to certify that I am identified with the Greek Orthodox Church, 208 South Sixth Street." Brethren, that is the exact address instead of yours. "I have been identified with this church for seven years, and I certify that no instruments of music made by the human hands are used in the worship, nor has there ever been such instrument used in the worship of this body of people in all their history." Don't you want their address? [Applause.]

Ladies and gentlemen, please observe the regulations as announced. Here is another statement furthering that: "As a Greek, I consider what is known as the American Revised Version as a faithful translation of our word 'psallo,' and also of 'psallendi' by the English words 'sing,' 'to make melody,' respectively. These two words to us in our tongue mean exactly what the word 'sing' or 'make melody' mean to the English-speaking people. [Signed] Chris Contos." I pass that to you for study. It is fair that I do that.

Now, that just shows, ladies and gentlemen, what a man will get into when he does not know what he is talking about. That is all—just playing for time. Why, I take it that Brother Boswell knew full well the practice of the Greek Church in general, and felt the force of my repeated reference to it. Something had to be done, and "necessity is the mother of invention;" and so let's play a grand-stand play, let's give him an address in Nashville, and then miss the address, perhaps, as given therein, according to the letter of the church.

Why, he says, Hardeman is not on scriptural grounds, and the reason that he is not on scriptural grounds is that he opposed instrumental music. Well, Brother Boswell, you said that we could render correct service to God without it. Suppose I did oppose it; am I not scriptural when you say that I can do it successfully and correctly without it? But he wants to know, and it is a fair suggestion, and I want to deal fairly with him. He says: "Brother Hardeman"—now mark—"do you have a right to oppose what I have a right to do?" I am going to say to you: No, if you have the right to do it, Brother Boswell, I have no right to oppose it; but your right to do it is the thing that is in question. You have no right to do that. Why? Because not one single word have you read from the Bible as direct authority, apostolic example, or necessary inference. Upon what, ladies and gentlemen, is that right based which proposes to be the right to introduce instruments of music? If he would furnish the proof of it other than say-so declarations, then my right to oppose it would cease; but in the absence of the proof I have the right to oppose it.

Now, let me present to Brother Boswell the negative of that, or rather the other side of the question. Brother Boswell, do you have a right to do that which I have a right to oppose? I claim that he does not. Now, the question: Do I have a right to object to instrumental music? If so, you have no right to do it. Upon what is my objection founded? It is founded upon this: that a thing to be scriptural must come under one of three heads—either direct commandment, and you know that there is not one in all the Bible; by apostolic precedent, which you dare not give; or necessary inference. But you say: "I am going to tell Hardeman about the temple at the last, so I will not be tormented very long in the reply." Why, ladies and gentlemen, I oppose the instrument, or the music made by man's hands, on the ground that it does not conform to the Scriptures in any way. It is not in God's direct command, it is not in God's book taught by apostolic example, it is not in God's book necessarily by inference, and, therefore, is weighed in the balance and found wanting. It comes outside of God's book, and hence I have a right to object thereto; and that being true, no man has the right to impose upon me a thing for which there is not the shadow of a shade of a reason beneath the twinkling stars.

Ladies and gentlemen, when you close the week and go back to your homes, what passage in the Bible has Brother Boswell referred to, what declaration has he made?

When he himself introduced the temple question and said that they worshiped back there in the temple where instruments were used, and when I asked him to show me, he has been absolutely silent. What has he had to say about the temple to-night? Not a word on earth about it. O, he is a promising young man still, and will tell you in the last speech of the debate—I suppose he will wait till next Tuesday night in the final rejoinder to tell you about all these things.

He has some criticism to make of me for referring to the school at Lexington and to the one to be founded, and says: "Why doesn't Hardeman address himself to the proposition?" Brother Boswell, you were the first man that got outside of the proposition and went to talking about schools, etc.; and when I get on the subject and show you some things, then you want to turn it loose. You had no business introducing it, Brother Boswell. And you are the first fellow who got to talking about divisions and about their faults, and now you say: "I wish Brother Hardeman would turn it loose. I know I started it, but I don't want to keep it up, and now I want him to help me turn it loose." He is the first man that began to talk about schools and to talk about divisions, and now he says: "Brother Hardeman, let's quit that." All right; if you have had enough of it, I will quit. Whenever a man says, "Brother Hardeman, let's quit that," why, I want to be easy and help him to turn it loose if he has a bad job on hand.

Now, in reference to the "creed in the deed," let me say that when God gave the land of promise to Abraham, he specified its border, its limitations, and stated exactly to whom it was given and for what purpose. All deeds to church property are intended to express the "creed in the deed." To this there is no exception. When a deed is made to a Roman Catholic Church, it is intended to restrict the use of that property to those holding the Catholic faith. The same is true regarding Methodists, Baptists, Presbyterians, et al. Suppose you try preaching sprinkling or pouring in a Baptist house without permission. Since division is in our ranks, not to put the "creed in the deed" is to invite a fuss and to wind up in a lawsuit. Brother Boswell says: "It is a most flagrant violation of the New Testament and the Restoration Movement." This is the opposite of the truth. If Brother Boswell had said that to play politics and carry on an effort to work up a majority vote in order to steal church property built by others was in violation of the New Testament and the Restoration Movement, he would have stated the facts in the case. These brethren who claim to be such missionaries have built precious few houses in Tennessee. Their tactics are to get possession of property built by others. This they have done by questionable methods. You say that Christ is your creed; but if you had proper respect for Christ and his word, you would never introduce the organ and other human inventions to the division of the body of Christ. Brethren, protect your property against those who seek to obtain it. Let some folks rage and imagine vain things. They seem mad because their plans no longer carry.

At last we have Brother Boswell's authority for the instrument. I have asked him if it was authorized by God or by man, and he dared not answer positively, passed over it; but he comes to-night and tells his authority. What is it? Why, he says: "Hardeman, my authority for the instrument in the worship is liberty." Then you have given up "psallo," haven't you? Now, how can both of them be authority? One of them is and the other isn't. Ladies and gentlemen, let me tell you, my brother seems to have the wrong idea of liberty. He thinks that it is license to run roughshod over all law and authority. We talk about the land of America as the land of liberty. It is. But does that mean you can go out and violate the laws of the land? Certainly not. When I talk about liberty, I mean liberty in harmony with the law. I am at liberty to serve God under his authority or I am at liberty not to do it. And beyond that I have no liberty. When God Almighty says for me to be baptized, my liberty is circumscribed there to do it or not to do it, and outside of that I have none. Yet his conception seems to be that if I have liberty I am licensed to act of my own accord, of my own will, to seek after my own pleasure.

Paul said: "If I seek to please men—myself being one of them—I cannot be the servant of God." The trouble with Brother Boswell is this: a lack of that spirit to take God at his word, believe just what he says, become and be just what he requires, live inside of the authority of God's directions, and trust him for guidance, rather than to exercise his own individual preferences in matters pertaining to things sacred.

But watch again some statements. He read to you from various authors, one of which just about capped the climax; but it is exactly the logical end to which the gentleman has been headed all the way. He is not as courageous as O. E. Payne, from whose book he has been reading. Why don't you accept his logical conclusion and deduction, which is this: Elder Payne walks out and says the Revised Version did not translate it right, and you seemingly haven't the courage to say that, and yet you read from the author and give him your indorsement when he said: "If the revisers knew Greek, they would have known so and so."

Isn't that a reflection upon the one hundred and one scholars selected by the world to translate it? And yet you give indorsement to the comment that ridicules them, which says if they knew Greek, which implies that they were smatterers, like McGarvey said you were. If the revisers knew Greek—ladies and gentlemen, there was but one logical deduction to make from Brother Boswell's argument—that the King James and the Revised Version were not correctly translated; and I have asked him orally, I have asked him the written question: "Brother Boswell, in the King James and the Revised Version, is the word 'psallo' translated correctly?" What is his answer? "I will tell you when I get ready." That is the answer. Why not march out and say "yes" or "no?" Why do you want to play around it and hesitate and postpone? Why not just come out, Brother Boswell, and say, "Hardeman, yes," or "no," and settle the question? Why, you have asked me several things. When you asked me if I worshiped over at Alamo at the commencement sermon, I said: "No." Suppose I had said, "I will tell you next Saturday?" I did not want to wait to answer that. If I have an answer, I will tell you now. But Brother Boswell's disposition is to say: "I will see you later; I am not prepared to-night to give answers." Ladies and gentlemen, when the time comes that I am afraid of my proposition, when the time comes that I am afraid to march out as an affirmant or take a definite stand

and answer simple questions, then I will draw in my sails and furl my banners and no longer pose as a representative of the affirmative side of the question.

"If the revisers knew Greek!" As much as to say they knew nothing about it, or else they would have translated it otherwise.

Let me repeat, ladies and gentlemen, the scholarship of the world was centered in the forty and seven gentlemen who translated the Greek into the English in King James in 1611. The richest, ripest scholarship of the ages was centered in the one hundred and one scholars that translated the Revised Version. What has Brother Boswell to say about it? With all the innuendo and the insinuation and the reflections possible, he read from an author, and thereby gave it his indorsement, to cast insinuating remarks upon the revisers. "If they knew Greek!" "If they knew Greek," they would have said so and so; and then, to cap the climax, at which I was astonished, why, he says, "Brother Hardeman, the Latin dictionary is far superior to the Greek lexicons," thereby taking out after the old Catholic "Vulgate" rather than that which our Lord Jesus Christ and the apostles spoke.

I want to say, friends, I hate to expose a man like that, but it becomes absolutely necessary. The idea of a man to-night posing as a representative of God's word, penned in Greek, and then saying that a Catholic Latin dictionary is superior to the Greek as used by Christ and by the apostles! I am surprised at a position forcing a good man to make such a statement as that. Ordinarily, out from under the shackles that bind him down to the impossible task, Brother Boswell would not say a thing of that kind.

But let me suggest to you this: He made the declaration, and a correct one, that when God Almighty commands a thing, it must be done. Amen! It is not a question of liberty, either. It isn't a question of the majority. It must be done. But the trouble is, Brother Boswell won't stick to his statement. Now, then, did God command people to "psallo?" (Eph. 5: 19.) Surely. What does it mean, Brother Boswell? "Accompaniment with a musical instrument." That is his statement. Now what? If that be true, and God commands it, then how can you worship God without it? There is a flat, plain, direct contradiction. Absolutely so. Brother Boswell, when God commands people to be baptized, it must be done. When God commands people to "psallo," it must be done. All right. What does "psallo" mean? "To accompany with an instrument?" You can't leave the instrument out, and hence your contention is wrong. Where is your lexicon that says you can "psallo" without the instrument? Absolutely none. And yet we have joined in "psalloing" here to-night. We have had the singing and the making of melody, but no instrument. Did the leader have an instrument? Why, Brother Boswell said last night: "Yes, the tuning fork." The first one I have seen here in this tabernacle the two years I have been here was to-night. Was it a tuning fork? Yes, sir. Was it a musical instrument? No, sir. Why? Music is a succession of harmonious sounds, and a tuning fork gives one single sound. Hence, it is not a musical instrument. The fact is, ladies and gentlemen, there has not been a statement presented by Brother Boswell that I have not wrested from him and exposed the position taken by him.

But he says: "Hardeman, just show now where God has ever taught us to sing in the congregation." Why, he says, it was a social matter. He doesn't know what the Greeks teach, seemingly, and will rush in where angels might fear to tread. He doesn't seem to know what the Bible says. I am glad to inform him of the singing of the congregation, and that thing he doesn't know. And there seems to be a whole lot of things some folks don't know. 1 Cor. 14: 26: "How is it, then, brethren? when ye come together, every one of you hath a psalm." What does "psalm" mean? According to him, a mechanical instrument. Then, brethren, when you come together, each fellow brings him a mechanical instrument. That is the idea. Heb. 2: 12: "Saying, I will declare thy name unto my brethren, in the midst of the church will I sing praise unto thee."

Now, what is it you want to know? He comes, ladies and gentlemen, and asks me what harm there is in a musical instrument. He says they are not dangerous. O, no, I am not afraid of musical instruments. I will say to Brother Boswell, by way of anticipation, in my humble home there are musical instruments. I am not prejudiced against them. He thinks that my opposition to musical instruments is because of the harm that inheres in the thing itself. Why, not so. I am not prejudiced against babies. I do not think there is any harm in immersing a baby or sprinkling water upon it. I do not think it will hurt it. Might scare it for the minute, but I do not think there is any harm in it. And, Brother Boswell, I do not think there is any harm in washing the hands, and I might just say to you privately I practice that; but here is the point: Would you permit me to bring these things into your meetinghouse and, as a religious rite, wash my hands? Answer that next week. No harm in the act of washing my hands; but if I were to take a basin of water into the service of God and, as a religious rite, were there to wash them and make the other fellow wash his, whether he wanted to or not, I would certainly be out of order and in violation of every correct principle.

Brother Boswell, there is no harm in the Catholics' counting their beads. I don't care if they count for hours. Nothing wrong in that. But will you let them come up to Georgetown and, as a religious rite, count beads with you?

I don't think there is any harm *per se* in the little crucifix and the burning of incense. I really like to smell it. But is that any argument why it should be brought into the service of God? It seems to me you should see the point in this.

A thing is right, ladies and gentlemen, upon one basis—namely, does God want it or not? If God says have it, it is right; if God doesn't say have it, it is wrong. But notice again. He says: "Hardeman, the Bible doesn't forbid instruments." Well, that's a bright idea. Neither, Brother Boswell, does the Bible forbid, in so many words, babies being baptized. The only reason that Brother Boswell practices instrumental music and denies infant baptism is because of a peculiar fancy of his own. The Bible nowhere says, in so many words, that "thou shalt not baptize babies." It is excluded, but by what? When God says, "baptize believers," he forbids babies by the ordinary law of exclusion.

Now, get it, when God says "sing" and "make melody in the heart," that forbids making it upon a mechanical instrument. The Bible does not, in so many words, say "thou shalt not burn incense." On the principle of Brother Boswell, you might come into the service with animal sacrifice, infant baptism, and counting beads; and if Brother Boswell objects, you stand back and answer: "Now, Brother Boswell, where does God say you shall not do these?" He could not show it to save his life. Absolutely not. And the same principle that answers for these answers for the instrument. I told you some time back there is not a single argument that can be made for the use of mechanical instruments but that I obligate myself to make the same argument in behalf of infant membership. Try your hand on the one, and I will answer it in a parallel with the other.

He says: "If a thing is scriptural, you can either do it or not, as your judgment may decide." Ladies and gentlemen, in the light of all reason and common sense, tell me, will you, how a thing can be scriptural and yet left to man's fancy at the same time? Such a statement reflects upon the sacred truth. Is it scriptural to baptize? Yes. Well, is it scriptural not to baptize? Of course not. Is it scriptural to circumcise the heart? Yes, sir. Is it scriptural to leave it off? No, sir. Is it scriptural to eat the Lord's Supper? Yes, sir. Is it scriptural to leave it off? No, sir. Is it scriptural to contribute on the first day of the week proportionate to our ability? Yes, sir. Is it scriptural, then, brethren, not to do it? Of course not.

And yet that is what Brother Boswell said. It is scriptural to have an instrument, and it is scriptural not to have it. And, as Brother McGarvey said, a man who reasons after that fashion can prove anything he wants to if you but give him rope.

I have asked Brother Boswell where he got his instrument of music, and I charged that he borrowed it from the denominational world. That is the history. Where did the denominations get it? They got it from the Catholics. When? The Catholics introduced it first into their services in the seventh century. Where did they get it? According to encyclopedias and history, from the pagan world round about.

Brother Boswell says himself it is a recent thing. I knew that. I knew that back in the days of the apostles they never heard of it. Quite recent. I knew that when Christ was here and Paul preached and the primitive disciples worshiped, there was no instrumental music. Brother Boswell is right when he tells you they had just recently found out about it. That is true. Do you not know that even in the denominational churches it did not become prominent until the thirteenth century, just a short while before Columbus discovered America? The denominations of the world had then been practicing organ music in their services but a short time. And that is the history of it.

You may commence with the first century, come on through the second century, and follow on down the line until the history of the apostles sinks beneath the line of the horizon, and in all of their teachings and practices there is not a hint of an instrument of music in their worship or in their service.

The proposition to-night appeals for argument and for support and yet finds none. This session has added nothing new to the discussion. Brother Boswell, in the time allowed, has continued to *vibrate* on "psallo" and to rehash the same old thing. He reads from Payne's book, and yet he has not the courage to accept the conclusion that Mr. Payne draws.

Where is the scripture, where is the commandment, where is the precedent, where is the inference? Let me say, ladies and gentlemen, not one single vestige can be found.

I thank you.

BOSWELL'S SEVENTH SPEECH

(Monday, June 4, 1923.)

Mr. Moderator, Brother Hardeman, Brothers, and Sisters: I believe that the affirmative speaker on a proposition has the right to determine his own method of procedure as long as he stays within the rules of order. At the very beginning of this discussion I stated that a leader upon the opposing side had made the statement that if one word could be found in the Scriptures that carried with it the right to use a mechanical instrument—though he did not say mechanical instrument—the right to use an instrument, meaning by that the mechanical instrument, the affirmative would be proved; there would be no necessity of further debate. We were in search of that one word; and so we have spent a good deal of time discussing the meaning of "psallo," giving first the primary meaning of the word from lexicons, then giving you the contemporaneous writers, and then the scholars.

We have, in the debate, somewhat changed our plan, and have already given you the commentaries, and I think in all of these we have found the word. I wish now to come to translations, and I shall get away from these just as soon as possible. Everything that has been said has been said with one great purpose in view—to prove that "psallo" means to sing with or without an instrument—and we have not allowed ourselves to be led away from our line of discussion.

Peshito Syriac (196 A.D.), perhaps the oldest among all the translations or versions of the Scriptures, uses in the passage which we have been discussing "zammar," from the Hebrew "zamar;" and that word carried with it instrumentation, mechanical. And, be it understood, all the time our argument was for a mechanical instrument; not to the exclusion of any other instrument, but a mechanical instrument.

"The Coptic" translates the word "play," if I do not forget. The version is here. It translates it "playing."

The German translates it by a word which means "to play."

"In the heart" is in the Greek, and, therefore, is in the translation.

The Norwegian—I have here a Bible which is almost torn to pieces; it is more than one hundred years old, and is a Norwegian Bible, and the word there means to "play." "Leger" is the word. If there is a Norwegian anywhere and you want to test it, you can test it by him.

The Swedish also translates it by a word which means to "play." "Playing" is the translation—"spelande," if that is the correct pronunciation, and I could not say it is, but it is translated "playing;" and so with the Danish "spelle," meaning "play;" the Dutch reads "psalmende," meaning "playing;" and so on with these several translations in the various languages.

I now present the English translations. The Twentieth Century translation is "making music." The King James and the Revised Versions translate it "making melody." The Rotherham translation gives it "striking the string." But I want to read you Moffatt's translation. I suppose no one denies the scholarship of James Moffatt. James Moffatt, in his "New Testament," a new translation, published in 1918, translates it in this way: "But be filled with the spirit, converse with one another, in the music of psalms, in hymns, and in songs of the spiritual life; praise the Lord heartily with words and the music, and tender thanks to God, the Father, in the name of our Lord Jesus Christ, at all times and through all things." Translating "singing and making melody in your heart," "praise the Lord heartily with words and the music," connecting "in the heart" with singing as well as with playing, just as they belong. "Repent, and be baptized . . . for the remission of your sins"—both repentance and baptism connected with remission of sins. Singing and playing in the heart—both in the heart. If the singing is in the heart, then there would be no vocal expression whatsoever. If singing is not in the heart, neither is playing. And I call attention to this fact: that several of the scholars and our other authorities, lexicons, etc., which I read last night, thinking that you would get this precisely, take the position that is taken here by Mr. Moffatt—that "in your heart" means *"heartily."*

I wish to call attention again to his statement in reference to the Revised Version and to the King James Version. Of course I accept the Revised Version; of course I accept the King James Version. But I do not accept the Revised Version or the King James Version as translating accurately everything that is in the Greek text.

Acts 3: 19 (King James Version): "Repent ye therefore, and be converted, that your sins may be blotted out, when the times of refreshing shall come from the presence of the Lord." The Revised Version is correct: "Repent and turn yourselves." Neither of us accepts the King James Version here.

Again, Rom. 1: 29 (King James Version): "Being filled with all unrighteousness, fornication, wickedness, covetousness, maliciousness; full of envy, murder, debate, deceit, malignity; whisperers." The word translated "debate" is "eridos."

2 Cor. 12: 20: "For I fear, lest, when I come, I shall not find you such as I would, and that I shall be found unto you such as ye would not: lest there be debates, envyings, wraths, strifes, backbitings, whisperings, swellings, tumults." Now, the King James Version translates the Greek words "eridos" and "eris," "debate" and "debates,'" and puts debates among all these sinful things. So if we were following the King James Version to-night, we would be among all those reprobates. But the Revised Version translates it correctly—"strife." So where we have "debate" in the King James Version we have "strife" in the Revised Version. But let me call your attention to this fact: that the Revised Version still carries "baptize" instead of "immerse;" and so, after all, there are some things in the Revised Version that neither of us accepts.

I am simply calling your attention now to the fact that the

Revised Version and the King James Version are not accurate in every regard.

But the claim has been made that the one hundred and forty-eight scholars who gave us the above versions have given their decision against the mechanical instrument in this word "psallo." Unfortunately, most of these men are dead, and dead men cannot testify; but there are men living who were living at the time this question was first raised, perhaps, and we have their testimony, and their testimony is certainly to the point. If we can discover a few outstanding scholars among those who translated the Revised Version who say that they did not intend to eliminate the mechanical instrument when they translated "psallo," we can reasonably claim that the others were of the same mind.

I read to you from M. R. Riddle, Professor of New Testament Exegesis, Theological Seminary, Hartford, Conn. Mr. Riddle was a member of the Revision Committee. He was one of the one hundred and forty-eight scholars, and Mr. Riddle says: "I have no recollection of any purpose on the part of the revisers to preclude the use of an instrument. My own opinion is that the word does not preclude the use of an instrument." And he means a mechanical instrument, or he would not have answered such a question.

Again, from Timothy Dwight, one of the revisers, Professor of New Testament Exegesis, Divinity School, Yale University. Mr. Dwight is not dead. He can speak for himself, and he says: "I do not think the revisers meant to imply by their rendering of 'psallo' that at the time of the writing of the New Testament the word precluded the use of an instrument. The use of such instrument is regarded, I think, by scholars, as altogether probable."

And so you discover that these one hundred and forty-eight scholars in the King James Version and the Revised Version have not rendered their decision contrary to all the scholars we have produced during this discussion.

Now, I call your attention to the fact that he has not criticized these scholars, has not denied their scholarship. The only one he did mention (if not the only one, perhaps he mentioned two or three others)—all were mentioned simply to cast a slur upon them.

Prof. W. B. Bacon, Professor of New Testament Criticism and Exegesis, of Yale University, answering for Prof. James Hadley, one of the revisers, now dead, says: "If the revisers so knew Greek"—and this is that quotation I made that the brother on the other side used as a hammer to make me out a smatterer of the Greek, when I call to your attention to-night that I have not uttered one single word concerning the Greek, except to call the names and tell you what the scholars have said. I took his advice when he said it is not "p-sallo," but "sallo." I did that to please the brother, knowing all the time that it is "psallo," for I wanted to please my brother one time. "If the revisers so knew Greek, they must have known that word in New Testament times did allow the use of an instrument. If not, their opinion is valueless." He does not say they were not Greek scholars; he does not say that Timothy Dwight and these other great men I have quoted were smatterers in Greek. He says that if they did not know, then their views are valueless—meaning by that that they did know it.

Then Prof. Casper Wester Hodge, of Princeton University, answering for Dr. Charles Hodge, one of the revisers, says: "No argument at all, I should say, can be made from this to prove in New Testament times that no instrument accompaniment was allowed." Speaking for a dead man, speaking for Charles Hodge.

And then Prof. Philip Schaff, who is now dead—before he died, Philip Schaff wrote this (and if he meant in translating that word "sing" to preclude the idea that it carried with it instrumentation, then what he says here contradicts what he meant there): "1 Cor. 14: 15: 'I will sing with the spirit, and I will sing with the understanding also'—a proof that the prayer was accompanied with song and harp also." So Professor Schaff, before he died, answered the statement of the brother, who makes the statement after the death of Schaff and tries to make that great scholar, Professor Schaff, line himself up against the scholarship of the world.

These translations I offer now are to prove what? To prove that instrumentation, mechanical instrumentation, is in the word.

And now I want to call your attention to just a few things in reference to matters that have gone before. I want to call your attention to the matter of Professor Calhoun. I read first what Brother Hardeman said; then I will read my answer that I made Friday night, that was published in the papers, that he could have seen if he had read the papers. Here is the statement. He said, referring to Professor Calhoun—here is what I said, according to Brother Hardeman: "The only answer that Brother Boswell attempts to make is as to the date of it." Which is equivalent to saying it is absolutely no answer at all. I did ask him the date. I did say the date was important, because you remember Hall Calhoun changed his mind. He used to stand with these brethren regarding the mechanical instrument in the worship; and so when he made a statement like that, and when I asked Brother Hardeman the date when that was written, he did not answer me, but said: "Suffice it to say it represents Brother Calhoun to-day." So I sent Mr. Calhoun—Dr. Calhoun—Brother Calhoun—Professor Calhoun—a telegram, for I had a letter from Brother Calhoun just before I came down here, and in that letter he told me he had complimented Brother Kurfees' book; but he says: "I believe in the use of the instrument in the worship, and practice it." And I know he does. Here is the telegram. I said: "When did you write it?" When he wrote it has all to do with it, my friends. He replied: "I made the statement in an article on worship which I wrote home many years ago." Here is the telegram. I offer this, my brother, as evidence that Brother Calhoun wrote that article when he did not believe in the use of an instrument in worship. Now, I want to bring the testimony of the brother himself. I want to answer that question. He says the only answer I attempted to make was to say: "When was it written?"

Here is my answer, reported in the paper: "The second question concerns the statement of H. L. Calhoun. I ask him when this statement was made. Was it before or after Brother Calhoun gave up his contention concerning instrumental music in the worship? Now, brethren, there is something in the date. The date here means much. I don't know when he wrote it. I don't know anything about it. I don't have to. I don't agree with him. I don't see why he asked it. I wouldn't be here discussing it if I agreed with him." And yet Brother Hardeman stood up here and said I simply asked about the date and did nothing more, and what he said meant only I made no answer at all. There is my answer, written down and published in the paper; and, my brother, you could have seen it if you had taken the time to read the paper. That is not all I said in answer to his questions—not all. Listen to the rest of it. In my answer to his questions I referred to Rom. 15: 9 and made the following point: The word translated "sing," in the Authorized and Revised Versions, is "psallo," and is from the Septuagint. The word in the Septuagint is "psallo." The Septuagint is the Greek translation of the Hebrew Scriptures, and the word in the Hebrew Scriptures is "zamar," and means to sing with an instrument, a mechanical instrument. Mechanical instrument is meant. And yet he said only last Saturday night that I had dodged the issue of the mechanical instrument. Mechanical instrument is meant.

I said that the Hebrew Scriptures were inspired of God; that the translators who made the Septuagint version translated the word "zamar" by a word that carried the same meaning; that if it did not, it was a mistranslation; that Paul was inspired; that if the word Paul took from the Septuagint did not carry with it the same meaning as "zamar" (and Paul quoted this translation), he mistranslated it; that if this were so, Paul could not have been inspired. But Paul was inspired.

Does that look like the only thing I said was: "What was the date?" Does that look like the only thing I said was to avoid the answer?

I say to him to-night that every question he has asked me was answered as fairly and clearly as that, and yet frequently he refers to my not answering some question and says that I am a "promising" man. I have not promised to answer that fling. I have fulfilled my promises.

Brother Hardeman replied by saying that the word used by the Septuagint did not perfectly translate it and it had to have another word to assist it. To this I replied that Paul did not use another word with it. To this he made reply that Paul used the other word in Eph. 5: 19; and on this I commented that as the Romans did not have the Ephesian letter, Romans having been written in 58-59, Ephesians in 62-63, if Paul did not use the right word in Romans, he was not inspired.

I believe Paul was inspired; I believe his word. I take his word as the inspired word of God. This quotation is a prophecy taken from the Old Testament; and if it were not translated specifically, then that prophecy was not given fully in the Greek. It refers to the time when Jesus shall come and when we shall sing praises to his name and play, as "zamar" has it.

Now, I call attention again to his misrepresentations. He quotes me as saying—I dislike very much to have to do these things, brethren; but every misrepresentation is made in order that another point may be made from it—he quotes me as saying: "Just show me where God ever taught us to sing in the congregation." I never said that. Get your to-day's paper and see what I did say. My statement was, my friends: "Can you find any congregational singing in the New Testament?" There is a difference in saying "singing in the congregation" and "congregational singing" in the New Testament. He quoted 1 Cor. 14: 15; Rom. 15: 9 to show "singing in the congregation," and then tells us that is "the congregational singing." I want to read to you Rom. 15: 9: "Therefore will I give praise unto thee among the Gentiles, and sing unto thy name." There is no congregational singing there. It is a prophecy—a prophecy taken from Ps. 18: 49 and brought over by Paul; and if Paul did not correctly translate it, then Paul did not bring the prophecy correctly over in the New Testament. You must either admit Paul correctly translated it or that Paul was not inspired. What a morsel that would be to the destructive critic!

Now, turning over to 1 Cor. 14: 14, 15, here Paul is talking about disorder in the church: "For if I pray in a tongue, my spirit prayeth, but my understanding is unfruitful. What is it then? I will pray with the spirit, and I will pray with the understanding also: I will sing with the spirit, and I will sing with the understanding also." He is describing what took place. What is it that took place? See verse 26, same chapter, "When ye come together, each one" of you—he quoted it last night, "every one" of you; and when he said "every one" of you, he said that meant everybody singing, and then he said that meant everybody had to have a harp. O, how skillfully that was brought in! But Jesus Christ said: "Go ye into all the world, and preach the gospel to the whole creation." Is that scriptural? Does that mean every one of you has to go? Does that mean you have to go into every single part of the world, each one of you? Such hair-splitting comment upon the word of God would destroy all the liberty and all the beauty and all the preciousness of it.

Disorder in the congregation—Paul is talking about disorder. He says: "What is it then, brethren? When ye come together, each one hath a psalm, hath a teaching, hath a revelation, hath a tongue, hath an interpretation. Let all things be done unto edifying." He says that each one of you is trying to do one thing, but all are trying when you come together to do the one thing at the same time. He says that the one who hath a psalm is to sing it by himself. That is what I meant by "singing in the congregation." If a man wished to sing a song, he sang it. The same rule was to be followed by those who spoke with tongues, who had a teaching, or an interpretation, or a revelation. Now, if "each one" means "every one," and "every one" must have a harp, then all must have a teaching, a revelation, an interpretation—must speak with tongues; and if it means that all must sing at once, "congregational singing," then all these other things must be done at once. Read your Scriptures, brethren. You say you will stand by the book. Take the book and read it. Stand by the book. That is where I am standing.

Again, Brother Hardeman took me to task for saying the Catholic Latin Dictionary is superior to Greek as used by Christ and by the apostles. I defy any man to find where I ever said that. Some of you have understood—why does he so often misunderstand me?

From this he slipped to the Vulgate, and accused me of accepting that version as better than the English, or Protestant, version—the King James or Revised. I said nothing of the sort. I quoted Prof. Walter C. Summers, of the University of Sheffield, England, who said: "The responsibility for assuming that 'psallo' can be used to denote singing without musical accompaniment [meaning mechanical] may fairly be thrown on those who put the view forward." Professor Summers then quotes from a Latin writer, and says the use is common in Latin; and Latin dictionaries are far superior to Greek lexicons. And then this is twisted into my indorsing the Catholic Vulgate and saying that it is better than the Protestant King James or Revised Version.

And his statement based on the quotation from Professor Bacon was misleading. It misrepresents Professor Bacon and myself. He says that I have reflected upon the one hundred and forty-eight scholars who translated the Bible. And, again, as to the smatterers in Greek, he tries to put that statement upon Brother McGarvey. He says that he did not say that I was a smatterer in Greek, but that Brother McGarvey said that. And immediately, when I quote Professor Bacon, he turns around and says I said it. What did Professor Bacon say? I have read what he said. The authority was open to him, but he did not ask to see it. There is the authority. He could have looked at it.

HARDEMAN'S SEVENTH SPEECH

(Monday, June 4, 1923.)

Ladies and Gentlemen: When I say I am delighted to come before you this evening, I but express an honest sentiment. I rejoice because of the presence of such a splendid company, the good feeling that prevails, and the interest that characterizes you as earnest, honest listeners to things that have been said. To the very best of my ability I shall call your attention to the address made and expose to you the many, many things therein that shall be weighed and found wanting.

I want to say to you, friends, that perhaps eighty or ninety per cent of the addresses made by Brother Boswell have been taken directly or indirectly from a book that I have in my hand, "Instrumental Music is Scriptural," by O. E. Payne. I mention this book because of the prominence it has had, although that prominence has not been acknowledged by the speaker who has quoted from it so very much.

Mr. Payne, in his book, takes the position that unless you have a mechanical instrument you cannot fulfill the obligation that God has imposed; and he not only defies the one hundred and forty-eight scholars of King James and the Revision, but he ridicules them and makes fun of them, and that is the point I am trying to-night to emphasize. If Brother Boswell is going to borrow Payne's thunder all the way through, why doesn't he go on and accept the legitimate and logical conclusion? I would hate to read the great bulk of my addresses from a man and then go back on him before I got through and reject the conclusions that are therein made.

Now, let me read you from page 97 of Payne, where he says: "Translators have no right to be arbitrary or capricious. Their duty is to render in harmony with the lexicons. Who will pretend that in translating 'psallo' as if it were equivalent to 'ado,' as is done in the Authorized and

Revised Versions, this course has been pursued?" Now, what is the statement? That in the rendition of "psallo" the Revision Committee pursued a course that was arbitrary and capricious and not in harmony with the lexicons.

But I read to you now from page 115 of the same book. After speaking with reference to the quotation that has been made, he has this to say: "The revisers, meeting a passage like the following, perhaps in order to save the prayer book"—now note the charge against the revisers—"perhaps in order to save the prayer book and throw dust in the reader's eyes," would have said so and so. What is the insinuation? That the revisers translated in order to save the Episcopalian prayer book, and they are charged with willfully translating so as to throw dust in the eyes of you people.

But I call attention to page 198. With reference to this same thing they have this to say along that line: "If Bible students generally were more familiar with the facts leading up to the revising, there would be less abject veneration for the mere vocabularies of either the Revision or its predecessor, and much more of intelligent reverence for and loyalty to the actual word of God."

"Let a few brief excerpts illustrate. The new Revision was born in the mother church of English Christendom. She made the Authorized Version, and had an hereditary right to take the lead in its improvement. She would never accept a revision from any other denomination. Then why should others accept mistranslations from her? One reason why the English revisers, the majority of whom belong to the Church of England (and dominated the renderings), more closely adhere to the archaic forms, is the daily use of their Book of Common Prayer. This is but a sample of the naked ugliness of the facts—spoiling the Bible to save the prayer book."

That is what that man from whom he has perhaps quoted ninety per cent thinks of the revisers of our Testament. I want to call attention to the fact that Dr. Philip Schaff, one of the ripest Presbyterian scholars of all the ages, was chairman of the American Committee; and this man, Payne, so much quoted by Brother Boswell, says that Philip Schaff, sitting as the chairman of that board, and Joseph Henry Thayer, author of the Greek lexicon, Congregationalist, of Manchester, sitting as secretary, ruined the Bible, threw dust in the eyes of you Presbyterians, you Methodists, and all the rest of us, in order that he might save the Episcopalian prayer book. That surely is the limit.

Now, I want to say further with reference to that book that it has been tested and reviewed, and I hold before you to-night a book that is absolutely and positively unreliable. It has been shown that in handling the authors, most of which he has quoted, this man misquoted them; that he added to what some said; that he left off part of what others did say; that he changed the capitalization and punctuation of some of their writings. Brother Kurfees, in a very able booklet, has reviewed Payne, and has exposed the corruption, defilement, and misrepresentations in his book.

Now, our dear Brother Calhoun—in July, 1922—says: "Dear Brother Kurfees: I write this letter to thank you for the very excellent and scholarly piece of work which you have done in reviewing Brother Payne's book on 'psallo.' In the interest of truth and scholarship, I think your review is all that can be desired." Signed by Brother Calhoun, July 20, just last year. But it is the most dangerous thing on earth for Brother Boswell to fool with letters and to give addresses.

I have a letter, ladies and gentlemen, from Brother Calhoun; and when he begins to talk about him, let me inform you I sat for two years as a student under Brother Calhoun. I know what his position was then, and I have been in touch with him by correspondence all along the line, and I know what he has taught every day, and read to you a letter of recent date comparatively. In 1916: "Dear Brother Hardeman: Replying to your letter of April 19, I would state, first, I do not believe that instrumental music is authorized by the word of God as a part of his worship. Neither do I think the Greek word 'psallo' furnishes any argument for the use of instrumental music." "Perhaps I ought to say, I think instrumental music accompanying the singing is not wrong. I think it, however, a matter of personal opinion or of preference, like the note books. Remembering with pleasure our former association and with love and best wishes, I am, very cordially yours, H. L. Calhoun."

Let me say to you, ladies and gentlemen, there is not a greater scholar, I think, to-night in all this land than Brother Calhoun. He was especially prominent as a student at Lexington, Ky., under Professor McGarvey. After that he taught at Henderson, in the school with which I was connected. He then went to Yale, and then to Harvard; and when Brother McGarvey died, the College of the Bible, of which Dr. Morgan has been, or even now is, a member of the board of trustees, in looking over their brotherhood to find a splendid man, of the highest type, chose Professor Calhoun, and there he stayed until that institution became rotten with infidelity. When Brother Calhoun exposed the matter, he was ousted, and is now at old Bethany College, and still believes just as the above letter says.

What does he say? "Brother Kurfees, when you exposed this book from which Brother Boswell is reading, in the light of truth and scholarship, I must say that you did all that can be expected."

"Brother Hardeman, I think that the Greek word 'psallo,' upon which Brother Boswell has based his argument, furnishes no evidence and no argument for the use of instrumental music in the worship." Brother Boswell, you are gone, absolutely.

When Brother Boswell told me to-night that he had answered the various questions to which I had called his attention, I was but surprised. When I first presented the list, he tried his hand on some two or three; but this audience knows that on some four or five Brother Boswell failed in his courage, of which he boasts, and said, "Brother Hardeman, ask them; they are of age;" and now he has the monumental effrontery, in the face of that statement, to say that "I answered all of them." I asked him Saturday night here five very plain, simple questions, and not one of them has he answered up to to-night, or even attempted; but he is still promising, I presume.

Now, he had something to say about the revisers on "psalloing," and then quoted from the King James and the Revised Version from Acts 3: 19 and other passages. I never asked him anything about that—nothing at all. That wasn't the point; and, besides, no distinction in fact between the versions. Here is the question I asked: "In the King James and the Revised Version, is the word 'psallo' translated correctly?" And you heard not a word with reference to matters of that kind. So I pass now from that to this thought.

He next called our attention to a number of translations of Eph. 5: 19, all of which I had, and more besides. I have twenty and six here on that table for your inspection. Out of this twenty and six translations let me suggest to you this: sixteen of them—sixteen out of the twenty-six—render this, "sing and make melody unto the Lord in your heart." One of them says, "sing and say the psalms." Another one says, "chanting and singing in your heart." Three of them say, "singing and making music in your heart." One of them says, "sing and praise in your heart." One of them says, "praising and playing in your heart." One says, "sing to the Lord with the heart." One says, "singing and dancing in your hearts unto the Lord." I wonder now is Brother Boswell going to take that last one seriously and as a matter that is absolutely literal.

I make the assertion that from start to finish, in the Bible, the Greek word "psallo" has reference to the use of music made, and that its use in the New Testament is figurative. It is metaphorical.

Now, let me call attention to some other things right along the line. He suggested to us that he has some letters from Professor Riddle and Dwight and others that say they do not think the revisers meant to exclude the idea of the instrument from the word "psallo." Ladies and gentlemen, it is not a question of what those men think, or what one or two think, after the thing has been done. This is the thought: When these one hundred and one men came with a solemn, sacred duty heavily laid upon them, selected because of their scholarship, and sat around a table as these brethren are and took up the original Greek and went to tell you and me what it means, they translated the word and said: "Sir, it means to sing and to make melody in your heart." And that is their scholarship, regardless of the opinions as to what some of the others thought they meant years afterwards.

It is strange that when Brother Boswell tries to quote an author, he only gives part of what he says. This he has done in the case of Professor Riddle. He was, however, reading from Mr. Payne, and perhaps did not know what Riddle said. I give the whole quotation: "The word 'psallo' occurs five times in the New Testament. The revisers render it twice 'sing praises,' twice 'sing,' and once 'make melody.' Originally the word meant striking the strings of a musical instrument, but afterwards got the more general sense of singing, the use of an accompanying instrument not being necessarily implied. I have no recollection of any purpose on the part of the revisers to preclude the use of an instrument. My own opinion is that the word does not preclude the use of an instrument."

When in his vigor and strength of mind, Professor Riddle commented on Eph. 5: 19, and said: "The original idea of the word—that of musical accompaniment—would hardly be retained at this time." ("International Commentary," edited by Philip Schaff.)

Any one can see what Riddle thought the word meant in the New Testament. The testimony of the revisers cannot be overthrown. Brother Boswell, your task is impossible, and, therefore, hopeless.

But let me notice now another thing. Brother Boswell failed wholly to get the quotation that I made from Heb. 2: 12, on singing in the congregation. He claims there's no authority for such. I called your attention, Brother Boswell, to Rom. 15: 6-9, and said it was the fulfillment of the prophecies found in Mal. 1: 11 and Isa. 52: 8: "Thy watchmen shall lift up the voice; with the voice together shall they sing." How is it? When they are together thus, they shall sing.

But the quotation I made the other night, which he failed to catch, was from Heb. 2: 12, where Paul quotes from the prophets, and gives this translation thereof, by the one hundred and forty-eight, saying: "I will declare thy name unto my brethren, in the midst of the congregation will I sing thy praise." There, Brother Boswell, you sing in the church, or in the congregation. Put down Heb. 2: 12. You missed it the other night.

But he said that Hardeman said when you come together "each one" hath a song, and then, if I recall, he said it is "every one." Well, as a matter of plain English, let me suggest, Brother Boswell, there are just four English words that are used in an absolutely distributive sense—"each" and "every," "either" and "neither;" and when these words are used, it is comprehensive. When you come together, therefore, each man and every man hath a song; and, according to his idea, each fellow would bring his banjo or his mandolin or his flute or have to have some kind of a mechanical instrument to assist. In Eph. 5: 19 I suggested to him that the Greek word "adontes" and the Greek word "psalantes," which are translated "singing and making melody," are in the plural number, and it means for each of the individuals in the congregation to sing or to "psallo." This cannot be done by proxy, Brother Boswell. You cannot "psallo" for the other fellow, because each one is to "psallo." Hence, if you had a congregation of five hundred, you would have to have five hundred instruments, or some of them would not be obeying God. There is no doubt about that conclusion, and your contention is ruined.

I call attention next to what Brother Boswell said: "Hardeman, you know 'each one' does not mean all of them." And he shifted from that and explained or illustrated by the commission, where God said: "Go ye into all the world, and preach the gospel to every creature. He that believeth and is baptized shall be saved." God did not say that to each member of the church, but he called unto him his apostles and said unto them: "Go ye into all the world, and preach the gospel." That charge was given to the apostles, and only indirectly does it come down to gospel preachers. Brother Boswell, you get your authority not directly from that, but you get it right where Paul said to Timothy:

"And the things that thou hast heard of me, the same commit thou unto faithful men, who shall be able to teach others also." There is the authority for your preaching and mine, and not from the Savior direct as given in the commission. So that is gone.

Note the next. In the observance of the Lord's Supper, the Bible said that after the supper they sang a hymn and went out. I wonder if Brother Boswell thinks that in the solemnity of that hour there was a mechanical instrument? At midnight Paul and Silas, in the prison cell, sang praises unto God. I wonder if there were instruments specially provided in their prison cell by which they could thus do?

Mark you, this man, Mr. Payne, from whom he reads, draws the conclusion—namely, that unless you have the instrument you cannot do the thing that God demands in "psallo." Listen: "The wonder is, whether, with so much conclusive testimony, very many of those who shall come to see that they have been mistaken, now see that instrumental music inevitably inheres in 'psallo,' and that, therefore, to employ it is mandatory." But Brother Boswell says: "You can and you can't." What does your author say from whom you quote? That you must do it. And, hence, Payne says: "We must unite in agreeing that if we forego musical instruments we cannot conform to the divine injunction to 'psallein.' "

The logical position is that if the mechanical instrument inheres in the word "psallo," if that means a mechanical instrument, then the conclusion is that you cannot "psallo" without the instrument, any more than you can baptize without immersion. Why? Because the word means to immerse. If you, therefore, do a baptismal act, you must immerse. Now, then, if "psallo" means a human instrument, then you cannot "psallo" without that mechanical instrument; hence, your proposition is lost again, for you have it on your chart that you can "psallo" with an instrument or without it. It is both scriptural and unscriptural at the same time. That man says when a thing is scriptural, that means you can either do it or not do it. Who ever heard of such reasoning?

Brother Boswell, answer this; put it down lest you forget: If a thing is unscriptural, can you either do it or not do it? Lying is unscriptural, but under the right of liberty a man can lie if he wants to.

Brother Boswell, stealing is unscriptural, even if it be stealing your Transylvania University. Stealing a meet-house is unscriptural. But that means you can either do it or not do it. Will the gentleman give attention to these things?

It is unscriptural to bear false witness; yet liberty says you can bear it if you want to.

Ladies and gentlemen, a citizen of Tennessee to-night enjoys splendid liberty, but the limitation of that liberty is marked by the law of the State; and whenever your liberty contravenes a declaration or a law, then you become the violator and a traitor to the government.

When a man comes out and accepts the Lord Jesus Christ as "Lord of lords, and King of kings," he is a servant of his, and there is no such thing as liberty to go beyond that which God has declared. God says "sing;" and when you play, you do that which God has not commanded or granted the right, and, hence, you have no liberty.

Again, ladies and gentlemen, I call your attention to this fact: Brother Boswell's time is rapidly passing. What about the argument that he made on the temple? Brother Boswell, have you any telegrams on that? Why don't you get the wires hot and call Brother Briney, the *Christian Standard,* and various others? Why don't you tell them that "my position is suffering at Nashville; I want authority for the temple worship with music—the temple in the days of Herod?" Why don't you say something about that? Three nights have passed since that was sprung, and you promised an audience of six thousand you would answer. Well, when? Next week, or next year? When are you going to answer it? Your proposition demands that you answer now.

Well, again, in this country the argument that is the stock in trade of those gentlemen who use the organ is that the organ is just like a tuning fork; and when he suggested the tuning fork and Hardeman told him the truth about it, he said I took it seriously. But such a statement doesn't excuse you. You made that assertion before too many people. The organ is like the tuning fork! It is not, because the organ is a musical instrument, and the tuning fork is not. Therefore don't stultify your conscience anywhere by misrepresenting those who oppose the organ. Further, you have made the proposition and the statement over this country that in the temple service, to which you have referred, they played musical instruments. Let's be careful along that line.

The next thing I introduced was the letter from one of the Greek Church members. I passed it courteously, as my duty was, to Brother Boswell. He has had it since Saturday night. To my certain knowledge he has been investigating that matter, and what is the answer thereto? He forgot to say one word on earth regarding it and passed it in silence; hence, that point is yielded by my opponent.

But now, ladies and gentlemen, to get some matters further and fresh before you, he says: "Why, Brother Hardeman, you make the organ a test of fellowship." I beg to say exactly the reverse. "Fellowship" means "joint partnership." When he asks me to partake of the worship with the organ, he asks me to become a participant therein; and when I say my conscience will not permit me to do it, he would have me stultify my conscience, or else charge me with responsibility for making a test of that fellowship. That which I do he does not question; but if I accepted what he wants me to do, I stultify my conscience in so doing. Because I won't do that, the ugly charge is made that you folks make it a test of fellowship. Not so. The man who demands it, the man who would ask his brethren to stultify their consciences in observing it, is the man who makes it a test of fellowship and stands in the way of unity.

I thank you.

BOSWELL'S EIGHTH SPEECH

(Monday, June 4, 1923.)

Mr. Moderator, Brother Hardeman, and Friends: I feel that I would be lacking in self-respect if I did not call your attention to the statement made by the speaker that I had stultified my conscience. I ask you to-night, my friends, what must be the desperate situation in which a man finds himself when he has to turn to a speaker on the other side and accuse him of stultifying his conscience? What can you say of a man, in argument, who, after having his attention called to a misrepresentation, will rise to his feet and make the same misrepresentation? He quoted me as denying "singing in the congregation." I said "congregational singing." His argument requires "congregational singing." He immediately arose and used the same expression, "singing in the congregation," and quoted that which proved my contention. Heb. 2: 12: "I will declare thy name unto my brethren, in the midst of the congregation will I sing thy praise." This is "singing in the congregation."

He tells us about Brother Calhoun. He says he has a comparatively recent letter—seven years old. I have a telegram dated "June 4, 4 P.M." I also have a letter from Brother Calhoun. Brother Calhoun takes the position on "psallo" that Brother Kurfees takes; but Brother Calhoun, his own great scholar, his own great and outstanding scholar, that he puts against the scholarship of the world, says he uses instrumental, mechanical instrumental music in the congregation, and thinks he has a perfect right to do so. Surely he is not a smatterer of Greek. Surely he won't discredit his own witness.

I do not know why he should call attention to the fact that Brother Morgan was a trustee in a certain college, and then tie it up with infidel teaching. I do not have to defend Brother Morgan. Brother Morgan has not been a trustee in that college for twelve years.

Brother Hardeman is so bent on doing everything just

exactly as the King James Version has it, I would like to ask him: Do you practice saluting the brethren with a holy kiss? I believe that he would back out on some of those to be kissed.

O, there are so many of these things I could pay attention to! But I cannot follow him into all these things and thus get away from my argument. Why does he not pay attention to what I said instead of telling you what Payne said? Why read from Payne and discredit Payne? I have not quoted anything Payne said. I have simply quoted the lexicons, the commentaries from Mr. Payne, the commentaries from Mr. Kurfees, and commentaries out of the Vanderbilt Library and from other libraries. I do not have to stand for all Mr. Payne said. I have not quoted him as authority for anything under heaven. Mr. Hardeman is the man that stands with Payne, so far as any instrumentation in the word is concerned. He says absolutely that the word carries instrumentation. He differs from Mr. Payne as to what that instrumentation is, but he is absolutely with Mr. Payne as to the meaning of the word. There is no doubt about that.

My friends, he gets terribly excited because I do not answer his questions just when he wants me to. I wonder who is leading in this debate? He is making the same speech over and over. It is sufficient to say that all this will appear in print. You can then form your own judgment.

I was quoting from Prof. Benjamin W. Bacon, Professor of New Testament Criticism and Exegesis, on the meaning of "psallo" at the time when the New Testament was written. He says: "Of the meaning of the word 'psallein' at the time, there can be no question. The meaning to 'play a stringed instrument' is primary; the application to 'sing,' secondary. If the revisers knew Greek, they must have known that the word in New Testament times did allow the use of an instrument. If not, their opinion is valueless." That is when he made the charge that I was a smatterer in Greek, making it the second time.

Now, he says, in regard to these revisers, that they knocked the mechanical instrument out of "psallo." Professor Riddle was one of them. He certainly knew what he meant. Timothy Dwight was one of them. He certainly knew what he meant. What do I care what Payne said about Philip Schaff, any more than I care what Mr. Hardeman says about me? And I expect there is just about as much fact in one as the other. Here is what Professor Schaff says for himself, "I will sing with the spirit, and I will sing with the understanding also;" and he says that the presence of "psallo" in connection with prayer in 1 Cor. 14: 15 is "a proof that the prayer was accompanied with song and with harp also." And Mr. Hardeman, in spite of the fact that Professor Schaff made this statement, says that he sat down with the Revision Committee and knocked the mechanical instrument out of the word "psallo." Do you believe it? I do not, any more than I believe the position that Professor Calhoun occupied before he came over on our side is correct.

In just a minute I will get to all these things he wants me to talk about—in a minute. I was showing that the mechanical instrument was the primary meaning of the word, and that that was the meaning during the New Testament times in all of the references; and I quoted more than thirty-three—quoted any number of references to show that, an abundant number; and in all the references a mechanical instrument is meant.

In this connection here he says what? Hardeman says: "When God commands people to 'psallo,' it must be done. All right; what does 'psallo' mean? To accompany with an instrument. You can't leave the instrument out, Brother Boswell." Who is that—Payne or Hardeman? It is Hardeman who says: "You can't leave the instrument out. Where is the lexicon that says you can 'psallo' without the instrument? Absolutely none—absolutely none." Brother Hardeman is the man who says he agrees with what Brother Payne says, as far as the meaning of "psallo" is concerned. I have never said I agreed with Payne. I do not agree with him in all of his conclusions. I have never used any of his arguments. Mr. Hardeman admits all that Mr. Payne says, as far as the word meaning instrumental music is concerned.

In this he parts company with Brother Kurfees and throws him in the wastebasket. Brother Hardeman says it means to play on the heart; that the heart is the musical instrument. Brother Hardeman, when the word "baptizo" was presented to the pedobaptists, they first fought the Greek meaning of that word, and next they did exactly what you are doing—spiritualized it. We have fought them from the meaning of the word. They have given that trench up, and yet Brother McGarvey says the man who can find instrument in "psallo" is a smatterer of Greek. Those on Brother Hardeman's side have found it, and it is bothering them.

We have come to Herod's temple. Now, remember, I had all the facts about Herod's temple before I began this debate, before I came down here. But Brother Hardeman had professed such a high opinion of what he knew about things that he scared me a little, and I thought I would wait a while. God put musical instruments in the first and the second temple. If they were not in Herod's temple, who took them out? Who had the authority to do it? Jesus never condemned them for disobeying God's command in not having them in the temple. Brother Hardeman argues from silence concerning the temple instruments. Silence is no conclusive argument. It is a most precarious argument. Any number of illustrations can be brought to prove this, but I have not time. Any one that knows anything about the laws of discussion knows that silence is the most precarious argument that you can use. At least, it is one of the most uncertain. Here is what the Bible says: "And he set the Levites in the house of Jehovah with cymbals, with psalteries, and with harps, according to the commandment of David and of Gad, the king's seer, and Nathan the prophet: for the commandment was of Jehovah by his prophets." There is your "Thus saith the Lord" for the instruments being in the first temple, in the second temple; and if they were not in the temple built by Herod, who put them out, and by what authority did they put them out?

No, I did not send a telegram to Jerusalem. I got my message from Jerusalem by the Holy Spirit, which is better than a telegram. And the Jewish rabbi of this city, Rabbi Stern, says that "God put them there. If they were not in Herod's temple, they were taken out without God's authority." Into that temple Jesus went; into that temple the apostles went. I have read you about Jesus' going into the temple. There I found the authority of Jesus for worshiping with instruments. The apostles went there, as we discover in Luke 24: 52, 53. We find: "They worshiped him, and returned to Jerusalem with great joy: and were continually in the temple, praising and blessing God."

Jesus went into the temple, as we find in John, and cleansed the temple. He did not put the instruments out. If they were not there, he did not condemn them for violating a command of God. So they must have been there. The apostles went up to the temple after the ascension of Jesus and continued in the temple daily. Peter and John were going up to the temple the ninth hour of prayer—the hour of prayer, which was the ninth hour. They went into that temple. Paul had a vow to pay. Paul went up to pay that vow. He was there arrested. When he stood before Felix, he said that he went up to Jerusalem to worship, and was worshiping God in the temple and purifying himself according to the law. You will find these references in Acts 21: 20-28; Acts 24: 11-18; Acts 2: 44-47; Acts 3: 1. Here is your apostolic practice.

Now, as we have been with the Hebrews, I think we shall go over to the Greeks. We received the following letter last night from Brother Hardeman: "This is to certify that I am identified with the Greek Orthodox Church, 208 Sixth Avenue, South, this city, and have been identified with it seven years, and that no instruments of music made by human hands are used in the worship, nor has there ever been such an instrument of music used in the church of this people in all history." Who would have the courage to go on the stand and deny that? The letter further says: "As a Greek, I consider what is known as the American Revised Version a faithful translation of 'psallo' and 'psallendi' of the English word 'sing' and 'make melody,' respectively. These two words, to us in our tongue, mean exactly what the words 'sing' and 'make melody' mean to the English-speaking people. Sincerely, Chris Contos." That is his letter. There isn't anything in there that is new. But we have another letter from the same gentleman, wherein he says: "Prof. George D. Zekidou, Greek Dictionary, page 1259, in interpreting the Greek word 'psallo,' says, 'Psallo,' epsela and (modern) epsalla." Now, my friends, this may be humorous, but it is serious. These are Greek words, and this is a letter from the same Greek gentleman who wrote the other letter, and he gives the definition as taken from the Greek Dictionary: "Epsalen, depilate, to pluck, touch, play by the fingers on a stringed [instrument] organ, singing to the cithara, and plain sing. Chris Contos." The other letter was saying nothing but what we already knew. Here he gives a definition out of a Greek dictionary. Of course the word "sing" carries with it whatever meaning "psallo" had.

Now, we have another one: "Nashville, Tenn., June 4, 1923. The Greek word 'psallo' means pull, touch, play the stringed organ with the fingers, plain sing. [Signed] Rev. Chas. Skoufis, priest of the Greek Orthodox Church, 300 Sixth Avenue, South, Nashville, Tenn." Reference: "Orthorgraphican Lexicon, by George D. Zekithoo, page 1259, Standard Greek Dictionary. And the distinguished gentleman sits here to-night, and he says: "The above was dictated by me personally. [Signed] Rev. Chas. Skoufis." Their own Greek language. He tells us just exactly what the word means. We have known that. We have understood that all the time. I warned Brother Hardeman about this last night. He would not take my warning. The Greek Catholics do not have congregational singing; they have male singers; and when asked why they have male singers, these Greeks, who know their language, say Paul says, "Let the women keep silence in the church," and, therefore, the women must not sing. Will Brother Hardeman accept the practice of his witness on this point?

Take his own witness; go into the Greek Catholic Church. They, I take it, would not use the instrument, because they came out of the Roman Catholic Church, and would not desire to do anything that they could leave off that the Roman Catholic Church practiced.

But here is another thing. The same Greek Church, who know their language, practice baptism, trine immersion, baptizing each candidate three times. So if we are going to take them as witnesses to-night, as to their practice in reference to "psallo," we must take them as to their practice regarding "baptizo" as well.

I have no objection to translating "psallo," "sing," because that word carries with it identically the meaning that is in "psallo." You can sing with or without an instrument, and anybody knows that.

Now, I want to get back to his questions.

"Can you baptize with or without an element?" No.

"What is the element in New Testament baptism of penitent believers?" Water.

"Can you circumcise with or without an instrument?" No.

"What is the instrument?" Never used one; ask a surgeon. I should think anything that cuts.

What have these questions to do with the subject, brethren? "Baptism" and "circumcision" are not analogous words to "psallo." They are not in the same class with the word we are discussing. Now, these questions are only to muddy the water.

"Can you 'psallo' with or without an instrument?" Not in its original meaning; but the New Testament meaning of the word is to sing with or without a musical instrument.

"What is the instrument?" By thirty-three authorities, whom he has not questioned or noticed—except one, Bacon, whom he perverted—I have shown it is a mechanical instrument. In addition to this mechanical instrument, Paul adds the spiritual element, "in the heart." "In the heart" is not in "psallo," but are added words. But these words do not exclude the instrument.

"What lexicon says you can 'psallo' without an instrument?" You say, "None"—that is, Brother Hardeman—"none, absolutely none." I have given you abundant authorities that say you can sing with or without an instrument.

He asked another question in his Saturday-night speech: "How can a thing be scriptural and unscriptural at the same time?" He has asked it again to-night. I have never said that. I do not know how a thing can be scriptural and unscriptural at the same time. The nearest thing I know is this: A church is scriptural; it is scriptural to have elders, and yet Paul told Timothy to appoint elders in every church. There were churches, then, existing that did not have elders in them. Timothy was to appoint elders. And so I suppose there are churches to-day that are existing—perhaps in this community, I do not know—that haven't elders; and yet these churches cannot be altogether unscriptural churches, because Paul said to Timothy to appoint elders in every church, and these elders were to be appointed in churches that did not have elders.

I do not think that this has anything to do with the question under discussion. But here is what I said: I said with or without is scriptural. I did not say anything is scriptural or unscriptural. I said with or without is scriptural. It is scriptural to sing with the instrument, it is scriptural to sing without the instrument. We have proved that by all these authorities which I have quoted. In fact, not a single authority other than Brother McGarvey—he has brought the splendid authority of Brother Calhoun; I love Brother Calhoun; I have been with him in congregations where an organ was used, and we have sung together with it. He only said that he does not believe that the instrument is inherent in the word itself, and that you cannot prove the right to use the organ that way. But he attacks the opposition to the organ on another ground.

Again let me emphasize the fact, because it has been brought to your attention so emphatically, that I am not standing behind Mr. Payne; I do not care what Mr. Payne says. My brother is standing with what he claims to be the position of Mr. Payne as to the meaning of the word, in that he says it calls absolutely for an instrument. The only difference between Mr. Payne and Mr. Hardeman is as to what is the instrument. I say to-night again that the instrument is the mechanical instrument. That has been demonstrated by these thirty-three witnesses. It has been proved that the word has the mechanical instrument in it by the testimony that has been brought to you from all these authorities through all these nights so far.

Then, brethren, I have proved absolutely—"therein and thereunto," if you please—absolutely we have proved the way which is scriptural. It is a command of God—yes, a command of God—to sing, to sing whether we use an instrument or not.

Last night he asked me this question: "What is a man going to do out there in the field plowing when he feels cheerful? Is he going to unhitch his mule and go and find a harp and come back and play on it?" I answer: If it means simply to play in the heart, then he would never utter a sound. That is all it says there. There would be no sound. If it carries sound with it, outward sound, and is a command and not an admonition, a man would have to sing every time he felt happy. If one is cheerful, let him sing. "Let him sing praises," is the translation in King James. That book was written in 44-60; Paul wrote Ephesians in 62-63, at least two or three years afterwards. Those who read James would not know what Paul had said in the Ephesians. If what Paul said made any change in it whatever, for fifteen years (it may have been twenty years), if the early date of James and the late date of Ephesians be taken, the readers of James would not know that the heart is the instrument, because James was written first and Ephesians was written afterwards. The readers of James would go by the ordinarily accepted meaning of that term and sing with or without the instrument.

So, my brethren, to-day, I simply say if a man was cheerful, he would do what God told him to do. If he was where there was no instrument to sing with, he would sing without it. If he was where he could get to an instrument and could play on that instrument, he would use that instrument; and in each case he would be carrying out the will of our Heavenly Father. The New Testament says sing; that is a command to sing; and if that means that every one must have a harp, it means that every one must sing; and every time a man does not sing, even though he might be as dumb as a post, you would fail to carry out the commandment of God. You cannot sit out there to-night with the song book in your hands, and because you cannot read the notes, you cannot follow the notes, refuse to sing. That does not absolve you, because, according to Brother Hardeman, you must sing and play upon the heart if that means a musical instrument.

I call your attention to-night, my friends, to the fact that we have endeavored so far during this discussion to bring to you the meaning of the word "psallo" and to show to you apostolic practice. We have found that that word carries with it instrumentation, mechanical instrumentation. We have proved that by scores and scores of witnesses. These he does not deny. The only thing he does is to stand up here and belittle and besmirch Mr. Payne, who is not here to defend himself and who has no avenue by which he can reach him, by and through which he can defend himself. And then he insinuates that all my power I have from "this man Payne," and by his insinuation and innuendo tries to answer my arguments. If he can destroy Payne in your estimation and show you that he is wholly wrong, you will throw "psallo" over with him, because "psallo" and Payne are in the same boat.

I have read the little book that he says is a refutation of Mr. Payne, and you have no right to take my word for it, nor have you the right to take his unsupported word for anything he says about Mr. Payne. If he says these things about Mr. Payne, he ought to produce the witness here upon the stand and prove his statements against a man who is not here. I refer not to Payne's conclusions, but as to what he said Payne did with these lexicons. Do you realize what he charged that man with, and then do you realize that he charged me with having done the same thing and of using the same thing? I have read the little book by Brother Kurfees. It does not refute Mr. Payne; in fact, I can show you in that little book that Mr. Payne is substantiated by Mr. Kurfees' review; and if Mr. Kurfees' review is such a deadener for Mr. Payne, why did Brother Hardeman repudiate Mr. Kurfees?

HARDEMAN'S EIGHTH SPEECH

(Monday, June 4, 1923.)

Ladies and Gentlemen: I trust this thirty minutes may be just as short as possible, and I will make it to you just as interesting as I possibly can, commencing just where my opponent began. I think it best always to take the speeches in order, that you may follow the line of thought suggested.

The first statement was, perhaps, not an intentional, but a misrepresentation of what I said, with the seeming intent of trying to gain some kind of sympathy or force against his opponent. Brother Boswell stated that I said he stultified his conscience. I beg to say to him and to you I did not. I said: "Sir, do not do that by misrepresenting us." But, ladies and gentlemen, he openly and above board asks me and my brethren all over this country to stultify our consciences by worshiping where there is an instrument of music. And unless we do so, we must be responsible for the test of fellowship. That thing I deny most positively, and denounce as absolutely the opposite of the truth. The man that injects the difference, the man that brings in the thing that causes the trouble, is the man that makes the test of fellowship. Before you introduced the organ we were in fellowship, in perfect accord, here in Nashville, with Brother Lin Cave and others, men whom I appreciate; all were together and were fellowshiping. What caused us not to be? Is it something, Brother Boswell, I have done? You have been absolutely unable to point it out. Gentlemen, it is something he has done. You have brought into the service of God that which was left out for fifty years after the Restoration Movement. It is that for which there is not a scintilla of authority, and you think more now of your human instrument, which you say you can get along without, than you do of my fellowship or that of ten thousand people in the city of Nashville. If you want fellowship, remove the barrier. Brother Boswell says: "I can do that and not stultify my conscience. I can worship with or without the instrument." Then, ladies and gentlemen, if that statement be true, and you accept his word for it, how do you account for his not removing it and, therefore, taking away the breach to the fellowship? There is but one answer—viz., he prefers his man-made instrument to the peace and harmony and oneness of the body of Christ in the city of Nashville. God said that six things he hated; one of them was a man that soweth discord among brethren.

I want to ask: What is the objective on the part of these brethren in this debate? What do they want to accomplish? They want, if possible, to show that they can use the instrument of music, so that they can go to other churches which they never builded and there enter in and get possession of them and introduce their man-made machinery, thereby either driving some out or make them stultify their consciences by adopting it. Brethren, remove your barrier, and we will all have fellowship, as in the days of old. Brother Boswell, the responsibility is yours. Take it out, and the fellowship will be restored. Put it in, and you make the test unless you ask me to stultify my conscience.

His comment on Heb. 2: 12 would be amusing but for the seriousness thereof. He says it is not "singing in the congregation," but it is "congregational singing." The passage is: "In the midst of the congregation will I sing thy praise." Brother Boswell, how do you reckon Christ does that? Does he come down personally, and all the members sit idly by, and Christ enters in to sing in the midst of it? Why don't you read Isa. 52: 8, "with the voice together shall they sing?" Who sing? They—the people. I said that was fully indorsed in Rom. 15: 6-9, and you paid absolutely no attention to it. But he calls attention to Mr. Riddell and Mr. Schaff again, who say that in the Revised Version they didn't intend to preclude the instrument; and he would have you think that they meant the mechanical instrument, but there is not one single word of authority or insinuation to that effect.

But he said: "Brother Hardeman read a letter from Calhoun of 1916, and that Brother Calhoun had come over on the Lord's side now." Well, I suppose there is a difference between the Lord's side and the side of the Lord, just as there is between congregational singing and singing in the congregation. Now note, ladies and gentlemen, Brother Calhoun never did believe, never has believed, does not believe to-night, that instrumental music is in the worship. He says that thing cannot be. And that is the source of his argument. Brother Calhoun says the instrument can't be in the worship, because it is not included. Brother Calhoun says that the word "psallo" gives no authority on earth in the church of God for mechanical instruments, and yet he says Brother Calhoun is on the side of the Lord. What side are you on, by the way? You are exactly the opposite of Brother Calhoun. O, yes, you are, Brother Boswell! Just keep quiet; you are. You say that "psallo" furnishes authority; Brother Calhoun says it is not so. Do you agree with him? [Mr. Boswell nods his head.] Why, he says, ladies and gentlemen, "I agree with Brother Calhoun." Brother Calhoun says that "psallo" gives no authority to use instrumental music in the worship. How is it that you claim to agree with him, and yet say that it does?

MR. BOSWELL: We both use the instrument.

MR. HARDEMAN: No, no; you claim "psallo" authorizes the instrument, and Brother Calhoun says it does not. Don't talk about "we both do." Brother Calhoun is exactly the opposite from you. Brother Calhoun says he doesn't believe that instrumental music is authorized by the word of God. What is he trying to prove? That it is scriptural. Does that look like we are together? What does "scriptural" mean? That it has scriptural authority. Of course, if a thing is scriptural it has scriptural authority. That is Boswell. Brother Calhoun, what about you? "The Scriptures furnish us authority." Now, the difference between Brother Calhoun and Brother Boswell is, one says it is and the other says it is not. That is the difference. They are nearly together. Just a *not* between. That is all.

But, friends, let me pass to the next, and I might answer it with a matter of pleasantry. Why, he said: "Brother Hardeman, when you go to hold meetings, do you greet the brethren with a kiss?" No; just the sisters, Brother Boswell.

Brother Boswell says that he has not quoted Payne's book, or has not quoted Payne. Now, here is the charge I made, and he will not deny it: Brother Boswell has read a large per cent of his speeches from Payne's book—not from what Payne himself said, altogether, but from what Payne has used of other authors. Those definitions, those commentaries he has been offering, he read from Payne's book. But Payne's book has been reviewed, and that review bears Brother Calhoun's indorsement, whom he says stands on the Lord's side. The review suggests and proves conclusively that Elder Payne is unreliable in the handling of an author; therefore the point I make is, when Brother Boswell has read from Payne's book what anybody says, it does not carry the weight of reliability with it. He says he does not indorse Payne and is not standing with Payne; but the Commission on Unity, composed of your moderator, Dr. Morgan, et al., does indorse him, I presume, because they gratuitously send these books out through the country. Brethren, if you do not indorse them, why send them out? Are you trying to palm off something by way of deception over the country? Are you trying to deceive people? Why, you sent me mine. I would have paid for it. But you gave it to me, mailed it gratis; and now Brother Boswell says he does not believe Payne. O, let's not practice deception one among another! Now, if you gentlemen don't believe it, call in your Payne books. I really believe you would be glad if the Payne book had never been written, for it sounds the death knell on that side of the question. But he says Hardeman stands with Payne. I stand with Payne on this one point: that the original meaning of the word "psallo" is to pluck, to twitch, to pull, to twang, or to play, the idea being of the instrument. That is the etymological, primary meaning of the word; but when it comes to the New Testament use of it, as all the lexicons suggest, it carries the idea with it of singing; and when you want to know what the instrument is, you can't go to the lexicons, but must go to the Bible. You can't take the lexicons and tell what the element in baptism is. The lexicon tells us what baptism means—viz., to immerse; but as to the element in which you immerse, you do not get that from the lexicon, but you get it from God's word, and God said that water is the element. Therefore from the lexicon I get what "psallo" means—to touch, to twitch, to twang; and then from God's word I learn what the element or what the instrument is, and God says it is the heart and not a man-made device.

I call attention again to the letters of the Greeks that are here to-night. Now, the facts are: These gentlemen went to Mr. Contos this afternoon and asked him very definitely regarding this letter; suggested to him: "Was it dictated to you?" "Did they secure your signature by way of implication without full knowledge?" When informed that of his own accord he wrote it, then they presented him a Greek lexicon and asked him to tell just what that Greek lexicon said, and he wrote out, translating the Greek as told by that lexicon into the English: "Psallo, epsallo, and (modern) epsalla—to pluck, to touch, to twitch, to play with the fingers, as a stringed instrument, singing to the cithara, to play and sing." Now, it is wrong, ladies and gentlemen, to introduce a man on a certain point unless you tell all the man said. Brethren, when you got through with the man and got his word, he told you to your faces: "I don't believe that the lexicon is right." Why didn't you tell that?

MR. BOSWELL: He didn't tell me.

MR. HARDEMAN: He said he did.

MR. BOSWELL: Then he did not.

MR. HARDEMAN: He said he didn't believe it.

MR. BOSWELL: I ask a point of order. The point of order is, he said: "If I went there, why didn't I tell what he said?" I said, "I did not go;" he said, "You did."

MR. HARDEMAN: I didn't mean you were personally. All of you are a oneness. We will agree on that. It doesn't make any difference who went, you or your representatives.

MODERATOR MCNEILLY: The point of order is sustained.

MR. HARDEMAN: All right; I accept your ruling, but somebody went.

MR. J. J. WALKER: I was there, and I deny it; here is the witness.

MR. HARDEMAN: Just hold the order a minute. I have this to say regarding it, ladies and gentlemen: After your conference, I saw Mr. Contos, and, upon my word of honor, in the presence of a brother who was there, Mr. Contos, in my room, said: "I told those gentlemen that I did not believe the translation correct." I am certain that I am stating it exactly, but I pass from that.

MODERATOR JOHN B. COWDEN: These brethren are insisting that they want to get this straightened out.

MR. HARDEMAN: Is Mr. Contos in the audience? [Mr. Contos answered present.] Will you make a statement, Mr. Contos? What have you to suggest with regard to it? Did I state it correctly?

MR. CONTOS: Yes, sir.

MR. HARDEMAN: Mr. Contos says that I did.

MR. COWDEN: We would like to hear these other witnesses that are present.

MR. J. E. GORSUCH (at the affirmative table): I went down there, and Mr. Contos didn't say that.

MR. J. J. WALKER: I was there, and he did not.

MR. HARDEMAN: All right; that is a matter between you and Mr. Contos.

MODERATOR MCNEILLY: In view of that situation, this matter is necessarily out of order, because the conflict there stands simply before the audience.

MR. HARDEMAN: Be it remembered, if you please, that the statement I made is correct. I am sorry to see you gentlemen embarrassed.

MODERATOR MCNEILLY: There is no implication against either Brother Boswell or Brother Hardeman at all. It is just a question of conflicting statements.

MR. HARDEMAN: Ladies and gentlemen, as a matter of fact, and with all kindness and courtesy toward the Greek Church, let me just suggest this: Aside from these gentlemen, every scholar in all this world knows that the Greek

Orthodox Church has never practiced instrumental music, and that is the point that has come up regarding the matter. They speak the original Greek; and, as Brother Boswell says, surely they ought to know their own tongue. As a matter of fact, these Greeks, whom I do not know, and whose intelligence and integrity I have no right to question, say by their action that "psallo" does not imply the mechanical instrument. They think the word forbids a mechanical instrument. Their very practice excludes it. In the year 608 there were some Greeks who tried to introduce the organ into the church, but in a synod in which there were some two hundred and eighty bishops it was repudiated as not being authorized by their mother tongue.

Brother Boswell says: "I knew all about the temple." That is a fact. He knew as much about it last week as tonight. He told the truth about that. But what has he learned about it? What does he know about it?

Now, he says that music was in Solomon's temple. That is a fact. So was animal sacrifice; so was burning of incense; so were the babies; and so was polygamy. All of them were together. He says it was in Zerubbabel's temple. All right. He asks: "Why wasn't it in Herod's temple?" I will tell you. From about 175 B.C. the Jews were engaged in a state of wonderful warfare, during which time Mattathias and his five sons fought for the maintenance of Jewish rights; and finally old Herod tried to secure their favor by the building of the new temple, the one in existence in Christ's day. There is not a man who can prove positively that Christ or the apostles or the primitive Christians ever heard the sound of a human instrument in any Jewish service upon the earth.

Well, he says, silence is a powerfully good argument. I think so, too; and since the New Testament says not a word about instrumental music, the organ must forever go, for there is not a shadow of a shade of an intimation of a mention of the mechanical instrument through all of the New Testament. If silence, therefore, is to be regarded, there is absolutely no hope for my opponent.

Another point I must notice. He says the Greeks practice three immersions. That is correct. I think they are wrong about that; but their wrong is not on the meaning of the word, but upon the interpretation of the commission. It is not a question of philology or etymology of words at all.

But he says Hardeman charged that he had been saying that the instrument is both scriptural and unscriptural. The point I was after is this: if a thing is scriptural, how can you both do it and not do it at the same time? That is the point. On the other hand and to the reverse, I asked him: If a thing be unscriptural, can you do it or not do it? Lying is unscriptural; stealing is unscriptural; murder is unscriptural. Brethren, how can it be unscriptural and then you be permitted either to do it or not to do it? That situation cannot possibly exist.

But I call your attention now to the fact that my opponent repudiates to-night, openly and above board, King James and the revisers. I asked if he indorsed them in their translation of "psallo." He passes it by. Ladies and gentlemen, your faith and mine rests upon the King James and the Revised Version. We read the Scriptures in English. Such I accept as the rule of faith and practice for Christian men and women. Destroy that, and you destroy the hope of the land.

With the few minutes now left, I call your attention to a chart. I want to base an argument upon it. In the Bible there are two classes of commandments—one of them designated on the board as a generic command, which means a commandment that does not carry the precise manner of its doing in the term; then there is the specific commandment. Illustrative of that, take the word "tree." That is a generic term. If you just have a tree in mind, any tree on earth would meet the demand in that case—the oak or gum or cypress—these become specific with reference to the tree and general with reference to that which follows. For instance, with reference to the oak, there are three subordinate kinds—namely, white oak, red oak, black oak. Under cypress, the species is gopher. Now, then, if God had told Noah to build an ark out of a tree, any tree would have met the demand. If God had said, "Noah, build an ark out of oak," any oak on the face of the earth would have done. If God had said, "Build it out of gum," the same would have been true. But, ladies and gentlemen, instead of God's saying, "Make an ark out of oak," or "out of gum," God specifically said to Noah: "Make an ark out of gopher wood." I am maintaining the thought that when God said make it out of gopher wood, had Noah made it out of any other than that, he would have been in rebellion against God. If Noah had gone and put up the studs out of gopher and then used oak on the balance, he would have disobeyed God. God said build it out of gopher wood, and you cannot build it out of another and obey God.

If God had said offer an animal, just any animal would have done. But animals are divided into quadrupeds and bipeds. Under the quadrupeds there are the cow, the sheep, the pig. If God had said to the Jews, "Offer an animal," then any kind of animal on earth would have done. But when God said, "Offer a sheep," the man that would presume to go and offer a pig was in disobedience to God. If any one had offered both a sheep and a pig, God's law would have been violated, for he said: "Ye shall not add to the word which I command you, neither shall ye diminish aught from it."

When God said in the commission, "Go," there is a general term—go by foot, go by horseback, go by automobile, go by train. But if God had said "walk," then the man who would presume to ride would be in rebellion against God. If God had said "ride," that would have excluded walk. And thus on down the line.

Now, if God had said, "make music," then any kind of music on earth would have sufficed. But out of the only two kinds of music there are, vocal and instrumental, God said "sing," and the man who makes instrumental music is in rebellion against God. When a man sings, he does nothing but what God says; when a man sings bass, he fulfills God's command; when a man sings alto, he is in obedience to God; but when, in addition to singing, he uses another and at the same time a coördinate term, he violates God's word and is in rebellion against high heaven. Brethren, there is no doubt about that. Just as Noah had to use gopher wood, just as the Levites had to use the sheep, and just as when we are to make music unto God we are to sing, there lives not a man on earth who can gainsay the argument as thus presented by the term. It is like the rock of Gibraltar—impregnable. Of the two kinds of music, instrumental and vocal, Lord, what do you want? God says: "Of the two, I say sing, and let the melody be in the heart and not upon any mechanical instrument." "Behold, to obey is better than to sacrifice, and to hearken to God's word is better than the fat of rams."

Just as the old Levite, if he had gone and offered a lamb, and then in connection with that, as an aid to his lamb, had sacrificed a horse or a mule, it would have been adding to God's word, and heaven's declaration and warning is not to do that. Faithfulness to God's word means this: Take God at his word, believe just what he says, become and be just what he requires, live as he directs, and trust him for the promises. "Not my will, but thine, be done."

"Lord, speak, thy servant will hear; command, I will obey." God said: "Sing and make melody in your heart." The man that sings and makes melody elsewhere is in violation and in rebellion against the word of God. Ladies and gentlemen, where is the scripture, where is the authority? As you pass home the fourth night, I beg you consider: Where—O, where—is the scripture that Brother Boswell has brought forth that authorizes instrumental music of a man-made type in the service of God? Where is the direct command? Where is the practice? Where is the inference? There is not a man on earth that can point his hand to one single scripture and say: "Here it is." But he said back in 2 Chron. 29. O, yes, but that is under the law of Moses. Back in those times David had eight wives; Solomon, seven hundred wives and three hundred concubines. That is the authority! And they had infant membership in the temple; there was the burning of incense; and yet they say: "There is the authority!"

I say to you, ladies and gentlemen, there is not a man on earth who can make one argument in behalf of instrumental music but the same argument can be made for infant church membership. I wish you would try that. Test it out, as we have the congregational singing, as we have the tuning fork, as we have the temple practice, else down is your proposition. It cries out in piteous tones for a man who can raise it up and find one word from God's book authorizing or even permitting the same.

When God gave the command to go and baptize, you cannot add to that, you cannot substitute for it, you cannot take away from it. So when he said, "Sing and make melody in your heart," it must forever stand.

I thank you, friends, very, very kindly.

BOSWELL'S NINTH SPEECH

(Tuesday, June 5, 1923.)

Brother Moderator, Brothers, and Sisters: It is a genuine pleasure to-night to have something new on the subject which we have been discussing—that is, new in this discussion. I call attention to the chart on the wall, placed there by the brother on the negative side of this proposition. There are just a few things to be said about that chart, and then we will leave it.

The chart—of course those who have read Brother Kurfees' book will recognize it as being one of the leading arguments in his book on this particular subject. I only take time to state the fact that the chart begs the question and asserts as being proof the very proposition under discussion. No one will deny that there are generic and specific terms, that there are oak trees and gum trees and cypress trees, and all these various trees under these generic terms, and he could have stretched that out to fill the side of the wall. The number of trees does not have anything to do with the subject. As a matter of fact, God said use gopher wood, and that is the only sort of wood that the builder of the ark was permitted to use. The same is true as far as animals are concerned. God never commanded that a pig should be offered. I suppose a child that has studied anything of the Old Testament would know that, and the prohibition of God would prevent the offering of any other sort of animal or kind of animal than that which God had specified. No one denies that. This has no bearing upon the question. If we were proposing to substitute something in place of something else, then this would have some bearing upon the subject; but it is not an argument that we have made that we have a right to substitute anything in the world for anything that God has commanded, and no one can put such words into my mouth. I could not possibly believe God's word and believe that I had any right to substitute anything in the world. I won't even go so far in substitution as to engage in that pleasant occupation that seemed so delightful to our good brother last night when I asked him the question: "What are you going to do with the statement of Paul in 1 Thess. 5: 26, where he said, 'Salute all the brethren with a holy kiss?'" And then with pleasantry—mind you, a pleasantry in answer to the question—he turned the whole thing off by saying: "I will substitute the sisters." Brethren, I ask you what sort of respect has any man for the word of God that would stand here and trifle with the word of God in any such way as that—"I will substitute the sisters." It would be just as proper for me to substitute a pig for a lamb as for this brother to substitute the sisters in place of the brethren. I don't want you to forget that, now. How could he answer that question? He could not have answered that question without letting down the bar. If he could do it, let him do it and stop a while with his substitution. That is a matter, then, of substitution; but bear in mind that there is no place for pleasantry when it comes to a command of God; and if you believe, Brother Hardeman, in the word of God, how could you reply with such a thing? I ask that question for you people to ask down in your own hearts. I defend God's word from substitution.

Now, on the chart we come down to "go," and then we have "walk." Well, let us take that word "walk." He gives that, but he does not put down there that you can walk with a stick or without a stick. You can walk with a stick, you can walk without a stick; and there is not a thing in the word that tells you you cannot walk with a stick, but you can walk without a stick. The word permits either way, and the same is true of "sing."

And so we come down to the question of music, and he has put "music" out there and made that the generic term, and then put "vocal and instrumental" under "music." We are not discussing vocal vs. instrumental music. That is not a part of this discussion. This discussion is, whether the word "sing" can include an instrument or not—whether or not you can sing with or without an instrument. He will not deny that you can sing with or without an instrument. This, I am sure, he will not deny. Of course I do not want to misrepresent him. He is giving this word in Ephesians a different meaning than it has in English, but the English word "sing" in Ephesians has exactly the same meaning that the Greek word "psallo" has in Ephesians, for it must translate that word.

And so with these remarks I pass from his chart to call your attention to a statement made the other night by Brother Hardeman that music of the organ was introduced in the year 670 A.D. And he gave you that as the time that musical instruments were introduced into church worship. If he will turn to Groves' Dictionary of "Music and Musicians," he will find this statement: "Julianus, the Spanish bishop, who flourished during that time—450 A.D.—says 'organs were in common use in the Church of Spain at that time.'" Thus Groves' Dictionary of "Music and Musicians" gives us the statement that organs flourished in Spain in the churches in the year 450—more than two hundred years before the time stated by our brother. St. Augustine in 400 A.D. encouraged the singing of songs with the lyre and psaltery. (Quoted from "Religion and Ethics," by Hastings.) Basil the Great opposed the use of the instrument in 364, proving that they were in use at that time in some of the churches. If they were not in use in some of the churches, there would be no force in opposing their use. Clement of Alexandria, 190, says: "If you are able to accompany your voice with a lyre or cithara, you will incur no censure." Showing that they were doing so at that time. Justin Martyr, in 155 A.D., opposed the use of the instrument in the worship, proving that some of the churches were using it. Now, there is no necessity of arguing that. I have stated historical facts, and all the argument in the world cannot brush out a historical fact; and so I will leave that and come to some other matters for our attention.

Notwithstanding my corrections of Brother Hardeman last night for saying that I said he could not find "singing in the congregation," when I said "congregational singing," he arose after that and again used the same expression, saying there is no difference; it is immaterial. Then he says Brother Boswell missed the whole thing and quoted Heb. 2: 12. Now, I do not claim to know it all. I do not claim to know everything that is in the Bible, but I do know that some people do not know it all. I do know that the Bible would be a good book for some people to read and study.

Let me quote the statement in Heb. 2: 12: "I will declare thy name unto my brethren, in the midst of the congregation will I sing thy praise." He quoted that correctly. Then he gives this as having reference to Isa. 52: 8: "The voice of thy watchmen! they lift up the voice, together do they sing; for they shall see eye to eye, when Jehovah returneth to Zion." Brethren, this is not the passage quoted by the writer of Hebrews. The writer of the Hebrew letter quoted from Ps. 22: 22. I will read it to you: "I will declare thy name unto my brethren: in the midst of the assembly will I praise thee." There is where it is found, in a Messianic prophecy, and the "they" is not there. He correctly places his quotation in Rom. 10: 15, where Paul says: "How beautiful are the feet of them that bring glad tidings of good things!" This quotation in Romans is taken from Isa: 52: 7, and the "they" in verse 8 has reference to the watchmen. The statement of Isaiah is of a fortified city. The Jews are in captivity. They see that God is sending them help. The watchers may be the people on the tower or the angelic hosts. They see help coming, and cry out: "How beautiful are the feet of those who are bringing this deliverance!" Then it says they shall shout, they shall sing. It has no reference whatever to the passage in Hebrews, and you cannot find it connected with that verse in any commentary. If he can, let him find it.

And let me say something here. It is all right to dispute the commentaries, it is all right to attack books; it is all right to do these things, provided you have witnesses back of you. But when any man stands up and makes charges concerning another man, whether he be present or absent, he ought to produce the proof.

Again, he seemed to be disturbed because I quoted so much from Mr. Payne. It is amusing, my friends, how a man gets a "Payne," and he had that "Payne" when he started, and he is not well of it yet. He says that eighty or ninety per cent of my addresses have been taken from Mr. Payne. He certainly ought to know Mr. Payne's book by this time. If he knows it so well as that, he must be reading it.

I am not defending Mr. Payne; but I am sure when the brother read from Mr. Payne, accusing Mr. Payne of taking the position he says he takes, he ought to have read to you, in justice to Mr. Payne, and should have read to you the bottom of page 51 and top of page 52, and thus give Mr. Payne a chance to speak for himself, when he cannot get a chance any other way.

To show you how much he knows about my addresses and Mr. Payne, I quoted seventeen lexicons. Of the seventeen lexicons I quoted, I quoted nine out of Brother Kurfees' book. Besides that, I quoted from about thirty original sources. Some of these were gotten from the library at Vanderbilt and many of them personal letters to other brethren from the scholars whose names I have read to you during these addresses.

And so his eighty or ninety per cent dwindles down to a very small number, after all. But what if I did take from Mr. Payne the quotations from the lexicons? If there was anything wrong with one of those lexicons, he ought to have pointed it out and not quoted another man as saying it is all wrong. He should have taken some of the lexicons Mr. Payne has quoted and indicated where he was wrong. To the contrary, he has said, time and time again, "I accept every one of your authorities;" and so he accepted Mr. Payne, with all his so-called "mistakes," premeditated or otherwise.

He says the lexicon does not specify the element in baptism. Mr. Campbell once said: "I will make the word furnish the water." Mr. Hardeman said that you have to go to the New Testament to get the element, and that you could not find it in the lexicon. I cited him to various New Testament lexicons, giving the New Testament meaning—"immersion in water." I have met his charges every time; I have brought the authorities every time. I have gone to his authorities and brought to you the refutation of the statements which he has made.

Again, if he was mistaken regarding this matter of the element in baptism, he might possibly be mistaken as to the instrument in "psallo." He was just as emphatic with the one as he was with the other. Now, the translations—he said he had twenty-six translations; it doesn't make any difference if he had twenty-six hundred translations. The question is: What do these translations say? I brought you one translation, and here it is—James Moffatt. I ask you to-night: Is James Moffatt a competent scholar? I ask you if James Moffatt knows the meaning of Greek. I present this: James Moffatt leaves out "in the heart" and says "heartily unto the Lord." I have produced one that has not in it "in the heart," but "heartily." I call on him to bring his twenty-six translations here and find me one that says without the instrument.

Herod's temple. It is an interesting temple. Let me read this regarding Herod's temple: "Instrumental music in divine service ceased with the destruction of the temple, and that was in the year 70. Music was prohibited generally in token of mourning for the destruction of Jerusalem, except on festal occasions, and especially at the marriage ceremonies. It appears that the organ was employed in nuptial ceremonies which took place in the synagogues." (Jewish Enc., Vol. 9, page 452.)

"The dispersal of the temple singers and the cessation of the performance of the musicians in the sanctuary influenced but slightly the synagogical cantillation, since the desire of many authorities that song should be abstained from in lasting mourning for fallen Zion was never generally heeded when it became a question of song in worship."

They said: "Cut out all singing, cut out all instrumentation, because Jerusalem has fallen." They continued to sing; but after the fall of Jerusalem, because of their mourning over Zion, the instruments were gone, driven from the temple. They went to the synagogue. "In the synagogue," reading from Smith's Bible Dictionary, Vol. 4, page 3135, speaking of the furnishing of the synagogue—"in it there was a chest of trumpets and other musical instruments, used at New Years, Sabbaths, and other festivals." Perhaps Mr. Hardeman will sweep Smith's Bible Dictionary out of the libraries of the world.

The following is taken from a quotation found in Mr. Kurfees' book. I want to prove now by Brother Kurfees that they had music in the temple. "The inference is pretty strong that they avoided some things that were Jewish—and instrumental music was a marked feature in the Jewish worship—but it is plain that (as with the Sabbath question) there was a great deal of blending at the edges between the two dispensations." Now, this is taken from Brother Kurfees' book, "Instrumental Music in the Worship." It is a part of a quotation made by him from "Latin Hymn Writers and Their Hymns." The quotation says that they had this feature, "instrumental music," this feature in the worship. You will find the quotation on page 150. On page 136 you will find this: "Be it observed, first of all, that instrumental music was no part of the worship in the ancient Jewish synagogue. It was never used in that worship. It is as much of an innovation in the synagogue worship of modern times as it is in the worship of the church of Christ. That it was used in the worship of what is called Judaism proper—that is, in the ancient temple worship—is a fact freely admitted by both Jews and Christians." Brother Hardeman says there was no "instrumental music" in the temple. Brother Kurfees says there was no "instrumental music" in the synagogue. "Instrumental music was a marked feature in the Jewish worship." If "instrumental music" was neither in synagogue nor temple in the year 50; if "instrumental music"—that is, not hymns alone—was neither in synagogue nor temple, where did the Jews worship? This is my question: Where did they worship if instruments of music were not in temple nor synagogue?

Now, Brother Kurfees says: "We are, therefore, irresistibly led to the conclusion that whoever, in order to find support for instrumental music in Christian worship, appeals to the fact that the apostles went into the Jewish temple, where such music was used in the Jewish worship, appeals to a record that does not contain a single statement, fact, or word in support of the practice." Admitting the use of instruments in the temple, Brother Kurfees is endeavoring to prove that the apostles did not go up to worship, but to preach. In this endeavor he makes the statement I have just quoted.

I am going now to prove it by Brother Hardeman himself. Brother Hardeman preached a sermon in this Tabernacle on April 20. I will read you what Brother Hardeman said, and out of his own mouth I am going to prove that instrumental music was in the temple. "For about three dozen times in the Old Testament instruments of music are mentioned in connection with the worship of God; but when you turn to the New Testament, not three dozen times, nor not even one time, is it thus mentioned, showing beyond the possibility"—now, listen; this sounds like him, doesn't it?—"showing beyond the possibility of a reasonable doubt"—sounds like his usual "you cannot prove it by anybody on the top side of the green earth"—"showing beyond the possibility of a reasonable doubt that while it prevailed throughout the days of David, and subsequent thereto under Judaism, that at the very inception and inauguration of the Christian dispensation and the church of the living God, it was purposely left out; and, therefore, the silence of the Scriptures regarding it ought to have some moment and weight upon those who rely upon the New Testament." When did the Christian dispensation begin? When was it inaugurated? On Pentecost, after the death, burial, and resurrection of Jesus.

Now, I have a task for Brother Hardeman. He made the statement—he has made this statement several times; now I ask him to make good with it: "I propose, or I make the proposition, to use any argument Brother Boswell made, or has made, rather, for the use of the instrument, to prove infant membership and incense." Now, if he can do that, there never was a better time under heaven to do it. I have used only two arguments—one, the meaning of the word "psallo;" the other, apostolic precedent. Now, if he proves it by any argument I have used, he will have to prove it by the meaning of a word or he will have to prove it by apostolic precedent. Give me the word and the apostolic precedent.

He says that liberty does not permit one to do that which God has said he must not do. I never said anything to the contrary. I never even hinted at the thing. He might wish to put an argument like that into my mouth, and has been hammering on it ever since this debate began; but I have never said it. I have never made any statement that even squints that way. My whole argument has been that the meaning of "psallo" and apostolic precedent give us the right to use an instrument or not use it. He is dissatisfied with my argument because I would not say something like that, I suppose, and wants to get away from it because of that same speech he made here in the Tabernacle, in which he said "the people who indorsed 'psallo' have shied away from it." I did not shy away from it, haven't for several nights. I have not got very far away yet.

Now, another question. Brother Hardeman has been saying all the time that I admitted that his position was correct. I now ask him to look over every speech I have made and find where I have said so. He will find this—where I have denied that; time after time I have said this: "My position is what? You can sing with or without the instrument. His position is that you cannot sing with a mechanical instrument." When I say "sing with an instrument," I mean mechanical instrument, and have always meant it. There is no use quibbling over that proposition.

Then I made this statement to tell him why I could not stand with him. I said: "The very principle that leads you to put the organ out and causes you to disfellowship your brethren is the principle involved—not the playing upon an instrument, not the singing with or without an instrument, but the principle involved, which is absolutely contrary to the New Testament and contrary to everything connected with the Restoration Movement. One of the things that we stood for in the very beginning was to oppose creeds of every sort. He has tried to give the impression that I was starting a college up in Kentucky, and that I was going to put certain things in the deed. No, sir, I am not going to put the "creed in the deed" of the college. A college and a church are two separate and distinct things; and if it were to go into the college, that would not prove that you had a right to put it into a church. But we have a better way than that. In Georgetown, Ky., we are standing by the Restoration Movement, and the Restoration Movement stood against the creed. Here is the thing that has split some of the churches. This has split churches that have no organ in them, and this is a thing contrary to the very spirit of Jesus Christ and contrary to the spirit of the Restoration Movement: "Put the creed in the deed." "It is the object of this building, this house, to encourage and build up churches that will in all work and worship use only what is ordered and required in the New Testament, rejecting all the innovations and devices of man, such as the use of the organ and other instruments of music in connection with the worship, and of any society other than the church of Christ in carrying out the word of God. In the event of any division arising over this or any other questions that may come up, the title of this property inheres to those, whether a majority or minority, who most rigidly adhere to the requirements of the New Testament."

Away has gone the fruit, almost the heart, of our movement—local self-government, the autonomy of the local congregation! Talk about your ecclesiasticism—this is equal to that of any missionary society! Such ecclesiasticism as this I will fight to the last breath in my body. There is no ecclesiasticism anywhere that is as deadly and that more completely takes authority out of the hands of the local congregation than this; for they have in the "creed in the deed" that even if there should be no dissenting voice to the use of the instruments and devices above mentioned, but should they be used as a part of the worship in the building or on said lot, "then said building and lot shall go to the control of the churches of Christ of said county." O, friends, that looks very much like a most unscriptural ecclesiasticism!

HARDEMAN'S NINTH SPEECH

(Tuesday, June 5, 1923.)

Brethren, Moderators, President, and Friends: It is very encouraging to-night to find a company of this magnitude gathered, evidencing your interest in these discussions. I do hope, ladies and gentlemen, that all of us may maintain that spirit and that decorum that is emphasized by the president moderator and will consider seriously and candidly the things that have been presented. We must answer these issues, not only for time, but for eternity as well. While it is unpleasant to see brethren that ought to stand together divided as we are and discussing our differences, I do hope that the ultimate result may be, not the furthering of that division, but the unification of God's people upon a platform where all can stand.

I want to suggest to you this as the next thought: Brother Boswell's mild attack upon the weighty chart is that I took it from Brother Kurfees' diagram. This I did, and his answer is but little short of none at all. The facts are, ladies and gentlemen, the man does not live who can meet the argument of the chart presented. It was only answered at, if I may thus say it. The chart was not intended to suggest the idea of substitution, nor was that the point made; but I want to call your attention to it, as you can see it. When God told Noah to build an ark of gopher wood, had he put up the framework out of gopher wood, and then braced it with white oak, not substituting, but adding to it, he would have been in violation of God's commandment. I believe that this audience can see that. Old Noah built the whole of the ark out of gopher wood. If he had supplemented it by bracing with black gum, or of maple, or of hickory, or any other wood than that which God declared, it would have been in disobedience to Heaven's will. When God commanded the Jews to offer a lamb, they might have gone and offered that lamb, and then if, in addition to that, they had offered a pig or a horse, it would have been in violation of God's law. Now, what was the argument thus made? It wasn't a question of substitution at all; but, to illustrate a principle, when God said build the ark of gopher wood, all other kinds were excluded; when God said offer a lamb, every other kind of an animal on earth was excluded; when God said, in the next place, that we are to go, he used a generic word and not a specific. Therefore we are at liberty under that kind of a commandment to fulfill it in harmony with our great right of liberty; and wherever, therefore, commandments are expressed in generic terms, man is allowed liberty to exercise his judgment. Brother Boswell said that to walk, for instance, does not forbid the use of a stick as a support or as an aid. Now, his argument is this: that the stick bears the same relation to walking that the instrument does to singing. I go, or I walk. "Now, then," said Brother Boswell, "if I take a cane to supplement or to aid me in the walking, I have not violated God's word." The argument is not fair or parallel; it does not illustrate. Why? Because, ladies and gentlemen, the terms "walk" and "stick" are not coördinate terms, tracing back and growing out of the same species—namely, methods of going.

Now, Brother Boswell would have had the parallel if he had said this: When God says "walk," a man can ride as an aid. If you will make that kind of an argument, I will grant you that it is parallel. Why? Because walking and riding are coördinate; but you cannot walk by using ride as an aid. When you put in the aid, you destroy the walk. Let us get the application. There is music. How many kinds? Just two. Are they subordinate one to another, as cane is to walk? O, no! They are coördinate terms. Out of these two coördinate expressions, God picked out one and said "sing." Therefore the instrument, which is the coördinate term, cannot by any process of logic be made as a supplement unto another equal, coördinate; and, hence, the argument still stands to-night absolutely untouched and untouchable.

But he said: "Brother Hardeman speaks lightly with reference to my quotation about greeting with a kiss." As he said with reference to the tuning fork, Brother Boswell actually took it seriously. Now, as a matter of fact, let me submit to you this: What does Brother Boswell do with the statement where God said, "Greet ye one another with a kiss?" I am sure that as between him and me there is positively no difference on the understanding of that passage. It refers purely to a custom still practiced in the East. But he said: "Hardeman, you want to substitute." O, no, my friends! But watch. I asked him time and again, and that has never been answered until this good hour: "Brother Boswell, when you play the organ in the absence of the singing, aren't you substituting then?" The singing has hushed, and nothing but the organ functions. Now, then, if you say it is an aid, I asked you repeatedly, what does it aid? If it is a supplement, what does it supplement?

I ask you: Does it aid the Lord's Supper, does it aid the contribution, does it aid the silence? And echo answers still: "Information from him you have had none." It is not a question of substitution, but addition.

Now, the Lord said eat the bread and drink the wine at the Lord's Supper; but I do not, from a physical point of view, fancy the taste of the dry bread that we have, and I seek to make that more pleasant to men. I take the Lord's Supper, the bread, just like he said, and I spread some butter on it, or some jelly, and make it a little bit more palatable. I have not substituted, but I have added that which God does not declare. I want to aid it. I still observe the Lord's Supper; but have I violated the command by the addition and by the putting into the pores of the bread the butter and the jelly? Let Brother Boswell answer. It is not a question or a charge of substitution, Brother Boswell. That is not the argument. It is a charge of addition. When God wanted men to worship the Lord and came down to the question of music, if he had said "make music," then liberty would have occupied the prominent place and we could have done as every man sees right in his own eyes. But God did not say "render music." Out of the only two kinds of music on earth, God picked out one of them and said: "Do this."

Now, then, when a man does something else in addition to that, my suggestion is that it is in disobedience to God's will.

But, passing from that, I call attention to this: Brother Boswell read some authorities which said the organ was in the church before the date I mentioned. I am certain tonight, ladies and gentlemen, that the preponderance, overwhelming, of historic reference thereto places it between the year 600 and the year 700. But he says: "I have found a man who said they had it back in 450." Well, suppose that is the date; that is just 450 years too late. But he said: "I traced on back and found one fellow that spoke and referred to having the flute in the year 190." Well, all right, Brother Boswell. Suppose you say, then, that it started in 190. Don't you know that all the apostles were dead then and the New Testament closed out? The thing you need to do is to find where it was permitted and used back in the days of the apostles. This you cannot do. Your best effort is only within 190 years of Christ.

It seems hard for Brother Boswell to understand Heb. 2: 12 and the point made. He said that I declared Isa. 52: 8 referred to that. Not so. I said that Isa. 52: 8 refers to Rom. 10, which he admitted; and I also alluded to this fact, which he has not observed: Christ said (Ps. 18): "In the midst of the Gentiles will I sing praise." Now, I asked Brother Boswell last night how it is Christ did that. I said: "Do you think Christ came in person?" The only time Christ ever sang was at the institution of the Supper, and the Bible said when it was over they sung a hymn and went out. That is the only time in which the Savior directly is connected. Not a word said about the instrument. They sang. Brother Boswell, did they also play? Paul and Silas sang praises unto God at the midnight hour. Did they, too, play?

But note the next. When he came to Payne's book, he asked me to read the bottom of page 51 and top of page 52; and I have read that, by the way, in which this statement is the conclusion: "With so vast a number uniting their voices as to the meaning of 'psallo,' the writer is not doubting that the candid will grant that it refers to the instrument, and that instrumental music in Christian worship is acceptable. The wonder is, whether, with so much conclusive testimony, very many of those who will come to see that they have been mistaken will now declare that instrumental music"—now note—"unavoidably inheres in 'psallo' "—that is, he cannot avoid it—"that instrumental music unavoidably inheres in 'psallo,' and that, therefore, to employ it is mandatory." "That instrumental music unavoidably"—cannot get on without it. His chart says you can with it or without it. "That instrumental music unavoidably inheres in 'psallo,' and that, therefore, its use is mandatory."

Now, Brother Boswell, to put my point to the test and see who has the "Payne," I want to ask you: Do you believe, as it is penned in the statement in this book, that the use of a mechanical instrument in connection with the singing is mandatory? Do you believe, as that says, that if we forego the use of the instrument we cannot conform to the divine injunction to "psallo?" Do you believe it or not? Tell us in your next speech. We will see who has the "Payne."

Brother Boswell insists that the element—water—is in the definition of "baptizo," and quotes from Thayer. Why, if you don't mind, you will get as reckless as Elder Payne. Thayer doesn't say, in defining "baptizo," that it means in water. Here is Thayer's definition. Now, you look there while I read from Payne, and we will see, on page 28. Next is given the definition of "baptizo" from Thayer, and here is what Thayer says about it: "*Baptizo*, to dip repeatedly, to immerse, to submerge." Now, after defining it, when he goes on to tell about the use of it, he says: "In the New Testament it is used particularly of the rite of sacred ablution, first instituted by John the Baptist." But he quoted Liddell & Scott: "*Baptizo*, to dip in and under water." What is the definition of it? "To dip, to plunge, to submerge." I have here the definition as given by twenty-four lexicons, and not one of them says in water. Ladies and gentlemen, it is known, without argument and as a matter of fact, that the word "baptizo" does not carry with it the element of water. But he said that Alexander Campbell once said: "I will make the word furnish the water." Yes, he so said; but his point was this: that it was used so much in connection with water that the affinity exists. In fact, whenever you mention "baptizo" in connection with the Christian religion, we think of water, because it was the element used. But the word means to dip, to plunge, to submerge, to overwhelm; and the element does not inhere in the word. If it did, then no other element could be used. But we read in classic literature of people being baptized in ignorance, they are baptized in sorrow, the Savior alluded to his baptism of suffering, there is the baptism of the Holy Spirit, or it may be a baptism of fire. The word means to plunge, or to dip; but the element must be found elsewhere. Now, just say in the New Testament it means to dip, or to plunge; but it does not mean to plunge in sorrow. It does not mean to plunge into drowsiness, though it may mean that. But in the New Testament God designates the element; and hence John says: "I indeed baptize you with water." Now, there is the element. But the water wasn't in the word, for in another statement it is said: "Christ shall baptize you with the Holy Ghost." Hence, there is in the word, to dip, to plunge; but the element has to be learned elsewhere.

Now, I asked Brother Boswell to-night, "How may men circumcise in the New Testament?" and he said: "Brother Hardeman, ask a surgeon." This shows your weakness and fear to meet an argument. The word "circumcision," ladies and gentlemen, primarily and in classic use means to cut around, and had reference to a mark in the flesh. It was originally and primarily performed by knife or some kind of a mechanical instrument, but in the New Testament there is the term and the doctrine of circumcision. What does it mean in the Bible, the New Testament? Back in Abraham's day it meant to cut in the flesh, physically, with a physical knife. Now, in the gospel age, there is the figurative or metaphorical use of the term. In Col. 2: 11 Paul talks about Christian people's being circumcised.

What is the use in the New Testament? It is a figurative use. It is a cutting around the heart and the lopping off, and the instrument in the Bible, the New Testament, is not a literal knife, but it is God's word, the gospel, the sword of the Spirit. Hence, there is a figurative use, as it refers to the New Testament. I suppose he may read a thousand definitions, all of which might be correct with reference to its literal use. The question is: How does the New Testament use the word "circumcision?" In its primary, physical meaning, it was performed with a mechanical knife, or device of man; but the word is used with the spiritual application, and the gospel, the old Jerusalem blade, is the instrument with which the act is brought about.

Now, then, the word "psallo" meant to pull, as to pull the hair; it meant to twang, as to pick a bowstring or a carpenter's line. It also meant to play, as upon a stringed instrument. But the word "psallo" does not carry with it the idea of any particular object at all. When you used "psallo," that meant to pluck; but it did not especially mean to pluck the hair; the hair had to be supplied by some other term. And when you use the word "psallo," it means to twang; but it does not mean to twang a bowstring. You must get the bowstring out of some other thought, etc.

Now, in the New Testament does it mean to pluck a hair? O, no! Brother Boswell says he doesn't think we ought to pull hair. I don't, either.

So, then, in the New Testament, when Paul tells us to "psallo," does he mean for us to shoot arrows? We agree that it does not mean that. Does it mean for us to twitch the carpenter's line? We both agree that it does not mean that. In the New Testament, when God says "psallo," does it mean to strike the chords or strings of an instrument? If so, no man on earth can show it.

What does Paul mean in the New Testament? The word "psallo" carries with it the idea of pull, or twitch, or twang, to pluck; but the instrument has to be learned apart from the word. And so, then, God said by the Greek word "psallo," "make melody," and added the element, or instrument, "in your heart." Just as you are circumcised in heart, metaphorically, let us "psallo" in the heart. Such is God's teaching.

Now, I want to read to you here from a little booklet by Brother Kurfees that speaks exactly the position that I believe to be true to-night. On page 13: "And let the reader never forget that from the very earliest usage of the word, while it retained and carried through all its subsequent mutations the original meaning to touch or strike some object, yet no particular object inhered in the word to the exclusion of all others." It does not, therefore, mean in the New Testament to pluck the hair, it does not mean in the New Testament to pull the bowstring, it does not mean to pluck a mechanical instrument; but in the New Testament that idea of plucking or twanging has reference to the chords of the heart, and hence it is a figurative or metaphorical use regarding the same.

So, then, I pass from that. Now, with reference to the instrument in the temple, let me say, ladies and gentlemen, in the quotation made from a sermon I preached, I did say, and say to-night, in the temple built by David there were instruments of music. Upon them, however, God later pronounced a woe. And in another temple, built by Zerubbabel, Ezra, et al., there were instruments of music. But in the temple built by Herod there is no positive proof that instruments of music were ever heard. But, as I have said, suppose that such could be established; then what? It would be no precedent whatsoever for us to-night, for in that same temple and practiced by the same people there was the burning of animal sacrifices and likewise of the incense. If it were a fact, therefore, that Christ and the apostles by their silence approved of the instrument, then by their silence they likewise approved of the sacrifice and the incense. Hence, we would have to bring these into the church as well as the instrument.

But, with reference to the Jewish synagogue, in the Jewish Encyclopedia, Volume 9, page 432, we find: "The modern organ in reformed synagogues, as an accessory to the worship, was first introduced by Isadore Jacobson at Berlin in the new house of prayer which he opened on June 14,

1815." Again, from the same book: "Instrumental music is quite a modern feature in the Jewish worship."

But he said: "Hardeman, how about infant membership?" Well, all right. Those who practice infant baptism claim to get it from the word. They say the word "baptizo" furnishes the authority for the sprinkling. Now, "Go ye into all the world, and preach the gospel to every creature." "In that," they say, "isn't the baby a 'creature?' Let us practice it." They turn to Lydia and her household, and they will find more babies in Lydia's house than you will find organs in the entire Bible.

Brother Boswell, your proposition is that instrumental music in the worship is scriptural. I want to ask you, in all candor, to-night, where is one single, solitary scripture upon which you rely?

I want to make this definite request: Brother Boswell, in your next speech point out the scripture, or those scriptures, definitely, upon which you base your claim. As yet not a single one has been quoted. I want to ask him, my friends, to quote one scripture on which he proposes to base the argument. If a thing is scriptural, it is not to be trifled with, and is a thing that you do not want to leave undone. When we are commanded to be baptized, I want to ask Brother Boswell: Can you either do it or not do it and obey the Lord? Observing the Lord's Supper is scriptural. May I ask: Can you either observe it or not observe it? To live a prayerful, upright life is scriptural. I want to ask: Can you either do it or not do it? To pray unto God is scriptural. Does that mean I can do it if I want to, and if I don't want to I can let it alone?

I have asked him to define the terms "scriptural," "unscriptural," and "antiscriptural;" but thus far no effort has been made, and I must insist that the suspicion as to his refusal is not wanting.

When a thing is scriptural, it must be done, and our only liberty is to obey God or reject his counsel. Such matters are not to be settled by a majority vote.

BOSWELL'S TENTH SPEECH

(Tuesday, June 5, 1923.)

Brother Moderator: The first thing I wish to do is to present two evidences here. He made the statement that the lexicon does not specify the element in baptism. I have Liddell & Scott, not Mr. Payne. It is a strange thing that he would condemn Payne's book and speak of him in the most disrespectful terms, and then turn around and quote from him and try to prove his position by him. "Baptiso"—he didn't say "baptizo," but "baptiso." "*Baptizo,* dipped in or under water." (Liddell & Scott.) That is the classical meaning. I now take Thayer's New Testament Lexicon, the one that he has exalted to the skies, and it is all he says. He read the classical meaning first, then read the New Testament meaning, and tried to make you believe that under the New Testament meaning Thayer was just giving an illustration. But Thayer first gives the classical meaning and then the meaning in the New Testament. He says: "An immersion in water, performed as a sign of removal of sin; an immersion in water." (Thayer's New Testament Greek Lexicon.) This is the lexicon from which he just read and in which he denied there was such a definition.

I did not pay very much attention to his chart. Now, as a matter of fact, the whole thing is predicated on an assumption. It is predicated on the assumption that "sing" is a specific word. "Sing" is a generic word, and means you can sing with or without an instrument. Everybody knows that, and why should I take up my time on it? Gopher wood—how many kinds are there? There is only one kind of gopher wood, but two sorts of singing—with or without instruments.

Again, friends, in reference to this, he says I made a mistake—that it was not a matter of substitution, but a matter of addition. What he charged was not a matter of substitution, but a matter of addition. All right. Gopher wood—there is one kind of gopher wood. The very thing we are discussing is that "sing," a translation of "psallo," has the two meanings in it. He wants to subtract, and the first law of interpretation is that the literal meaning, if possible, must be taken. You must take the literal meaning of the word if possible; and we have had all these scholars, all these authorities, telling us that the literal meaning is to play with a mechanical instrument, mechanical musical instrument. But God added the other instrument, the heart; and so we play on the musical instrument and play and sing with the heart at the same time. This has been my contention all the time, brethren, all the time.

Now, I did not say much regarding his question as to the organ's playing when there was no singing. He says I did not answer his question: "What about when the organ is playing when there is no singing?" Well, I will tell you. If you do not like that practice, you could do just as he did down at Alamo. Do not worship, simply do not worship; sit there and enter into the service in every other way, but do not worship. But I did answer. Here is my answer: I said: "Grant that to be wrong; it does not prove that you are right when you say put the organ out." I never defended that custom in this debate. It is not a part of the debate. The thing we are discussing is, whether or not we can sing with or without a mechanical instrument. Whether a man makes a mistake, whether a man does the thing that is wrong or not, in this, does not enter into this discussion. The abuse of a thing does not prove that the use of it is wrong.

Then, as we go on in this discussion, I ask him this question: What does the word mean in Rom. 15: 9, where "zamar" is used, from which "psallo" is translated; in the translation of the Hebrew into Greek, what does "zamar" mean? You cannot get the instrument out of "zamar."

He says Jesus at the Supper did not use an instrument, thus using the argument of silence to prove his proposition. How does he know? But did it ever dawn upon his mind that the word used here is not "psallo?" Paul and Silas were singing in the prison, but the word used there when it says they were "singing hymns" is not "psallo." It is not the word we are discussing at all. We are discussing "psallo." We have not gotten away from that word yet. However, I have not said you cannot sing without the instrument.

You cannot add to the literal meaning of the word. It is, as I said the other night, not Brother Boswell, but Brother Hardeman, that has accepted Payne. I never have stood for Payne. Mr. Hardeman accepted every single one of these authorities. Not only so; he says the idea inheres, the meaning inheres, in the word. It is up to Mr. Hardeman to get the figurative meaning into the word. You ask if I indorse all that Mr. Payne says. I answered you time and time again: No, I never have. I have consistently said that I did not.

Again, you ask me: "Can you do a thing that is unscriptural in a scriptural way?" Foolish question! No. If God says, "Do not lie," do not lie; if God says, "Do not kill," do not kill. But the whole argument here is: Does God say sing without an instrument? Do not beg the question. Meet the question fairly and squarely, as I have tried to get you to do during this entire discussion. I have stood right here, and I have insisted on meeting the proposition and not asserting that no man on the top side of God's green earth can get rid of such and such a thing.

Listen: He says that—well, now, what did he say? The reason I asked him what he said is, he forgets it so often himself. How do you expect me to remember it? Now, here is what he said. I have it down here. He said: "Yes, it was in Solomon's temple; it was in Zerubbabel's temple." But he says: "Who knows whether it was in the temple in Jerusalem or not?" Why, Mr. Hardeman knows. Listen to his own words: "Showing beyond the possibility of a reasonable doubt that while it prevailed throughout the days of David and subsequent thereto under Judaism, at the very institution and the inauguration of the Christian dispensation and the church of the living God it was purposely left out." Why, he himself said it continued up to the day of Pentecost, and he said that without any hesitation. But he is learning. If he will read Mr. Payne a little bit more and get a little bit more in harmony with him than he is, there is no telling where he will be after a while.

He got away from Brother Kurfees, and here he comes back. I will be frank with him and tell him if he had stayed with Brother Kurfees all the time he would have been a great deal better off, and I think his brethren feel that way about it. I do, anyway.

Now, last night he said the most peculiar thing I ever heard a man say who believes the Bible, the New Testament. He says you do not get your authority from Jesus Christ to go into all the world and preach the gospel. O, brethren, it is there! He said it. He said you get it from Paul, who gave it to Timothy, and you get it from Timothy. Why, he said the apostles were directed particularly and specifically to do it, and then Paul said to Timothy: "You go and preach it, and tell others the same thing, and let them preach it." I wonder if he remembers the commission? "Go ye therefore, and make disciples of all the nations, baptizing them into the name of the Father and of the Son and of the Holy Spirit, teaching them"—teaching whom? the nations that you disciple and baptize—"teaching them to observe all things whatsoever I have commanded you." And Jesus told them to go, and they were to teach those whom they discipled and baptized to disciple and baptize others, and so on to the end of time. And if you do not get your authority to preach the gospel from Jesus Christ, where under heaven do you get it? If I did not get my authority directly out of the commission of my Lord Jesus Christ to preach the gospel, I would have no authority to preach it. I am surprised at a statement like that from one who has stood up here and said: "Do you believe the gospel of God?" I ask you people to-night who are listening to preachers: Are you listening to the preacher who gets his authority from Timothy or the one who gets his authority from Jesus Christ, who said: "All authority hath been given unto me in heaven and on earth?" I make statements here to-night that have been made. They are in the record. They can be found.

I ask him again, and propose to accept his challenge, that

he prove by my own arguments infant membership and the burning of incense. My argument was—the two of them, the meaning of the word and apostolic precedent; but he immediately left that proposition and went off on another line and spoke about those who believe in infant church membership. So that got my challenge out of the way. He spoke of those who believe in infant baptism, and then he mentioned the household of Lydia, and said that there were more babies in Lydia's home than all the organs in the Bible; and then—a remarkable thing—he skipped over 670 years with his organ, clear down to 1800 and something. If what he read to-night is correct—the first date—then the date he read the other night cannot be correct. You cannot have the organ introduced first on one date and in one church and then introduced on a different date at another time. That is one thing you cannot do. He made these statements when he tried to bring in the infants and the burning of incense on the ground of my two arguments.

Brethren, I will not stop to discuss his statements about putting butter and jelly on the bread at the Lord's table. Absolutely no analogy at all, simply trying to cloud the issue and get away from the question. That is all there is to it. He pretends to get you around the Lord's table and to plead with you along that line. Brethren, if you put the bread on the table and then put the butter and jelly on it, that would be adding to the elements; but if you take the word "psallo," which means sing with or without the instrument, there is no addition; it is in the word. There is nothing added at all. God put it there; God put it there.

Now, here is a thing in that same April speech; and as he said about the same thing then as now, I think I shall let him answer his own statement about the babies. He said: "If instrumental music is to accompany the worship, then from every point of authority or reason, harmony or consistency, babies ought to be entitled to church membership, and must come in upon the very same ground and from practically every point of view." I will introduce Brother Hardeman now to answer his own question with his own statement. He says: "But some one says: 'Infants are prohibited or forbidden upon the ground that God said baptize believers, and the fact that he said baptize believers cuts out and prohibits all others who are not that.' Well, I think that is correct." He knows it is correct, and knew it when he made the previous statement.

He brought in beads the other night. He has brought in counting beads. "Some one said: 'Now, Brother Hardeman, the Bible does not forbid it; and, therefore, we are at liberty to use it, and it is permissible.' Well, is that a safe principle? Now, friends, the Bible has nowhere said, 'Thou shalt not count beads as an act of religious worship;' and if the principle prevails, then it is permissible for our Catholic friends to come into the service of God Almighty and institute there the counting of beads; and if I should protest, with an air of triumph, and even defiance, he would say: 'Hardeman, where does God say you must not count beads?' Well, I would be up with my work on that." O, can't you see that God never did put beads in the worship? He has put instruments there, and he has permitted that. Can you see any analogy there? He has also used the same argument as to incense. Turn to Revelation, and there we are told that the incense is the prayers of the saints. Incense was in the worship as a type. It has been set aside because fulfilled—the type in the antitype prayer.

And here is a remarkable one. He said the other night that he could prove polygamy scriptural on the same ground; and I can read this most remarkable statement, next to the one where he said he did not get his authority from the Lord Jesus Christ. I shall read you this most remarkable statement: "Then the Mormon elder, in days gone by, might have paraded down the aisle with some three or four or five women in his wake as his wives. Where in the Bible does a command say that a man must not have three wives at a time? Well, I don't know, absolutely." One of his funny words—"absolutely." Now, listen: He said he didn't know where to find it in the Scriptures—could not tell what to do about that matter. I told you he ought to read his Bible. 1 Cor. 7: 2: "But, because of fornications, let each man have his own wife, and let each woman have her own husband." He might have quoted that to the Mormon elder. Eph. 5: 31: "For this cause shall a man leave his father and mother, and shall cleave to his wife; and the two shall become one flesh." He might have quoted that to the Mormon elder. And yet this opponent of mine stands up here and says you cannot get polygamy out if you put the organ in. He says if a Mormon should come down the aisle with four or five wives he would "absolutely" not know what to do to keep him out. How about the words of Jesus? "And there came unto him Pharisees, trying him, and saying, Is it lawful for a man to put away his wife for every cause? And he answered and said, Have ye not read, that he who made them from the beginning made them male and female, and said, For this cause shall a man leave his father and mother, and shall cleave to his wife; and the two shall become one flesh? So that they are no more two, but one flesh. What therefore God hath joined together, let not man put asunder." (Matt. 19: 3-6.) There is the authority; there is the authority to direct him. Where did I get it? Got it from Jesus Christ, where I get my authority to preach.

No wonder a man does not know how to meet a thing like that, when he does not get his authority to preach the gospel from Jesus, but gets it from Timothy! Take these statements, my brother, and put them together and see the weakness of the arguments that are made against the position I am occupying. I have been standing by this position from the very beginning and asking that he examine these authorities. He has called two of my authorities in question—Liddell & Scott and Thayer. I brought the authorities here and laid them on the table. He has not criticized any of the other authorities or referred to them directly, except one—Professor Bacon—and that one he perverted. He has ridiculed Payne's book—the book he keeps by his side, the book he reads, the book he stands for, and one of the greatest books ever written on this subject. I am not afraid to say that. But I do not stand for all its statements. I never have. He has tried very hard to get me lined up with his statements, but I have positively refused to do so. There are the authorities on the table.

Again, he has spoken about twanging the chord, shooting the arrow, and all that. Let me say to you to-night that Brother Kurfees admits, Brother Hardeman admits, that music is in the word. He said to-night—I want you to get this now; I like to come along and tell you what he said—he says, "God nowhere says make music;" and then he turns right around and says, "God said make melody in your hearts;" and I have shown you that some of the translators, his own among them, translate it "music" instead of "melody." God said "psallo." The English translation of that word is "sing." "Psallo," according to the authorities, means to sing with or without the instrument. If it does not mean that, now is the time for him to produce the authority that says to the contrary. He will give you two—Brother H. L. Calhoun and Brother McGarvey. Beg your pardon, I thought I heard something. [Laughter.] Now, brethren, sisters, I am delighted to have you laugh a little bit, if it does you any good, because I frankly tell you it is just as religious to laugh as to cry. There is nothing wrong with a laugh, provided you feel more like yourself when you laugh, and I certainly do.

I call your attention again to the statement as made by Brother Hardeman in reference to his chart. Now, I am doing this just to please him, not that I think it is such an unanswerable thing, after all, but just that I may call attention to it again, lest you get away from the fact, that "sing" is a generic word; that it means to sing with or without an instrument; and you do not have to know Greek to know that. There is not any one here that does not know that the word "sing," in English, means that you can sing with or without an instrument, and you do that thing time after time. You sit down to your piano and sing; you sing with the instrument; and you get up from your piano and stand there and sing. You sing without the instrument. Now, the English word "sing" is generic and not specific. The English word does not mean only to sing without any accompaniment; it means to sing with or without the instrument. The reason I am emphasizing this thing is—I am glad I had the few minutes left to emphasize it—is that he has ignored it from the very beginning.

In every speech I have made I have presented proof; I have called upon him to produce authorities on the other side or to impeach the witnesses I have brought. I have asked him every night to show that this is a specific word; and yet, after all these four nights that we have been speaking, and the first speeches that we have made to-night, he comes to you this last night and says: "Here is the word 'sing,' and it is specific." Not one single authority to prove it but his own say so! In spite of all that has been said in days gone by, and then to-night he comes again and says the word is specific, and not a scintilla of proof or evidence to prove it! We are not up here just taking my word or his word. We could settle this question to our own satisfaction, each of us, to-night, if that were the case. The thing for us to do is to stand before you, present our proposition, make our arguments, give our authorities, and leave it for you to decide the question. I have followed that procedure, I have given my authorities, I have presented my witnesses. I have given you my arguments night after night. These arguments have not been met, but in every case he comes to you and begins the same speech over and over and over.

Now, I think you will find that out a little bit more certainly when you read the book. I knew this was going to be published. I have been exceedingly careful, because I knew that this book after a while would be staring me in the face; and I have been careful all the time of my authorities, been careful of my arguments, been careful of my references to my brother, because I know that this book is going to be read by thousands of people in order to find out all about this discussion; and when you read it, these arguments I am giving to you to-night will stand out clear, well defined, and settled. But I am afraid of this, my brethren: that after you read one speech of the brother who has been speaking against me, you won't have to read the others, except sections throughout the whole book, because every time it is this: "Bring me proof of this." And every night it has been the same thing over and over and over. It has not been because he has not had time; it has not been because he did not have the authorities up there on my chart to study and refute. I do not know why he has done so, except it be the fact that he got over on Payne and left Brother Kurfees, because there is no doubt about it, my friends, that he absolutely repudiated Brother Kurfees as to the meaning of the word "psallo."

Brother Kurfees said the word lost its primitive meaning entirely; that from 145 on to about 1100 it did not have any idea of instrumentation. Now, Brother Hardeman comes along and says it never did lose it; it has always had it; but that the instrument is the heart. It has had the meaning to play on the heart. I assert that there is nothing substituted in the word "sing" when you use the organ with it; there is nothing subtracted from the word "sing" when you use the organ; in fact, any instrument that you wish or desire can be used. The proposition defended by me has taken nothing away, and nothing is added to the meaning of the word. The word carries with it the meaning of instrumentation—metaphorically, to play on the heart; literally, to play upon a musical instrument. And then God gives in his inspired word the new application. There is your change in the use of the word, there is your added spiritual use of the act indicated by the word—that it shall be spiritual—that is, with the heart; and you can use the instrument or not use it.

HARDEMAN'S TENTH SPEECH

(Tuesday, June 5, 1923.)

Brethren, Moderators, Ladies, and Gentlemen: I really regret to have to expose Brother Boswell. He said in the last words of his speech that Brother M. C. Kurfees said that the word "psallo" lost all idea of its primitive meaning, and that Hardeman has turned him down. To the contrary, I just read in the speech before a word from Brother Kurfees, on page 15 of Kurfees' book, his own language. I want you to get a sample of this man's reliability, and we are going to have to place him in Elder Payne's class in spite of all that can be done. He seems beside himself. Now, listen: Brother Kurfees says: "And let the reader never forget that from the very earliest usage of the word, while it retained and carried through all its subsequent mutations its original meaning to touch or strike some object, yet no particular object inhered in the word to the exclusion of the other."

If you do the right thing, you will write Brother Kurfees a letter and tell him you misrepresented him. Read that as a matter from Brother Kurfees. I just read it in my last speech, and then you got up and said: "Hardeman turned him down." "It has lost its original meaning." That is just Boswell. And I can only apologize for him on the ground that in his last speech he was jumping in every direction, grabbing at straws, and so wonderfully wild in his declarations of matters stated. Now, ladies and gentlemen, as a matter of fact, when he says that I am making the same speech, be it remembered that I am following in his footsteps. I am in the negative of this discussion. He said the other night, in very classic terms, that he hadn't "quite petered out," but he has given evidence to-night that ought to be conclusive.

I think Brother Boswell is a splendid man. I know he is a good preacher, because he said he was. He said that some of his brethren back in Georgetown said he could beat Alexander Campbell, and maybe he can. If so, I recommend that he spend his time in preaching rather than debating.

Brethren, hear it. The word "baptizo," as defined primarily by Mr. Thayer from the book that Brother Boswell read, does not carry with it the meaning that he mentioned. Thayer's definition is to dip, to plunge, to immerse, or to submerge; and in the primary meaning the idea of the element is not there. Why, look at the ridiculousness of that! If the element is in the word "baptizo," and it means to dip in water, then when Christ says, "I have a baptism to be baptized with; and how am I straitened till it be accomplished!" it could mean nothing but water baptism. But such is not so. Christ alluded to the baptism of suffering, to the submerging in sorrow that should characterize him while agonizing on the cross. I suggest to you that I really regret to have to meet such as that from a man who has the reputation of my friend here to-night.

With reference to the word "psallo," let me say again: It means to pluck, or to pull, or to twitch, or to touch, or to sing. Now, then, it has these meanings.

Question: In the New Testament, which one of these meanings does it have?

Does it mean in the New Testament to pull the hair? No, sir.

Does it mean, in the New Testament, to pluck the string? No.

Does it mean, in the New Testament, to twitch the carpenter's line? No, sir.

What does it mean in the New Testament? It is a figurative use, like circumcision, which he forgot to mention; and hence I just have to go over and over, trying to get him to refer to it.

In the New Testament, what does "psallo" mean? It means to make melody, and Paul tells the instrument. Now, watch the instrument. "With the heart." That settles it. What does Brother Boswell say? "With a mechanical instrument."

Does any dictionary on the face of the earth suggest that it has to be purely a mechanical instrument? Not one.

And, ladies and gentlemen, there is absolutely no consistency in Brother Boswell's repeated statement. "Psallo" means, in the New Testament, to strike the chords of the heart. You cannot have your arbitrary position. You cannot do what God says by either with or without. Brother Boswell, when God says make melody with the heart, you cannot make that melody and leave out the heart; and hence it is ridiculous, my friends, when he says "with or without."

What is the thought about "with or without?" Now, here is the ridiculous statement: to say that this one word means two opposite things. What is the relation between *with* and *without?* One is positive and the other negative. One points in one direction and the other in the other, and yet here is a word that means going in both directions at the same time! A ridiculous—yea, foolish—statement! Such a word never so meant. I want Brother Boswell to give just one other word in all of the lexicons that means both with and without at the same time. Ladies and gentlemen, that is a plain contradiction of terms. The idea of a lawyer pleading a case and defining the terms and saying: "Now, gentlemen of the jury, Bill Jones killed Sam Smith with and without a shotgun."

How do you plow corn in Kentucky? *With* and *without* a mule? How do you hoe cotton down in the land of Dixie? *With* and *without* a hoe?

There is a plain contradiction of terms here, because *with* and *without* are opposite the one to the other. Now, if they were synonymous, one might be used to supplement the other; but these words are not synonymous. It is a matter of impossibility for one word to have opposite meanings at the same time. Your contention that "psallo" means with and without an instrument is ridiculous and will appear foolish to every schoolboy in our land.

When Brother Boswell goes to eat, does he do it both with and without his mouth? When he goes to digest his food, does he digest it both with and without his stomach? Why, I know that is a thing ridiculous, and that is what your chart is—absurd. Brother Boswell, that is the term that fits the chart. It is "doubleness of speech" (duplicity) and positively contradictory in its statement regarding "psallo."

But he refers to the Alamo business again. Just to make myself clear, let me say this: I went to Alamo recently and preached the commencement sermon in the Methodist Church. They had a piano in it. They had a few people on the stage, as a choir. The congregation never sang a song. The choir did the singing. He wants to know if I sang or worshiped God in the singing. I have answered: "No." Therefore, I did not worship God at all in that part of the service.

But he said: "Hardeman, the ridiculous thing you got off was that you don't get your authority to preach from Christ." He seems unable to quote Brother Kurfees, and he can't quote me. Brother Boswell, I said I didn't get it direct from Christ in the commission. Neither did you. When Christ gave the commission (Mark 15: 16), he appeared unto the eleven apostles. You weren't there, Brother Boswell. [Applause.] "He appeared unto the eleven as they sat at meat, and upbraided them. . . . And he said unto them, Go ye." And you thought that meant you, didn't you? Well, I will prove to you that you are not in that company or else have departed. He said to them: "Teaching them to observe all things whatsoever I have commanded." And that thing you are not doing, for he commanded people to sing, and you teach them to play in addition. Your authority for such a practice comes not from Jesus Christ. If so, put your finger on any statement he ever made authorizing your practice.

I said that we get our direct authority from 2 Tim. 2: 1, 2: "Thou therefore, my son, be strong in the grace that is in Christ Jesus. And the things that thou hast heard of me among many witnesses, the same commit thou to faithful men, who shall be able to teach others also." There is the authority, and it comes indirectly from Christ Jesus, our Lord, through Paul to Timothy.

Now, then, does Brother Boswell mean to insinuate that because Paul handed it down to Timothy it has not the authority of Christ? It has his authority, but indirect.

Brother Boswell, let us hear you preach on the operation

of the Spirit. Do you preach a direct or indirect operation? I know you will say it is indirect. Now, do you thereby deny the authority of the Spirit? O, no! If you preach like I think you do, you just deny the direct operation and preach that God does it. But how? Indirectly through the gospel. Just so our authority to preach comes from Christ, but indirectly. But you just needed something to say, and hence your effort to cloud the thought.

When I deny the direct and immediate operation of the Spirit, sectarians charge that I deny the work of the Spirit. But they no more misrepresent the facts than does Brother Boswell in his vain effort to set aside the truth.

It seems that Brother Boswell can't get a thing under heaven right. He says that Hardeman once said that the instruments were introduced in the seventh century, and the last time he said it was in 1815. That is but a sample. Brother Boswell, how absent-minded you are! No wonder you forget when you want to quote what I said! You get lost and go to rambling around. Here is what I said: "It was introduced into the churches of Catholicism in the seventh century and into the Jewish synagogue in 1815." And yet you think that it is a wonderful contradiction and that Hardeman is lost.

No, no, Brother Boswell; by no means. I said, ladies and gentlemen, in the sermon from which he read, that back in the days of Abraham, and subsequent thereto in the days of David, there was the same authority presented for the introduction of the organ as for infant membership and polygamy. I was making the argument that the instrumental-music folks contend that because David used instruments, therefore we ought to have them now. David also practiced polygamy and allowed infants in the congregation. Brother Boswell has not made that argument, but it would be far better and more reasonable than to say that "psallo" means two opposite things at the same time. I am sorry he is unable to get the point made in that sermon.

In the New Testament, God has never said: "Thou shalt not baptize babies." God has never said: "Thou shalt not have instruments in the service." But if the fact that God said "baptize believers" excludes babies, and both of us think it does, then the fact that God said "sing" excludes mechanical instruments, and the fact that God says "the husband of one wife" excludes the polygamist in his practice.

God did, at one time, authorize the burning of animal sacrifices; but nowhere in the New Testament is it declared: "Thou shalt not." Hence, on this hypothesis, we are at liberty to have the animal sacrifices, because God has not directly prohibited them. That is the argument.

But he passes on then and says there will be incense in heaven. Yes, and there will be babies in heaven. Why not make the other part of it, as usual? You say there will be harps in heaven, but the revisers—those "who threw dust in the eyes of the readers and spoiled the Bible to save the prayer book"—don't say so.

I come to you with this other thought: There were forty and seven men who translated the Bible in King James; there were one hundred and one who translated the Revised Version—making one hundred and forty-eight in all. I read from twenty-six translators the other night, making one hundred and seventy-four. Hear it! One hundred and forty-eight scholars, of the highest type, the very cream of the world, gave to you and me that Bible, the book upon which our faith is founded. When they came to the word on which my brother hangs his trembling cause, they translated it. Now, what did they tell you people that it meant? They said that the word "psallo" means to sing, and not one time did these scholars say to play. Their translation is supported by these other twenty-six, making a total of one hundred and seventy-four.

Friends, do you believe that Prof. Philip Schaff, the learned Presbyterian, as president of that board, and Prof. Joseph Thayer, as secretary of it, allowed the Episcopalians, as charged by the opposition, to spoil God's book in order to save the Episcopalian prayer book? If that be true, and if our Bible is incorrect on "psallo," then how do you and I know that it is correct on any other thing? Hence, we are out in the midst of the ocean and left without chart or compass, to drift amid the rocks until by and by we pass over the precipice into the fathomless depths of the boundless beyond. Why? Because the translators, one hundred and seventy-four, have deceived us, or put "dust in our eyes," and did it in order to obscure our vision and save the prayer book. Do you believe it? Who can accept a man's statement whose cause is weighed in the balance and found wanting? But I ask: Does my brother before you believe any such? Do you, friends of his—and I mean religious friends—believe our English Bible in Eph. 5: 19? Brother Boswell has in reality rejected our Bible on that point.

Where is the scripture upon which my opponent relies? Name one passage that he has brought forth in support of the proposition that instrumental music is scriptural. His proposition seems to have been that instrumental music is lexicographal. He changes the term. But on the proposition that instrumental music is scriptural, not one single, solitary passage of scripture is produced. And I ask him in the last address: Brother Boswell, turn to one passage; just tell this audience, so that they can take it home with them. You are the representative here of a splendid body of people, who know not to-night what passage you rely upon to prove your proposition. Brother Boswell, tell me privately just what passage proves your contention. If you will do so, I'll quit calling on you over and over and over.

Let me suggest to you this: The Restoration Movement was, to my mind, the grandest movement that ever challenged the attention of mortal man this side of the cross and the apostolic period. When Barton W. Stone, Thomas Campbell, Alexander Campbell, and other great men looked about and saw the confusion in the religious world, they decided such was wrong and contrary to the genius and the spirit of our Savior's prayer, when, in the shadow of the cross, he lifted up his voice and said: "Father, I pray that they all may be one, as thou, Father, art in me and I in thee; may they be one in us, that the world may believe that thou hast sent me." Actuated by that splendid sentiment and by that humble appeal from the lips of the Son of God, they started out to find common ground on which Christian people could unite. First of all, they laid down the Bible, and the Bible alone, as their sole authority. No man had to make a sacrifice of faith in giving up his creed. He could give up his opinion, it is true; but none were called upon to sacrifice their faith. Could not all people accept the Bible? Indeed so. Then all could accept immersion as the scriptural act demanded by the Greek word "baptizo." Hence, they laid down that scriptural ground. No one denied that to be a Christian only was sufficient. Party names were, therefore, rejected. Then when it came to the worship, it was this: Let us meet together and teach and encourage and instruct. There is common ground. Let us pray together, and all could agree. Let us take of the Lord's Supper without addition. They all could stand on that. Let us contribute of our means, every man according to his ability; and upon that they could stand. And then let us sing psalms and hymns and spiritual songs, making melody in our hearts unto God. They accepted that as the basis of Christian unity; and for fifty years, as one solid phalanx, under the blood-stained banner of Christ Jesus, our Lord, they marched against the powers of denominationalism and sectarianism in every form.

When men wanted to be like their sectarian neighbors, like their denominational friends, they introduced, in 1858, a man-made instrument with which to worship God. They sought no longer to worship God purely out of spirituality, but now by machinery; and when they brought that instrument into the service of God, they drove the wedge that split asunder a once happy, harmonious, and united people. They say to me and others: "If you can't partnership with us in it, you can get out." When I oppose that for which there is no authority and that which divides the body of Christ, I am styled a "mossback," an objector, and a disturber of the peace. That is the spirit of the brother's appeal all over this land and country where such things have prevailed.

And to-night, notwithstanding Brother Boswell has said that you can worship acceptably without it, he would rather hold on to his organ in Nashville than to have the fellowship of ten thousand Christians. In the name of high heaven, why not give up your man-made machinery, give up your innovations, and let us, heart to heart and hand in hand, as brethren, without bitterness and without strife, settle at least one point of difference. Perhaps others can be agreed upon. Then we will not be afraid nor ashamed, Brother Boswell, to preach the full gospel of Christ in Nashville, Tenn.

When we come to quote the commission, let us not be afraid to say: "Go ye into all the world, and preach the gospel to every creature. He that believeth and is baptized shall be saved." When we come into the midst of sectarian people, let us not shun to declare the gospel because somebody else happens to be present.

There is but one safe ground in all this wide, wide world. That is the Bible, and the Bible alone; God's word, and that alone. Here is common ground on which every child of God can stand and not stultify his conscience. Do that, and I pledge you to the best of my ability I will stand gladly with Brother Boswell to-night. I like these brethren. I do not like their doctrine. I do not like their spirit, but I appreciate them personally, and I would like to be able to worship with them. They say: "Hardeman, that which divides us is unnecessary; we can worship with or without the organ." Then, if you mean that, Brother Boswell, why not worship without it and let us worship with you? Brethren, there is the test that stands confronting them to-night; and I want to say, as I have said to this audience before, I would rather stand as that character who took the Roman spear and pierced the body of Christ on the cross than to be responsible for introducing a wedge that has driven asunder and divided the spiritual body of Christ Jesus, our Lord. And woe unto that man, whosoever he be, in the final judgment! For God hates a man that sows discord among his brethren. We are taught to mark them and avoid them. I charge, as a matter of fact, that such men as Brother Boswell have gone over this country dividing the churches over that which he admits is nonessential. That is a bad spirit, unsupported by the word of God.

I thank you.

BOSWELL'S ELEVENTH SPEECH

(Tuesday, June 5, 1923.)

Brother Moderator: Brother Hardeman said he would rather be the Roman soldier that divided the body of Jesus Christ than to be the man who divided the brotherhood of the church. Brother Hardeman has his preference.

The introduction of the organ, however, is not the cause of the divisions in every case. Churches have been divided because of putting the "creed in the deed." One thing is certain: Vine Street Church never yet has put it in the deed that you "cannot be a member of this church if you do not worship with the organ." They never have done it, and they never will do it.

Another thing I want to call attention to is: Brother Hardeman has said time and again that I am trying to prove that you can sing with or without the organ *at the same time.* He has put that "at the same time" in there; I never did. There is no reason for my putting it there. It is not a part of this argument, and no man would be fool enough to make such a statement as that. He asked me: "How can you digest your food with and without a stomach at the same time?" The man must have forgotten about his head, thinking about his stomach, to ask such a question as that. I ask you this question: Can you love your wife and take her a sack of flour at the same time? Just as good on my side as the other is on his, and not worth much.

Now, Brother Hardeman says that the Revised Version—that the men who translated the Revised Version—repudiated the idea of the instrument in "psallo." I read to you again from Mr. Riddle: "I have no recollection of any purpose on the part of the revisers to preclude the use of the instrument. My own opinion is that the word 'psallo' does not preclude the use of an instrument." The mechanical instrument is what he means. He was a member of the Revision Committee. A member of the Revision Committee, Philip Schaff, before he died, said: " 'I will sing with the spirit [quoting 1 Cor. 14: 15], and I will sing with the understanding also'—a proof that the prayer was accompanied with song and harp also." Timothy Dwight, a member, testifies to the same thing. So we have these men, who answer that they are not guilty of Mr. Hardeman's charge.

He says I have never quoted any scriptures. If any have been quoted anywhere, he says, he does not recall them. I am sure that Rom. 15: 9 has been quoted; I am sure that 1 Cor. 14: 15-26 has been quoted; I am sure Eph. 5: 19 has been quoted; I am sure Col. 3: 16 has been quoted; I am sure James 5: 19 has been quoted.

Brother Hardeman says that the Revision Committee swept the harp out of Revelation. I wonder when was the last time he read the book? Listen, in the fifth chapter and the eighth verse: "And when he had taken the book, the four living creatures and the four and twenty elders fell down before the Lamb, having each one a harp, and golden bowls full of incense, which are the prayers of the saints." There is the Revised Version, and yet he tells you they took it out. Rev. 15: 2: "And I saw as it were a sea of glass mingled with fire; and them that come off victorious from the beast, and from his image, and from the number of his name, standing by the sea of glass, having harps of God." There is another of his misrepresentations.

Now, he asks me to write a letter to Brother Kurfees, apologizing for misrepresenting him. Why, if Brother Hardeman would write me a letter for all the misrepresentations he has presented to you regarding me, he would have to get him a stenographer and keep her busy for the next month.

Listen: He said Brother Kurfees did not say that "psallo" had lost its meaning. I shall read you what Brother Kurfees says on page 60 of his book, "Instrumental Music in the Worship:" "But we have already seen that before the beginning of the Roman period—i. e., B.C. 146—the above-mentioned classical meanings were no longer current in the language; and, of course, a lexicon limited to the time when *psallo* had no such meanings could not correctly say that it had them at that time. For this reason they do not appear in Sophocles' Lexicon at all."

There are other quotations to the same intent he can read in Brother Kurfees' book. He did not tell you that Brother Kurfees wrote the statement he quoted after he read Payne. He changed his mind when he read Payne, for he found out there was more in that word than he thought there was. My quotation is from Brother Kurfees before he read Payne, and his is from Brother Kurfees after he read Payne.

As to "baptizo"—he immediately jumps to "baptizo"—he read you something which I read again, under the New Testament definition of "baptizo:" "An immersion in water"—reading in the very place he read before—"to cleanse by dipping, to submerge, to wash, to make clean with water." He read the very thing he read before.

Another question he says I never answered for him is about circumcision. Read the report and see if I did not, and see if he quoted the question as he asked it. He never said one single word about circumcision in the New Testament when he first asked the question. Here is his question: "Can you circumcise with or without an instrument? What is the instrument?" That is his question as recorded in the report and as I have it down. Not a word about *the New Testament!*

He said he didn't get his authority from Jesus Christ, because Jesus gave it to the apostle; and he said: "Brother Boswell, you were not there, were you?" Then he said he got his authority from Paul. Were you there, Brother Hardeman? The day you find yourself standing up with Paul, you will find me right down there with the apostles. He says he got it indirectly from Jesus, but he gets it directly from Paul. Now, I will say this much, brethren: I have never knowingly done a man an injustice in my life; I am man enough to do the right thing; and if he did put "indirectly" in his statement, I am perfectly willing to say: Brother Hardeman, it is there, if you put it there. I would not misrepresent you, and I am man enough to take back a misrepresentation if I made it. But after I have done that, he is right where he was before. I do not want to misquote him under any circumstances.

Brethren, I have not time to preach you a sermon here on the Restoration Movement and on the Bible, and the Bible alone. I always thought my creed was Christ. I always thought the Restoration Movement stood for the creed that needed no revision. Jesus Christ is the creed. He is the one in whom I believe; he is my authority; he is my all in all. I exalt him, my brother. If I were going to write a deed, a creed, to put in a church deed, I would put this: "Jesus is the Christ, the Son of the living God." I would put him there as born of the virgin, as bodily raised from the grave, as God in the flesh upon this earth. I would not leave all that out and put the organ in, either for or against.

Now, I must close. My time is drawing to a conclusion here. I am glad to have met you, brethren; I am glad to have been with you. I thank you for your courtesy.

I want, just in a few minutes, to summarize some things I have tried to say, and I sincerely trust—and just here let me say, even if I have to leave out some of my arguments—brethren, if during this discussion I have said a single unkind word, if during this discussion my mannerism upon this platform has been the least offensive, I ask your pardon. I have stood for what I believe is right. I brought you the testimony; I stand upon all the word of God; and if I know my own heart and my own past reputation, I would not intentionally wound the feelings of any one.

I have said we proved it by the word; we have proved it by apostolic precedent. I want to read you just a few words here from three or four writers. Brother Hardeman admits the instrumentation; he and I differ only upon the instrument itself. He says it is the heart, and the heart alone. I say that we sing and play in the heart figuratively, but that we have the right to play on the mechanical instrument. It is in the word. We can sing with or without, but not *at the same time.* I have quoted authorities for that. He has not denied a single authority; he has accepted every one of them. I have shown by thirty-three authorities that the instrument is there; that you can sing with or without the instrument. He has brought two to the contrary—Brother McGarvey and Brother Calhoun; and these two brethren he sets up against the scholarship of the world.

And so I shall turn and immediately read to you what the eminent scholar, Mr. Moule, says: " 'In your heart'—both voice and instrument were literal and external, but the use of them both was to be spiritual, and so in the heart." (Cambridge Bible.)

Prof. J. Heinrichs, Northwestern Baptist Seminary ("Commentary on the Psalms"), says: "In later times, such as the New Testament, 'psallo' had come to signify the singing of any hymn, with or without an instrument."

Cheyne testifies that "in your heart" means "with your whole heart."

Philip Schaff testifies to the use of the mechanical instrument.

Westcott: "In the heart, the outward music was to be accompanied by the inward music of the heart."

And had I the time, I could read to you statements of thirty-three men, scholars, who testify to the same thing, outstanding scholars.

And now I close with this: You and I want an infallibly safe way. When it comes to the subject of baptism, I call in good old Brother Benjamin Franklin, who preached that wonderful sermon on the infallibly safe way. He took that which had the most authority; he did not take that which some one else said might do as well; he took that which had the greatest amount of authority in and out of the word of God. And so to-night you and I, believing in God's word, standing by it as the inspired, infallible word of God, take that which has the most authority, because we want to be on the safe side.

Brother Hardeman says you cannot use an organ; the position that we have taken is that you can use it, but you need not to use it if you do not want to. You can sing with or without it. We have brought you the scriptures, we have offered you the authority to prove it; and so to-night I am asking you as a Christian brother, I am asking you as one who has tried to present to you from the beginning to the end of this discussion what God has said, as one who has tried to bring you all the material from the outside possible to find and to present as much as possible in so short a time, I am saying to you: Stand, brethren, on the infallibly safe way; take God's word for it as found in Ephesians, in Corinthians, in Romans, in James, and in Colossians; take his word as found there; take the meaning of that word as given by the Scriptures themselves; take the meaning of that word as given by the scholarship of the world; take the meaning of that word as given by the thirty-three who testified directly as to whether it can be done with or without; and if to-day a man should come to you and tell you the meaning of a certain word, and you had two men, good men, fine men, but who were not qualified in that particular field—because no one will ever say that J. W. McGarvey was recognized as an authority on Greek or Calhoun an authority on Greek—which would you take, these thirty-three or the two?

HARDEMAN'S ELEVENTH SPEECH

(Tuesday, June 5, 1923.)

Brethren and Friends: I hope you will be patient for just a moment. When Brother Boswell expressed his feeling toward the audience and his appreciation of you in every way, I made those sentiments mine and now lend a hearty support thereto.

Now, let me call attention to this: Brother Boswell suggests that he has thirty-three scholars upon which he relies—thirty-three, a wonderful host! Ladies and gentlemen, I hold in my hand the Revised Version of the New Testament. Brother Boswell, there are one hundred and one scholars to your thirty-three, selected for their scholarship, and in all the translations they never one time ascribed to the word that which you say it means. I said, further—and I want you to bear it home with you—that it is ridiculous, absurd, and preposterous to say that the word "psallo" means two opposite things, and that in the same period.

Watch the scriptures that came finally at the close, on which he relies to prove his proposition. 1 Cor. 14: 15: "I will sing with the spirit, and I will sing with the understanding also." What does that word come from? You one hundred and one scholars, plus forty-eight, plus twenty-six—a grand total of one hundred and seventy-four—what do you say about it? We translate it "sing," and hence Brother Boswell says: "That is my scripture." Well, try again. Rom. 15: 9: "Therefore will I give praise unto thee among the Gentiles, and sing unto thy name." Not one time "play!" Col. 3: 16: "In all wisdom teaching and admonishing one another with psalms and hymns and spiritual songs, singing with grace in your hearts unto God." Brother Boswell needs a passage that says "playing." Again, Eph. 5: 19: "Speaking one to another in psalms and hymns and spiritual songs, singing and making melody with your heart to the Lord." James 5: 13: "Is any cheerful? let him sing praise."

And not one solitary time in all the translations, by the representative scholars of the two committees who gave us our Bible, do they say as Brother Boswell contends. Their statement, like the other translations, is to sing and make melody in the heart, not on a mechanical instrument.

In reference to the harps as mentioned in Revelation, let me give you the whole story as told by John. John's entire picture is this: "I saw, in fancy's vision, a sea of glass; I heard something." John, what was it you heard? "I heard a voice." How was it, John? "It was *as* a voice of many waters." John, did you hear the waters? "O, no; but I heard a voice *as* of waters." What else? "I heard a noise *as* of thunder." Did you hear thunder? "O, no; in that cloudless day, God's perfect sunlight, there would be no storm clouds to gather, but I heard a voice; it was *as* the voice of mighty waters, it was *as* the voice of thunder; it was a voice *as* of harpers harping with their harps." Thus was the comparison made to waters, thunder, and harpers.

MR. BOSWELL: Point of order. He is quoting a scripture I never quoted, and he says that I quoted that scripture. I arise to a point of order.

MR. HARDEMAN: No, I said I will give you the whole scripture. I will get to that picture; just hold.

MR. BOSWELL: I want to insist on my point of order. I call for a ruling on my point of order right here. Mr. Moderator, he cannot say a thing until I have heard that point of order. Don't let him say anything now.

MODERATOR MCNEILLY: He must wait until the ruling on the point of order.

[After a consultation between Moderators Srygley and Cowden, Moderator McNeilly said: "The point of order is sustained."]

MR. HARDEMAN: At Mr. Cowden's suggestion, I was going to give the whole story of what John saw and the comparisons he made. If they insist, I shall leave it off. Let me say, however, that the whole story of the harps is in Revelation, from chapter 5 to 15, and that the Revised Version, when it came to the specific language, makes a comparison of these harps, as it does of the thunders and waters.

The other items mentioned in the last address I do not care to notice. It is but a rehash of that to which you have patiently listened.

The debate is now over, and I must hasten to the train, which leaves at 11 sharp. Ladies and gentlemen, brethren and friends, I want to express to you my highest regards and genuine appreciation of your kindness and courtesies in every way. I can truly say to-night that I leave you, Brother Boswell, and his direct friends, with not one single unkind feeling toward any. I want to thank you for every consideration you have ever given me since, more than a year ago, I came, as a stranger, into your midst.

And now may I announce that, through the exceeding kindness of a very dear friend, I expect to leave our beloved country on the 17th to visit that far-away land made sacred by the footsteps of patriarchs and prophets, priests and kings, Christ and the apostles. I want to travel over Judean hills and gaze upon the valleys of Samaria. May I ask that the prayers of you, my friends, accompany me. Gratefully, I bid you good-by.

www.ingramcontent.com/pod-product-compliance
Lightning Source LLC
LaVergne TN
LVHW091048080826
845145LV00002B/672

* 9 7 8 1 5 8 4 2 7 0 2 3 2 *